EVERYBODY'S SHAKESPEARE

EVERYBODY'S
SHAKESPEARE

REFLECTIONS

CHIEFLY ON THE TRAGEDIES

MAYNARD MACK

[signature]
1/7/12

½ PRICE - E.V.
$5.98 + .55

UNIVERSITY OF NEBRASKA PRESS

LINCOLN & LONDON

© 1993 by Maynard Mack

All rights reserved

Manufactured in the United States of America

Acknowledgments for the use of

previously published material appear on pages xi–xii.

First Bison Book printing: 1994

Most recent printing indicated by the last digit below:

1 2 3 4 5 6 7 8 9 10   10 9 8 7 6 5 4 3 2 1

Library of Congress Cataloging in Publication Data

Mack, Maynard, 1909–

Everybody's Shakespeare: reflections chiefly on

the tragedies / Maynard Mack.

p. cm. Includes bibliographical references (p.)

and index.

ISBN 0-8032-3161-x (cl : alkaline paper)

ISBN 0-8032-8214-1 pa.

1. Shakespeare,

William, 1564-1616 – Tragedies.

2. Tragedy. 1. Title.

PR2983.M326 1993 822.3′3–dc20

92-25122 CIP

Third cloth printing: 1994

∞

For Robert & Virginia Knoll

CONTENTS

PREFACE

THIS book is addressed to all or any who enjoy Shakespeare and read for pleasure. "Common Readers" we were once called, and with deserved respect. Today, in academic circles, it is alleged that our style of reader has vanished without trace. But I take this to be a self-serving illusion, witness the staggering number of books on all imaginable subjects, sometimes including even commentary on literature, sold weekly in bookstores. What has actually happened, it appears, is that Common Readers have prudently lost interest in the tribal wars and Byzantine pedantries that now balkanize professional students of literature into new-critics, new-historicists, neo-marxists, feminists, structuralists, psychoanalysts, deconstructionists, and other cells of the elect, each claiming sole possession of the truth and each purveying in its windier moments prose indecipherable (to paraphrase Polonius) and nonsense unlimited: Heidegger cannot be too heavy nor Foucault too light.

No such claim to special clairvoyance is made for the essays included here. They aim no higher than to be read as thoughtful opinion derived from long acquaintance with the plays and expressed, I like to think, without jargon. They were written to be delivered orally at various times to various audiences, normally very mixed audiences containing as many Common Readers as professionals, as many young readers as old. (Some have since been expanded.) Two of the eleven are recent. One of these, later printed privately, is now "published" for the first time. The other is quite new. The remaining nine, having appeared separately in books and journals, are collected here with minor changes for a readership that I hope will resemble the audiences to whom they were originally presented.

Throughout, my effort has been to focus on those aspects of the plays that seem to me to concern us not as ideologues or literary critics but as human beings with a certain interest in how great works of art manage to affect us as profoundly as they do. I am sufficiently naive to believe that men and women occasionally emerge in all fields with the kind of insight we call genius. Shakespeare is one such, in drama possibly the greatest of all such, and offers much to which, in the 1990s as in the long past, we can profitably listen. If but one word in the following commentary helps but one person to listen more intently, the book has served its purpose.

*

Like Prospero's island, the mind of anyone who has enjoyed the high privilege of teaching Shakespeare during much of his life is full of voices. Voices of the great scholars, great critics, great reviewers, great actors and directors. Since in this many-sided conversation it is often most difficult to be sure which voice is one's own, may any whom I have here echoed unawares without acknowledgment forgive me and accept this belated thanks. May also Professor Michael W. Young of the University of Nebraska English department hear and receive my paean of praise for his gallant services as editorial assistant during the final preparations of this book for print. And may it likewise be known, as always, that the greatest of my unpayable debts is to my wife, our children, and their spouses for the charity that suffereth much and is kind.

For the convenience of readers, the text of the plays throughout this book is that of the Pelican Shakespeare (*Complete Works*. General editor, Alfred Harbage. Penguin Books, 1969). Citations of quoted passages give act, scene, and number of first line.

ACKNOWLEDGMENTS

C HAPTER 1 was originally printed as "Our Legacy from Shakespeare" in *Pros and Cons: Monologues on Several Occasions*, privately printed for Florence B. Mack at the Yale University Printing Office, 1989, pp.74–82. Chapter 2 originally appeared as "Engagement and Detachment in Shakespeare's Plays" in *Essays on Shakespeare and Elizabethan Drama in Honor of Hardin Craig*, edited by Richard Hosley, University of Missouri Press, 1962, pp.275–96. Reprinted by permission of the University of Missouri Press. Chapter 3 was first printed as "Rescuing Shakespeare" in Occasional Paper, no.1, International Shakespeare Association, privately printed at the Oxford University Press, 1979, pp.1–30. Chapter 4 was published as "An Introduction to *Romeo and Juliet*" in *The Tragedy of Romeo and Juliet*, edited by Maynard Mack and Robert Boynton, Portsmouth: Heinemann/Boynton-Cook, 1981, pp.1–20. Chapter 5 appeared as "An Introduction to *Julius Caesar*" in *The Tragedy of Julius Caesar*, edited by Maynard Mack and Robert Boynton, Portsmouth: Heinemann/Boynton-Cook, 1981, pp.1–16. Chapter 6 was published as "The World of *Hamlet*" in *The Yale Review*, 41 (1953): 502–23. Chapter 8 was originally subtitled "An Essay on Some Characteristics of *King Lear*" in *The Yale Review*, 54 (1964): 161–80. Chapter 9 appeared as "An Introduction to *Macbeth*" in *The Tragedy of Macbeth*, edited by Maynard Mack and Robert Boynton, Portsmouth: Heinemann/Boynton-Cook, 1981, pp.1–14. Chapter 10 first appeared in *Shakespeare's Art: Seven Essays*, edited by Milton Crane, published for The George Washington University by The University of Chicago Press, 1973, pp.79–113. Reprinted by permission of The George Washington University. Chapter 11 was originally titled "The Jacobean Shakespeare" in *Jacobean Theatre: Stratford-upon-Avon Studies*, 1, edited by John Russell Brown and Bernard Harris, London: Edward Arnold, 1960, pp.10–41.

CHAPTER ONE

ÉVERYBODY'S SHAKESPEARE

I

SHAKESPEARE is the only writer in world literature who actually comes close to belonging to the world. Of course there are whole peoples who have never heard of him, whole peoples who may have heard of him but have never read him or seen a play of his onstage. And of course some parts of Shakespeare are more accessible than others. Still, his plays continue to be produced, occasionally or regularly, in many dozens of languages and countries on all the continents of the world. However far cultures and values may differ, there are events and characters in plays like *Macbeth* and *Othello* and *Romeo and Juliet*, not to mention *King Lear* and *Julius Caesar*, to which at least some members of any culture can respond save possibly those who deprecate all works by dead Anglo-Saxon white males.

For the many who have roots in the European tradition or have become familiar with that tradition, and most especially for those to whom the English language is not strange, Shakespeare is a constant presence. Every time we open our mouths, if only to remark that somebody *cudgeled his brains, wore his heart on his sleeve*, made an *abrupt* answer, *caught* a cold, *painted from life*, *discharged* a debt, gave a *lack-lustre* performance, discovered himself to be *fretful, fancy-free, heart-sore, dog-weary*, or about to *breathe his last*, we are drawing on Shakespearean inventions. And there are thousands more. To *Hamlet* alone, some of you will recall, we are in debt for *flaming youth, to the manner born, rich but not gaudy, more honored in the breach than the observance, it smells to heaven, the glass of fashion, hoist with his own petard, the dog will have his day, ay there's the rub,*

I

this mortal coil, there's *method* in my *madness, brevity is the soul of wit, the whips and scorns of time, more matter and less art, caviar to the general, the witching hour, The undiscovered country from whose bourn No traveler re-turns* — one could go on and on, but there is no need to. Shakespeare's contributions to our common speech inhabit us like the air we breathe.

Or consider his people. Though all of us have difficulty remembering who appears in what play, here again many of his inventions have become part of our common mental furniture. How could we talk at all about certain kinds of feminism without Lady Macbeth and Cleopatra? Or at the other end of that spectrum, without Jane Nightwork and Doll Tearsheet? Or about certain kinds of wives without Portia and Desdemona? Certain kinds of young lovers without Petruchio and Kate? Certain relationships of child to parent without Cordelia and Lear? Or even about the inequities of military service without Bullcalf, Mouldy, Shadow, Feeble, and Wart? Delicious chaps all. We may be acquainted with only a few of this teeming multitude, or with many; but those we do know, as Bernard Shaw once said, we know to such a degree as we know few if any persons alive.

Or consider finally those eloquent moments that his plays have etched on the whole world's consciousness, moments that speak to the human condition as such. So Hamlet, you will remember, stands in the grave-yard of the world with the skull of Yorick in his hand — "I knew him, Horatio" (5.1.173) — and thinking of all the whited sepulchres he has uncovered in that world, cries out with an anguish that remains as unre-solved for us as for him: "Now get you to my lady's chamber, and tell her, let her paint an inch thick, to this favor she must come. Make her laugh at that" (5.1.180).

So likewise, in *Measure for Measure,* Isabella faces the typical hypo-crite-plus-bureaucrat, Angelo, with the one argument that is morally unanswerable in the transactions of the helpless with the powerful, and the one most often heard in Shakespeare's plays — which in itself tells us much about him:

Alas, Alas;
Why, all the souls that were were forfeit once;
And He that might the vantage best have took,

Found out the remedy. How would you be,
If He, which is the top of judgment, should
But judge you as you are? (2.2.72)

Or, as Hamlet at about the same time was putting it in *his* play: "Use every man after his desert, and who shall scape whipping?" (2.2.516).

In *King Lear* there are many such moments. Let me remind you of one, when the old king, now recovered from madness and kneeling beside the body of his dead child, tries to register on his exhausted brain the finality of his loss. This is surely the most universal of Shakespeare's moments and one that every reader of these lines has experienced, will experience — must experience:

No, no, no life?
Why should a dog, a horse, a rat, have life,
And thou no breath at all? Thou'lt come no more,
Never, never, never, never, never. (5.3.306)

2

These are some of the ways in which Shakespeare presses upon us even if we have never read or seen his plays; and there are others. Often, he comes to us through his intermediaries. If tonight we go to the theater, for instance, to see a typical modern production, the chances are excellent that we shall meet with some device of stagecraft that survives mainly because he revealed its power: a thrust stage, a theater in the round, a dramatic action that flows without scene-breaks. And not only with some device of stagecraft. Here is a minute sampling of plays by distinguished dramatists of this century: Edward Bond, *Lear*; Bertholt Brecht, *Coriolan*; Friedrich Dürrenmatt, *King John*; Eugène Ionesco, *Macbett*; G. B. Shaw, *Caesar and Cleopatra*; Tom Stoppard, *Rosencrantz and Guildenstern Are Dead*; Peter Ustinov, *Romanoff and Juliet*. I cite only a few of the best known. And I omit altogether the musical stage, in which would have to be included at the very least *The Boys from Syracuse*, *Kiss Me, Kate*, and *West Side Story*.

Or suppose like the Marx brothers we decide on a night at the opera.

If all the librettos based on Shakespeare were available in one repertory, we would be obliged to attend an opening every night of the week for six months to hear all 180 of them even once — 70 of them written in this century. There are only 6 of the 37 plays, in fact, from which at least one opera has not been composed; and while the quality of many is distinctly B-flat, a rough dozen of them would have to be named in any list of operatic masterpieces: most notably, Verdi's *Macbeth* (1842), *Otello* (1887), and *Falstaff* (1893), and Benjamin Britten's *A Midsummer Night's Dream* (1960).

I will spare you my eleven-hundred-page bibliography of ballet and orchestral music inspired by Shakespeare and press on from the opera house to the library.[1] You take down your brand-new anthology of twentieth-century verse, and what do you find? Titles like "Ben Jonson Entertains a Man from Stratford," "When I Read Shakespeare," "King Claudius," "Elegy of Fortinbras," "Juliet's Garden," "Edmund to Edgar," "Cleopatra to the Asp," "Cleopatra Topless," and so on *ad nauseam*. No escape from Shakespeare there.

And none in fiction either. For you already know what happened last week when you looked down that shelf: *Brave New World, Glimpses of the Moon, Pale Fire, The Sound and the Fury, Tomorrow and Tomorrow and Tomorrow* — one blasted Shakespearean title after another, all of them reminding you that for writers in this century his works have become not merely a Swiss bank account of golden allusions and opinions, but a sort of extended credit system enabling one to imply a great deal without having to say it. How much meaning, for instance, Faulkner manages to convey before we even turn the first leaf of his story about the feeble-minded Benjy by relating it to Macbeth's verdict that life is a tale told by an idiot, full of sound and fury. Or again: with what a powerful sense of waste and loss Frost invests his New England farm-boy who bleeds to death after losing his hand in a buzz-saw, in this case by referring us through the poem's title "Out, Out" to that same *Macbeth* passage only a few lines earlier: "Out, out! brief candle!" (5.5.23).

What all this adds up to, of course, is that Shakespeare is not only witty in himself, but (as Falstaff once said of himself) the cause that wit is in other men. And, sometimes, alas, the cause that other men think wit is in them. How else account for the extraordinary number of school and college plays with titles like: *As We Certainly Don't Like It*; or again, *Katherine and Petruchio: The Shaming of the True*; or *Macbeth—a Twisted Tale from Shakespeare*; or, finally, to sup full with horrors, *The Lamentable Tragedy of Omelet and Oatmealia*, in which the supporting characters are—I kid you not—Fraudius, Postum, Baconius, Toastem, and Milk—Milk being Omelet's mother.

From the same conviction—that if you can't swim you can at least muddy the water—have been hatched also those now literally thousands of efforts to out-Shakespeare Shakespeare by rewriting his famous speeches. Some are so embarrassingly fatuous that I could only bear to utter them if I were on the Donahue show—like, for instance, "All the world's a bar, and all the men and women merely drunkards," or "Friends, Romans, countrymen, lend me your ears. I will return them next week." Or—the most unkindest cut of all—"To urn or not to urn" (i.e., is it better to be cremated or buried?).

Yet there is one specimen of this kind of thing that you might not forgive me if I failed to bring to your attention. This is the version of "To be or not to be" that the King teaches the Duke in *Huckleberry Finn*. The King and the Duke, you may recall, are the pair of rascals who share the raft for a while with Huck and Jim, stealing a bad living through all sorts of shell games for suckers in the shore towns, including the occasional recitation of bits of Shakespeare raggedly remembered. In this parody, for once, genius met with genius, and a small masterpiece resulted, not only catching the wonderful raw ignorance and appetite for instruction that characterized the American frontier in those days, but illustrating as well just how Shakespeare's intermediaries do help perpetuate him, planting the original again in our minds and making us turn back to see what it really says. Here are a few lines from that soliloquy, as the Duke commits it to memory for his evening performance—a mishmash of lines and phrases from *Macbeth* as well as *Hamlet*.

To be or not to be; that is the bare bodkin
That makes calamity of so long life; . . .

Till Birnam Wood do come to Dunsinane, . . .
And makes us rather sling the arrows of outrageous fortune
Than fly to others that we know not of. . . .
There's the respect must give us pause:
Wake Duncan with thy knocking? I would thou couldst; . . .
But soft you, the fair Ophelia:
Ope not thy ponderous and marble jaws,
But get thee to a nunnery — go!

3

Turning now to something far more important in the ways that Shakespeare speaks to us and for us, I want to touch on three particular effects of his that I call judgment, hope, and challenge. Let me begin with judgment. What I am using that term to mean I can best convey by referring to some marvelous verses by the German poet Rilke on a headless archaic statue of Apollo: a work of art the poet reads so intensely, so consumingly, that he suddenly realizes it is reading *him*, and not with entire approval. Translation does the poem scant justice, but I shall quote it in translation anyway:

We cannot know his high unheard-of head,
Where his eyes' apples ripened. Yet the torso has
Retained their glowing, as
A street-lamp might, where his gaze, not yet dead,
Only turned low, still shines. For else, the breast
Would not blind you.
Else would this stone, disfigured and too small,
Stand mute under the shoulders' lucid fall
And not gleam like a great cat's skin, and not
Burst out of all its contours, bright
As a great star: there is no part of him
That does not see you. You must change your life —
    Du musst dein Leben ändern.

It is not uncommon, I think, when in the theater we sit in judgment on a play of Shakespeare's, to sense — as in the poem — that we too are being judged. Claudius feels it, sitting at the play-within-the-play that the Prince provides for him in *Hamlet*. Rosencrantz and Guildenstern feel it too, in Tom Stoppard's re-rendering of that play as a looking-glass for us in *Rosencrantz and Guildenstern Are Dead*. The two schoolmates of Hamlet, you'll remember, wander about in a text that dwarfs and baffles them. They sense dimly that their situation abuts on a larger and more significant situation, but they fail to make the necessary inferences. And they fail again even when one of the players in the play-within-the-play stops to explain to them how the plot comes out. The king, he tells them, "decides to despatch his nephew to England — and entrusts this undertaking to two smiling accomplices — friends — courtiers — to two spies." But Rosencrantz and Guildenstern miss the point. They don't so much as notice that the actors playing the spies are dressed exactly like themselves, though Rosencrantz is moved by the sight of the player playing *him* to say: "I know you, don't I? I never forget a face."

Stoppard's intention in all this, I have always supposed, is twofold. First off, he wants us to see that, whereas the people in Hamlet's world play for keeps and therefore achieve the insights that tragic experience sometimes brings, Rosencrantz and Guildenstern content themselves with an address to life in which one creates no significance and makes no difference. When the intent of Claudius's letter procuring the death of Hamlet in England becomes known to them, they do not act to alert the Prince to his danger. No. Far be it from them to intervene in the goings-on of a world that seems continually to raise questions and deny answers.

What Stoppard asks us especially to see is that their response is not unimaginably far from being a reflection of our own. Living as we do today in a universe in which the significance of individual lives is doubted and heroic endeavor of any sort is quickly written off as a symptom of some early anal or oral maladjustment, how far are we — the play asks — from sharing their vacuity? To give life meaning requires a notable investment — in T. S. Eliot's memorable phrase, "the awful daring of a moment's surrender Which a lifetime of prudence can never retract."[2] Yet to boggle at that investment, Stoppard suggests, is to be blind to the planet-sized difference between the fate of Rosencrantz and Guildenstern as they simply vanish without trace at the close of their play and the fate of Hamlet as he achieves his tragic readiness at the close of his: "If it be now, 'tis not to come; if it be not to come, it will be now; if it be not now, yet it will come" (5.2.209). As a thoughtful critic has lately remarked, "For Hamlet, placing himself in the hands of Providence and the powers of his own resolution, there is the glory of a noble and tragic death. For Rosencrantz and Guildenstern mutely disappearing into nonexistence, there is only the vacuum of ignorance and despair."[3]

4

Yet if Shakespeare's plays invite judgment, they also invite hope. The English actor Robert Speaight speaks somewhere of an old farm woman in North Wales who happened upon him one afternoon as he was looking into a copy of Shakespeare (perhaps he was learning his part for an upcoming production: I don't now recall), and when she saw what book he had, she said understandingly: "He be such a comfort, Gwyllym, be'ent he?" — Gwyllym being William — William Shakespeare.

I think we know what she meant. After the hatreds, the betrayals, and the murders, after Richard III and Iago, Edmund and Goneril, Macbeth and Claudius, here is a man who can nevertheless close his career with a comedy of forgiveness — in fact, with four comedies of forgiveness, *The Tempest* being the last. Hatreds, betrayals, and murders are implicit in that play too, but they remain implicit, because he who might the vantage best have took *did* find out the remedy. In the end, Prospero eschews vengeance, and at a crucial moment unfolds before the play's lovers a betrothal masque, in which a company of nymphs and reapers dance. That dance has always interested me because I suspect it expresses in its own visual and kinetic terms the psychic processes that make pardon and conciliation — what Freud calls sublimation — possible. In the intricate configuration of their movements, the two groups join divine and human, female and male, water and earth, spring and summer, virginity and fruition. And their dance suggests, at least to this reader, the release of powerful opposites in a patterned act that enables them to be creative, not destructive.

8

That act also points forward, I believe, to a corresponding release at the play's end, when Ferdinand and Miranda are "discovered" playing chess. Chess, we all know, is a war-game, and that, I take it, is the significance of its appearance here: it is a war-game, a *mimic* war, strictly hedged about with rules, and thus a token of our ability, at our best, to channel our aggressions into art and play, and live for life rather than for power, as Prospero himself has been learning to do. At this point, Miranda playfully complains that Ferdinand plays her false and this, we know, is what Antonio did to his brother Prospero and what Sebastian meant to do to *his* brother Alonso. Ferdinand replies, because he loves her, that he would not do so for the world, and she replies, because she loves him, that even if he did, it would seem fair play to her. Thus the chess game, like the masque before it, has something of the character of a ritual dance, in which aggressive and potentially destructive energies are reconciled — patterned into an order in which there is no winning or losing. For in love you must lose to win, and in winning you gladly lose.

The breathtaking beauty of that moment, unforgettable when Miranda looks up from the game and, seeing so many unfamiliar faces crowding in upon her, utters the now famous exclamation:

How beauteous mankind is! O brave new world
That has such people in't! (5.1.183)

is matched by its equally heartbreaking fragility, underscored for us by the presence of so many hardened offenders. Yet it is with reference to these very people and this moment that Prospero resolves not merely to forgive, but to give up freely his special power:

I'll break my staff, . . .
And deeper than did ever plummet sound
I'll drown my book. (5.1.54)

For Prospero to come to this frame of mind after all that has been done to him — and, more important, for Shakespeare to come to it despite the unflinching gaze he has bent for twenty years on the Antonio and Caliban in all of us, ignoring nothing and disguising nothing — this, it seems to me, is hope indeed. Shakespeare may laugh or anguish at what we are, but he never loses faith in what we may be.

5

Finally, and very briefly, the challenge. Shakespeare's depiction of what it means to function as a genuinely humane and human being in a harsh and often wholly incomprehensible universe constitutes that challenge. In the comedies, this usually takes the form of an invitation to join the human race — a task not so easy as it sounds since it requires the ability to stand back from oneself and laugh. We are to accept the follies and frailties of our species, including our own, with whatever tolerance, grace, and wit we can muster — enter the game, make our bets, avoid being onlookers only, and *live*, with all considerate gusto.

In the tragedies, the challenge runs a little deeper. In these plays, there is always present some hint or glimpse of a lost or vanishing world, impractical by the standards of the world that is supplanting it, yet a repository of value beside which other worlds look small. In *Richard II*, we might call this John of Gaunt's world: his vision — half memory, half dream — of an England that bred its kings to selfless service and true chivalry. In *Julius Caesar*, perhaps it is the measured life of the Roman Republic, of whose private graces we are given some hint in the deep affection between Brutus and Portia. In *Hamlet*, it is the garden before it went to weeds, before the serpent Claudius invaded it, when Ophelia was still the "rose of May" (4.5.157) and Hamlet still the ideal soldier, courtier, scholar, "Th' observed of all observers" (3.1.154). The extreme graciousness of Duncan possibly serves a similar purpose in *Macbeth*. He cherishes and nourishes his thanes, the play tells us, as a good husbandman cherishes and nourishes his fields, and his thanes in turn cherish and nourish him. Even when he is dead, Shakespeare presents him as a rich possession: "His silver skin laced with his golden blood" (2.3.108).

But I need not labor the point. We encounter here a recurring feature of Shakespeare's dramaturgy, and one that is not, I submit, a piece of sentimental nostalgia, but a device of his imagination. In these old worlds, threatened and crumbling, or lost and lamented, he keeps alive for us, however qualified it may be by its surroundings, some gleam of human *possibility* that the progress of the play itself — always a truer image of our actual lives — resolutely ignores.

The Olivier film of *Hamlet* (I choose Olivier's film because of all the filmed *Hamlet*s his still seems to me the most thoughtful) caught this dimension of Shakespearean tragedy beautifully in its closing frames. For though in some sense ruin and defeat lie all over that littered stage, so does a sense of mission accomplished, indicated in the moment when Olivier's Hamlet falls back, dying, upon the throne that should always have been his; but indicated more significantly when, for a soldier's burial, to the booming of the great cannon, he is carried up the staircase past each of the symbols that for us in the audience both recapitulate the play and relate his experience to our own.

At the first level, you may recall, he is carried past the symbol of Ophelia, a sprig of rosemary-for-remembrance lying where she left it on a chair — a reminder that our lives too are fashioned out of memory interleaved with hope. At the second level, he is carried past the royal bed, and we realize that whatever our theological beliefs may be there is a sense in which all of us are born guilty — "Virtue," says Hamlet, "cannot so inoculate our old stock but we shall relish of it" (3.1.117) — born guilty, and into times that are always out of joint. At the third level, he is carried past the throne-room, where the murder of Gonzago was re-enacted, and where it was unforgettably brought home that it is our lot, too, to sit at a play within a play — some of us bewildered, some of us watching each other narrowly, some of us perhaps wondering whether or at what moment we shall be exposed, and some of us crying out from time to time (like Claudius) for light, light, more light. And so, at last, up into the darkness and the cold, to that shadowy castle platform between two worlds where it all began, and where we first heard those two words — the opening words of the play — which pose for all of us the overwhelming question about ourselves: "Who's there?"

And there, I think, in that question of identity, is where Shakespeare's challenge is found. Wrapped, as we are, in a riddle inside an enigma at the heart of a secret in the middle of a mystery, what kind of courage and magnanimity can we summon up for the conduct of our lives?

CHAPTER TWO

AUDIENCE AND PLAY

I

OST of the transactions that take place between an audience and a play are ultimately grounded in two familiar psychological states that I shall call engagement and detachment. To some extent these principles underlie our experience of any art;[4] but Shakespeare's handling of them seems to me characteristically many sided, as he explores their implications for the audience–play relationship, applies them to individualize and evaluate his characters, incorporates them as aspects of his style, and even, I am inclined to think, sets going at certain moments under his surface dialogue a kind of brooding debate between them, to which we are also meant to listen, as in a passacaglia to the figured bass. The subject is a large one and deserves a book. All I wish to do here is to touch on some of the signs of what I take to be Shakespeare's interest and sophistication in these matters.

Little as we sometimes may be aware of them, engagement and detachment are crucial to our experience of either stageplay or film. When engaged by what is taking place before us, we are in some sense rapt out of ourselves, snatched by the poet "To Thebes, to Athens, when he will and where" — as Pope says, translating Horace in *To Augustus* (347). As engagement increases, the spectator's passions become "raised" — I quote now from James Shirley's preface to the first folio of Beaumont and Fletcher[5] — and "by such insinuating degrees" that he "shall not chuse but consent, and go along with them," till at last he finds himself "grown insensibly the very same person" he sees.[6] If such *ekstasis* intensifies, the spectator may discover that he or she is advising the personages

13

onstage in tones audible throughout the theater, like Partridge at Garrick's *Hamlet* in *Tom Jones* (Bk.16, chap.5) or the modern movie-goer's "Oh no!" as the monster gains on the fleeing girl. The maximum possibilities of engagement do not stop there. A radio audience in the thirties, it will be recalled, panicked when listening to an Orson Welles program dramatizing an invasion from Mars. Several spectators are reported to have been carried out in a dead faint from Peter Brook's production of *Titus Andronicus* at Stratford-upon-Avon in 1955, when Titus appeared to chop off his own hand. And we are told that at a performance of Aeschylus's *Eumenides* in 458 B.C. the sight of the chorus of Furies caused several women with child to give birth right in the theater of Dionysus. The theoretical absolute of such responses is probably the case where a member of the audience leaps onstage and wrings the villain's neck.

These are curiosities. But they remind us that the playwright's task is not simply to create illusion: he must know how to control it too. Several reasons spring to mind. Jean-Paul Sartre urged one of them in his address before the Sorbonne in 1959, in which he said (deploring what he called a bourgeois debasement of the theater) that if drama does no more for us than encourage unmitigated identification, it becomes an exercise in narcissism — a means not to self-knowledge, but to self-indulgence.[7] This is a criticism applicable to much of Hollywood's and Broadway's annual product. Brecht makes a related but different point with his *Verfremdungseffekt*, his "alienation" principle, which he declares a necessary counterweight to engagement.[8] When one is carried away, he points out, one is no longer reflective: we have the experience, but we miss the meaning, as T. S. Eliot would say.[9] Therefore in any kind of drama where events not only exist as events but figure forth a meaning, as events do in poetic drama (witness Lear's storm, Hal's victory over Hotspur, Malvolio's imprisonment in darkness), an appreciable degree of detachment is imperative.

Finally, for testimony of a third sort, we may turn again to Shirley's preface, which goes on to add that in the same moment you find yourself grown insensibly the person you behold, you also "stand admiring the subtle Tracks of your engagement."[10] The essential condition of dramatic experience, and in fact the Renaissance view of art generally, has rarely been better put. The work, though composed to be experienced as a Second Nature, is likewise to be experienced as art; the mirror remains a mirror, and our pleasure in the face we see in it comes as much from the fact that we know it to be a reflection as from the fact that it is a face we know.

What the modern theater seeks to recapture in the work of a few advanced dramatists, Shakespeare's theater had as free gift from its history, structure, and conventions. This is not the place to rehearse the commonplaces about the Elizabethan stage. The crux of the matter, as we all know, is that this stage and the style of drama played on it enjoyed a system of built-in balances between the forces drawing the spectator to identify with the faces in the mirror and those which reminded him that they were reflections. There was the bare stage itself if nothing else, the open daylight, the jostling visible crowd, a style of acting that, however we may describe it from our meager information, had "more of recitation" in it than ours, as Coleridge apprehended long ago[11] — not to mention two hazards that Shakespeare himself periodically deplores, the huffing actor who is only for a part to tear a cat in, whose conceit lies in his hamstring, and the timid actor, "a little o'erparted," as Costard says of Nathaniel in *Love's Labors Lost* (5.2.578), "Who with his fear is put beside his part" (Sonnet 23). All these factors must have pulled enormously in the direction of detachment. No wonder that a situation which came readily to Shakespeare's mind in his early days should be that of the audience whose detachment has got altogether out of hand: the young lords and ladies watching "The Nine Worthies" in *Love's Labors Lost*; Theseus, Hippolyta, and the lovers watching "The most lamentable comedy and most cruel death of Pyramus and Thisbe" in *A Midsummer Night's Dream*; Christopher Sly beginning to go to sleep at *The Taming of the Shrew.*

On the other side, pulling manfully toward engagement, were the "well-graced actor" (to borrow the phrase that York applies in *Richard II*, [5.2.24]), a few props, some splendid costumes, and the power of a poet's imagination to involve the imaginations of others. An unequal contest, one would say — yet the imagination evidently held its own, and if we re-call *A Midsummer Night's Dream* we can see that Shakespeare knew per-fectly well why. *A Midsummer Night's Dream* has qualities that prompt one to regard it as a loving and perhaps even fully conscious study of what the imagination can and cannot do. In the play itself, we are al-lowed to contemplate its operations at their most persuasive, drawing us to accept the corporeal solidity of invisible and indeed imaginary pres-ences like Puck, Oberon, and Titania, and to view them, at the poet's will, as simultaneously vast meteorological forces, pert mischievous mannikins, and onstage actors of the normal human-family size. On the other hand, in the play-within-the-play and the preparations for it, we are shown how imagination can be trammeled by not trusting it, as the mechanicals do not trust it when they look in the almanac for moonshine and decide to use a man to present a wall. For them, as for Sir Philip Sidney and all champions of the unities of place and time, play and reality are so far from being distinguishable, the spectator's engagement is presumed to be so complete, that a moonlit night at "Ninny's Tomb" (3.1.87) requires a moonlit night in Athens (or still another actor), place must be constrained not simply to one city but to approximately six feet on either side of a wall, and if a lion appear on-stage, he must be accom-panied by a prologue to tell he is not a lion, or else stick his actor's head out of the lion's mouth to reassure the ladies. One wonders whether Bottom's play is not in part a wry retort to some of those "lisping . . . fantasticoes" and other formalists (like Tybalt in *Romeo and Juliet*), who doubtless sometimes sat on Shakespeare's stage or near it and com-plained that things did not go by the book. It is quite possible that Bottom's asshead was not invented for him alone.

2

All of Shakespeare's plays show him keenly aware of these processes of audience engagement, and in a few instances he seems actually to make their nature part of the subject matter of his scene. At the extreme end of his career, we have, for instance, Miranda in *The Tempest*. Watching the great storm and the "brave vessel . . . Dashed all to pieces" before her eyes (1.2.6), she clings to the assurance, as we do too when sitting at an exciting play, that this is only the work of a great magician: "If by your art, my dearest father, you have Put the wild waters in this roar, allay them." Yet she responds to what she sees with emotions whose reality she cannot doubt: "O, I have suffered With those that I saw suffer! . . . O, the cry did knock Against my very heart. Poor souls, they perish'd. . . . O, woe the day!" (1.2.1).

In the middle of Shakespeare's career, we have Claudius at "The Murder of Gonzago" (3.2). He too identifies, feels real emotions set astir by what he knows is only an image in a mirror; but because in his case it is his own image, he is so gripped by the thing it is and the question how it came there that he breaks the audience-play relation altogether and rushes from the room clamoring for light. Whenever the identity to which the theater engages us concurs nearly with some part of the identity we bring to it, engagement is at a peak. Probably most of us can think of plays or films that at some time in our lives have held for us this status of semirevelation.

Finally, toward the beginning of Shakespeare's career, we have Sly in *The Taming of the Shrew*. Even in the anonymous play *A Shrew*, but much more in Shakespeare's version, we confront in Sly's experience after being thrown out of the alehouse what appears to be an abstract and brief chronicle of how stage illusion takes effect. Sly, having fallen briefly into one of those mysterious sleeps that Shakespeare elsewhere attributes to those who are undergoing the power of a dramatist, wakes to find the identity of a rich lord thrust upon him, rejects it at first, knowing perfectly well who he is ("Christopher Sly, old Sly's son of Burton-heath. . . . Ask Marian Hacket, the fat ale-wife of Wincot, if she know me not" (Induction, 2.16), then is engulfed by it, accepts the dream as reality, accepts also a dressed-up players' boy to share the new reality with him as his supposed lady, and at last sits down with her beside him to watch the strolling players put on *The Taming of the Shrew*. Since Sly's newly assumed identity has no result whatever except to bring him face to face with a play, it is tempting to imagine him a witty paradigm of all of us as theatergoers, when we awake out of our ordinary reality of the alehouse, or whatever other reality ordinarily encompasses us, to the superimposed reality of the playhouse, and find that there (at any rate, so long as a comedy is playing) wishes are horses and beggars do ride. Sly, to be sure, soon disengages himself from the strollers' play and falls asleep; but in Shakespeare's version — the situation differs somewhat in the source play *A Shrew*[12] — his engagement to his identity as a lord, though presumably broken when the play ends, stretches into infinity for anything we are ever told.

This way of considering Sly is the more tempting in that the play as a whole manipulates the theme of displaced identity in a way that can hardly be ignored. For what the Lord and his servants do in thrusting a temporary identity on Sly is echoed in what Petruchio does for Kate at a deeper level of psychic change. His gambits in taming her are equally displacements of identity: first, in thrusting on himself the rude self-will which actually belongs to her, so that she beholds what she now is in his mirror, and he (to quote his man Peter) "kills her in her own humor" (4.1.167); and second, in thrusting on *her* the semblance of a modest, well-conducted young woman —

> 'Twas told me you were rough and coy and sullen,
> And now I find report a very liar,
> For thou art pleasant, gamesome, passing courteous —
> (2.1.245)

so that she beholds in another mirror what she may become if she tries, in the manner of Hamlet's advice to his mother:

> Assume a virtue, if you have it not.
> That monster custom, who all sense doth eat
> Of habits devil, is angel yet in this,
> That to the use of actions fair and good
> He likewise gives a frock or livery
> That aptly is put on. (3.4.161)

Petruchio's stratagem is thus more than an entertaining stage device. It parodies the idolatrousness of romantic love which, as Theseus says in

A Midsummer Night's Dream, is always seeing Helen in a brow of Egypt; but it also reflects love's genuine creative power, which can on occasion make the loved one grow to match the dream. Lucentio, possibly because identity for him is only skin-deep, as the nature of his disguises seems to show, takes the surface for what it appears to be (like Aragon and Morocco in *The Merchant of Venice*), and though he wins the girl discovers he has not won the obedient wife he thought. In Geoffrey Bullough's words, he falls victim to "the last (and richest) 'Suppose' of all."[13]

3

One of the most notable conventions of the Elizabethan theater for fostering a balance of engagement and detachment was that which proclaimed the stage to be the world and the world to be a stage. Shakespeare constantly alludes to this interplay of fact and dream, as critics have pointed out. Sometimes he used it to supply the distancing that enables us to enjoy an action without qualms, as when he reminds us (through Fabian in *Twelfth Night*) that this is only a stage play just before Malvolio's humiliation in the dark room — "If this were played upon a stage now, I could condemn it as an improbable fiction" (3.4.119). Or, in line with Brecht's thinking, he will use it to make us sit back and reflect on the meaning of what we see. Thus when Brutus and Cassius, their bloody hands contrasting absurdly with their cries of Peace, tell each other that as often as future ages re-enact this lofty scene, "So often shall the knot of us be called The men that gave their country liberty" (3.1.117), the allusion invites us to remember what kind of liberty in fact ensued. Or, he may use it to draw attention to a manifest implausibility and so sterilize its power to annoy. Edmund's scornful comment at the approach of Edgar in *King Lear* (whom he is about to gull with implausible success) — "and pat he comes, like the catastrophe of the old comedy. My cue is villainous melancholy" (1.2.130) — functions in the same propitiatory way.

However used, the effect of the stage and world comparison is to pull us in both directions simultaneously, reminding us of the real world whose image the playhouse is, but also of the playhouse itself and the artifice we are taking part in. If the traveling players in *Hamlet* solidify the realism of the play by the lesser realism of the fictions they bring to it, they also nourish our sense of the play as an artful composition made up of receding planes where almost everybody is engaged in some sort of "act" and seeks to be "audience" to somebody else. Conversely, if we sit looking down with detached superiority on the lovers watching Bottom's play in *A Midsummer Night's Dream*, because they in turn look down with detached superiority on the antics of Pyramus and Thisbe without realizing that they are watching the very image of their own antics the night before, we are forced by Theseus's remark about the best in this kind being but "shadows," and the worst no worse "if imagination amend them" (5.1.210), to understand that there is another play afoot, in which we are actors as well as spectators, and embraced by a still larger irony than our own: Puck's — Shakespeare's — the Comic Spirit's — perhaps even that "high heaven's" before whom (we are told in *Measure for Measure*) we play such fantastic tricks "As makes the angels weep" (2.2.121).

Strongly supporting such verbal allusions to the metaphor of stage as world were the stratagems of the Elizabethan theater for narrowing the psychic distance between tiring-house and galleries and pit. On the one hand, to varying degrees, the audience could be involved in the play. If the play were written for a private occasion, this might be brought about by merging the occasion in some way with the content, as Shakespeare is generally believed to have done in *A Midsummer Night's Dream*, where the blessing of the fairies on the house of Theseus probably fell also on the house in which the play was played, and on the real bridal couple, or couples, whose nuptial, like his, had been celebrated by the play-within-the-play.

Something analogous takes place in *Troilus and Cressida*, when Pandarus at the end dissolves the barriers between the onstage and the playhouse audiences; and this sort of effect could be obtained at almost any moment in a theater which took for granted the relation of personage to spectator implied in the soliloquy and the aside. Coriolanus, and the tribunes in *Julius Caesar*, vilifying the Roman mob; Henry V before Harfleur haranguing "You noble English" (3.1.17); King Lear scourging a social system that only his offstage audience could be supposed to have experienced; Prospero reminding others than Ferdinand and Miranda that we are such stuff as dreams are made on — at every such moment, it can have required nothing more ingenious from Shakespeare than optimum use of the spatial relations of his theater to bring the audience to that alert sense of participation and revelation which Joyce calls epiphany.[14]

And over and through all this, as we know, still floated the traditional theatrical notion of man (proud man!), on his little space of earth, working out his destiny between the painted Heavens of the canopy and the Hell opened into by the trap. A variant of this notion was already present in the architecture of the Roman theater, if we may believe Vitruvius, who saw in its circularity an emblem of cosmic harmony that included "the twelve celestial signs, which astrologists calculate for the music of the stars."[15] It was more deeply and centrally embedded in the mystery plays, whose subject was precisely the salvation of men, including those who came to watch and those who took part, and whose spectators, on at least one occasion,[16] occupied the same scaffolds with the angels, thus dramatizing their common involvement in the unfolding story. Perhaps the efficacy of the architectural symbolism of the Elizabethan theater had weakened by Shakespeare's time; but the sense of the player as universal man, suffering and acting as epitome of the race, was evidently still strong enough to support and give special poignancy to those invocations (and sometimes, apparitions) of the extra-human audience in which his plays abound: "Angels and ministers of grace, defend us!" (*Hamlet*, 1.4.39). "O heavens! If you do love old men . . ." (*King Lear*, 2.4.184). "Come to my woman's breasts And take my milk for gall, you murd'ring ministers" (*Macbeth*, 1.5.45). "Behold, the heavens do ope, The gods look down, and this unnatural scene They laugh at" (*Coriolanus*, 5.3.183).

4

This was one way of bridging the gulf between tiring-house and audience: to bring the audience into the play. Another way was to bring the tiring-house and all that it represented into the play. What I refer to is the habit of recapitulating on-stage, as part of the drama, elements which derive from the conditions under which plays are prepared for performance. For example, the actor's impersonation of another than himself becomes, if moved into the play and supported there by make-up box and wardrobe, the disguised character. The actor's speaking as if he were unconscious of his auditors, moved into the play, becomes the overhearing episode. In the plot of *Much Ado*, Shakespeare has seven such overhearings, acted or described, and the play as a whole may be viewed as a comic study of the psychology of perception: how the eye and ear may be tricked, and how they may trick themselves.

Though any play has the option of drawing into itself these elements of the theatrical situation, it is notoriously the Elizabethans who exploit them with gusto, and Shakespeare most of all. One is struck, for instance, by how often he places among his dramatis personae an author surrogate — either a commentator like Edgar, Enobarbus, or Menenius, or a stage-manager like Oberon, Rosalind, the Friar-Duke Vincentio, Prospero, Richard III, Prince Hal, or Hamlet (to mention only a handful) — who assumes within the play the explanatory and choral functions, or else the incentive and implicating ones, which are properly the author's. In *1 Henry IV*, these onstage evocations of life behind the tiring-house facade are extended to include the casting process, when Hal objects to Falstaff's impersonation of the King. In *Love's Labors Lost*, they include an actors' quarrel, when Hector and Pompey, played by Armado and Costard, almost come to blows about Jaquenetta's pregnancy during the performance of "The Nine Worthies." In view of the probably topical nature of *Love's Labors Lost*, Shakespeare may be glancing in this latter circumstance at some particular altercation as well known to his contemporaries as the stage tussle of the opera divas Cuzzoni and Faustina was to John Gay's, when he fixed it forever in the amber of *The Beggar's Opera*.

Typical too are the versions of rehearsal in Shakespeare's plays. In *1 Henry IV* alone, Falstaff rehearses Hal for the next day's encounter with the King, Hal rehearses Poins for the little joke on Francis, and Bardolph and his crew have been rehearsed for their part in the great fib, even to the point of hacking their swords and slubbering their garments with nosebleed. Often the variants of the rehearsal motif are less overt. In *As You Like It*, Rosalind manages to rehearse Orlando in a romantic lover's attitudes and speeches while pretending to cure him of love. Iago's manipulations of Roderigo, while not rehearsals, have something of rehearsal in them. Edmund all but rehearses Edgar in the bloody farce they are to act before Edgar flees. And Cleopatra, like any modern director, perhaps like Shakespeare with Richard Burbage, teases, cajoles, insults, and comforts Antony, until he warms and swells and rises to the roles her mind cuts out for him. "Still he mends," she says to Charmian in his hearing:

> But this is not the best. Look, prithee, Charmian,
> How this Herculean Roman does become
> The carriage of his chafe. (1.3.83)

At a few places in the plays, our attention is drawn explicitly to the most vexing problem of the Elizabethan acting company's art: how to mime reality in its grander forms without riveting attention on the inadequacy of the means. One can hardly read, for instance, the Chorus's caveat in *Henry V* —

> Where (O for pity!) we shall much disgrace
> With four or five most vile and ragged foils,
> Right ill disposed in brawl ridiculous,
> The name of Agincourt . . . (Chorus, Act 4)

— without thinking of Hal's reflection as he watches Falstaff gird for his part as Henry IV: "Thy state is taken for a joined-stool, thy golden sceptre for a leaden dagger, and thy precious rich crown for a pitiful bald crown" (2.4.362). So, in an age prolific of regal and martial grandeur, it must have often seemed to other spectators than Hal.

And then came the other half of the process. After the putting-on, the taking-off; from being Henry V or Antony or Richard II to being simply Richard Burbage. In More's treatise of the Four Last Things, there is a touching passage on this subject, comparing the man of proud estate, soon to be snatched by death from all his comforts, with the actor exchanging at the play's end his lordly costume for the shabby clothes in which he came:

If thou shouldest perceive that one were earnestly proud of the wearing of a gay golden gown, while the lorel [ragamuffin] playeth the lord in a stage play, wouldest thou not laugh at his folly, considering that thou art very sure that when the play is done he shall go walk a knave in his old coat? Now thou thinkest thyself wise enough while thou art proud in thy player's garment, and forgettest that when the play is done, thou shalt go forth as poor as he. Nor thou rememberest that thy pageant may happen to be done as soon as his.[17]

In the world that was a theater and the theater that was a world, such sudden metamorphoses came often into Shakespeare's meditations, as we know from comments put into the mouths of Richard II, Hamlet, Prospero, and the King in *All's Well*, who comes forward in the epilogue to tell us: "The king's a beggar now the play is done" (5.3.331). One is driven to speculate whether we may not possibly have a relic of such another meditation in the great scene in *Lear* where the old king is moved to strip off his robe to become like naked Poor Tom:

Thou ow'st the worm no silk, the beast no hide, the sheep no wool, the cat no perfume. Ha! here 's three on 's are sophisticated. Thou art the thing itself. (3.4.98)

Even if these words owe nothing to the reversal of butterfly into worm — the richly costumed actor into the poor bare forked animal that Shakespeare saw about him every afternoon at the Globe — they must have brought a shock of recognition to the actor who spoke them first, as they have to audiences ever since.

By bringing into the play the actor's as well as the audience's world, the Elizabethan theater could hold a fine poise between elements making for engagement and those making for detachment. Not simply because devices that drew the audience into the play were matched by others that insisted on the consciousness of artifice, but because devices on either side could be used so as to exert an influence in both directions. Use of disguised characters, for instance, which tends to stress dramatic artifice, made it possible for boys who were acting girls to become boys again, and so intensify realism. Soliloquy, which insists that we acknowledge the presence of an actor, has yet such psychological intimacy that it encourages maximum identification of spectator with persona, as Shakespeare's tragedies amply prove. Likewise, in the conditions we have been discussing, the ineradicable awareness of a man moving on a scaffold could be made to merge at chosen points with awareness of a larger scaffold, so that the dream one watched melted imperceptibly — for the time being — into the dream one lived.

5

If it should ever come to pass that an actor experienced the absolute degree of engagement to his role — say, the role of Macduff in *Macbeth* — he would presumably come back on-stage at 5.8.54 with a real head on his pike, that of the actor playing the usurper. He would have become so "lost" in his part that he failed to differentiate it from fact.[18] This is the condition attributed to Don Quixote by Cervantes, and the condition parodied in Beaumont and Fletcher's Ralph, who is so subdued to his idea of himself as Knight of the Burning Pestle (in the play of that name) that he takes the appurtenances of a barber-surgeon to be those of a cruel destroying giant. The incident is hilarious, and the moral we are evidently to draw from it, as from *Don Quixote*, Part 1, is the usual lesson of comedy: that overengagement to any obsessive single view of oneself or the world is to be avoided. In Theseus's words in *A Midsummer Night's Dream*, once a man gets into the grip of his imagination, "How easy is a bush supposed a bear!" (5.1.22). Yet the problem is not so simple as Theseus thinks. Ralph's mad mistaking of the barber-surgeon's professional identity, again like Quixote's mistaking of the nature of his world, makes a point about the barber-surgeon at a deeper level of identity, as his romance-name Barbaroso seems intended to confirm. Thus through misconception and even self-deception we may stumble into truth, and find the beginnings of wisdom in an intensity of vision the world calls mad.

Some such speculations on the narrowness of the gulf that separates comic from tragic writing are in order as we turn to consider Shakespeare's manipulation of engagement and detachment as aspects of character in action. His tragic persons, on the whole — Brutus, Othello, Lear, Timon, Macbeth, Antony, Coriolanus — are exemplars of engagement. They have an heroic, single-minded commitment to some absolute in themselves or in the sum of things, or both, to which their hyperbolic speech is vehicle; and against them, characteristically, are ranged all the personalities and forces which favor a less intransigent address to life, the tempters representing orthodoxy or expediency, for whom, also, something is to be said, and who say it in a correspondingly lesser idiom, often in Shakespeare a racy understating prose.[19] Even Hamlet, the least engaged of all the Shakespearean heroes (because disengagement is in a sense his problem), is made to seem heroically engaged when placed against the extreme detachment of Horatio; though Hamlet's detachment is likewise placed favorably against the too easy engagement of Fortinbras and Laertes. That Hamlet does not manifest the extreme engagement of Othello and the rest, but seems to stand back, withholding something, a man of multiple not single directions, is perhaps the reason that our feelings about him (he is, I think, alone among the tragic heroes in this) contain no jot of patronage. He is never anyone's dupe; there are no springes he does not finally uncover. He is, in fact, partly an *eiron* figure, one whose ironic perspective includes and encloses the perspectives of others, and his language shows it. The other heroes, hyperbolists, use the confident language of the *alazon*, the eiron's reversed image in the comic mirror; but Hamlet's speech is mixed. All but its most inflated resonances have an undertone of *eironeia*, the eiron's native tongue. For the most part, too, the other heroes support ironies that are thrust upon them; Hamlet, though sometimes thrust upon, knows how to return the thrust: he mines beneath the mines of others and hoists them with their own petard.

In Shakespearean comedy, the characters most sympathetic are those who, like Hamlet, combine both principles. But the total moral weight of comedy inclines generally toward the detached man, as that of tragedy inclines toward the man engaged. One is somewhat higher in the comic scale if one is Jaques, say, in *As You Like It* — even though detachment, as his Seven-Ages speech and his role in general show, has made him a type of comic vampire feeding curiosity on the acts and feelings of those more vital than himself — than if one is simply Silvius in that same play, engrossed by a single convention. Or again, one is higher in the scale if one is Feste than if one is the Orsino or Olivia of the opening scenes of *Twelfth Night;* if one is Puck rather than Demetrius in *A Midsummer Night's Dream;* Costard rather than Armado in *Love's Labors Lost;* Benedick rather than Claudio in *Much Ado about Nothing.* But only somewhat higher. What is really high in Shakespearian comedy is to be the Rosalind of *As You Like It,* who both indulges love and schools it; the Berowne of *Love's Labors Lost,* who can commit himself to the folly of Navarre without failing to recognize it for what it is; the Duke Theseus of *A Midsummer Night's Dream,* who is sympathetic with imagination even while skeptical about its influence; the Viola of *Twelfth Night,* who is man enough to please Olivia, woman enough to marry Orsino; the Benedick of the end of *Much Ado,* who has learned to eat his scoffs at love and marriage with a grin. To this group belongs notably *As You Like It's* fool Touchstone, who can ridicule the life of nature as wittily as the life of nurture —

> That is another simple sin in you: . . . to offer to get your living by the copulation of cattle; to be bawd to a bellwether, and to betray a she-lamb of a twelvemonth to a crooked-pated old cuckoldy ram, out of all reasonable match. If thou beest not damned for this, the devil himself will have no shepherds (3.2.74)

— and who, though he sees Audrey for what she is, can accept her like a prince in a fairy tale (like Bassanio, in fact, choosing the leaden casket in *The Merchant of Venice*):

27

A poor humor of mine, sir, to take that no man else will. Rich honesty dwells like a miser, sir in a poor house, as your pearl in your foul oyster. (5.4.56)

Touchstone is a good reminder that Shakespeare's plays exhibit foolery of two kinds, the dry and the sly.[20] This has often been noted, and the change from Bottom and Dogberry to Touchstone and Feste and the Fool in *Lear* has been credited to the replacement of Will Kempe in Shakespeare's company by Robert Armin. There is no reason to quarrel with this speculation, so long as we are aware that both styles of fooling appear in Shakespeare's plays of every date, and would almost necessarily appear there even if Armin and Kempe had never lived, for the reason that they represent the two bases of all humor, the intentional and unintentional. Dogberry's humor, in *Much Ado*, obviously unintentional, is dry. It arises from an engagement to present self and present purposes so single-minded as to inhibit freedom of intellectual and emotional maneuver, and its badge in Shakespearean comedy is normally malapropism. This need not be of the glaring type illustrated in Bottom's "There we may rehearse most obscenely and courageously" (*A Midsummer Night's Dream*, 1.2.96), or Dogberry's "If I were as tedious as a king, I could find in my heart to bestow it all of your worship" (*Much Ado*, 3.5.19). Juliet's Nurse manifests malapropism of a subtler kind when, in her effort to reproduce the indignation of a great lady at sexual insult, she drops into the treacherous idiom of: "And thou must stand by too, and suffer every knave to use me at his pleasure!" (2.4.146). Much of the humor of Mistress Quickly in *1 Henry IV* comes from ringing the changes on this style of malapropism, as she walks repeatedly into semantic traps: "Thou or any man knows where to have me, thou knave, thou!" (3.3.123). Still more sophisticated is the form malapropism takes in Malvolio, who does not misuse language like Dogberry (though he does use it at least once with unrealized equivocations — *Twelfth Night*, 2.5.80 — like Quickly and the Nurse), but abuses it by wrenching it, in the letter laid out for him by Maria, to mean what he wants it to mean:

"I may command where I adore." Why, she may command me: I serve her; she is my lady. Why, this is evident to any formal capacity. There is no obstruction in this. And the end; what should that alphabetical position portend? If I could make that resemble something in me! Softly, M, O, A, I. . . . This simulation is not as the former; and yet, to crush this a little, it would bow to me, for every one of these letters are in my name. (2.5.126)

The deception to which Malvolio here falls victim, by crushing the simulation a little, is not far different from that which victimizes Macbeth, when he too crushes to his will the riddling speeches of the Witches; or from what King Lear allows to happen when he reads duty in the flattering phrases of his elder daughters, ingratitude in the blunt speaking of Cordelia; or from what takes place in Othello when his whole vocabulary begins to shift and slide under the erosion of Iago's insinuations. Here again the attributes of comedy and tragedy throw light on one another.

At the opposite pole from Dogberry's stands Touchstone's humor, which is intentional and "sly." It therefore has for its badge the pun, which is a voluntary effect with language, as malapropism is involuntary. Instead of single-mindedness, pun presupposes multiple-mindedness; instead of preoccupation with one's present self and purposes, an alert glance before and after; and instead of loss of intellectual and emotional maneuverability, a gain, for language creatively used is freedom. The alazon shows his innate hubris by using words and the concepts they represent without regard for their properties, like a bad artist —

Dost thou not suspect my place? Dost thou not suspect my years? O that he were here to write me down an ass! But, masters, remember that I am an ass. Though it be not written down, yet forget not that I am an ass. No, thou villain, thou art full of piety, as shall be proved upon thee by good witness. I am a wise fellow . . . and which is more, a house-holder, and, which is more, as pretty a piece of flesh as any in Messina, and one that knows the law, go to! and a rich fellow enough, go to! and a fellow that hath had losses; and one that hath two gowns and everything handsome about him. Bring him away. O that I had been writ down an ass! (*Much Ado*, 4.2.68)

The eiron honors his materials and, circling them with the golden compass of his wit, marks out a world:

> Therefore, you clown, abandon (which is in the vulgar, leave) the society (which in the boorish is, company) of this female (which in the common is, woman); which together is, abandon the society of this female, or, clown, thou perishest; or, to thy better understanding, diest; or, to wit, I kill thee, make thee away, translate thy life into death, thy liberty into bondage. I will deal in poison with thee, or in bastinado, or in steel. I will bandy with thee in faction; I will o'er-run thee with policy; I will kill thee a hundred and fifty ways. Therefore tremble, and depart. (*As You Like It*, 5.1.46)

7

The intellectual action of Shakespearean comedy may frequently be read as a continuing debate between sly and dry voices, complicated, in the so-called romantic comedies, by a third voice, that of romantic convention. The pattern appears at its simplest in *A Midsummer Night's Dream*, where the lovers speak the convention, Bottom and his companions run riot through language like those dry fools of the cinema who find themselves in a house where everything they touch comes apart in their hands, and Theseus, though no jester, shows the disengaged catholicity that belongs to "slyness." For these groups in *Much Ado* may be substituted Claudio and Hero, Dogberry and Verges, and those virtuosi of language, Beatrice and Benedick. *As You Like It* has Rosalind, Touchstone, and, within limits, Jaques, for its sly voices, Audrey and William for its dry ones, and for its conventionalists the hyperconventional Silvius and Phebe (who are themselves a species of dry fool), as well as the more moderate Celia and Orlando. *Twelfth Night*'s dry fools are Aguecheek and Malvolio, who share common failings despite their differences in temperament and status and are both on the make; Feste, and in some respects Toby, Maria, and Fabian, are its sly fools; Orsino and Olivia are the conventionalists (but again with a list toward the "dry").

Patterns in plays, like patterns of nerves in the body, reward study, since they can bring to us a clearer understanding of how the organism works. But they need to be studied *in situ* as well as in abstraction, and when one puts them back into context, one usually finds them to be more perplexed than one supposed. None of the groupings just mentioned, for example, will quite stand. Beatrice and Benedick, though they have the language skills of sly fooling, become dry fools during the arbor trick. Claudio and Pedro, who participate in the slyness of that occasion, go dry when tricked by Borachio. Dogberry and the Watch, the apparently unredeemable dry fools, manage for all their maladroitness to deviate into sense: they really have, to tell truth, "comprehended" the villains, and the villains really are "aspicious" (3.5.43) for a happy ending. Similar readjustments must be made for the other plays. Nor may we even claim, always, that the voice of the eiron strikes a more responsive note in us than the alazon with his dunderhead. Aguecheek could hardly be a "dryer" fool, as Maria insists, yet there is so endearing an enthusiasm in his candidacy for the role (2.5.75) that the heart goes out to him, as it does yet more to Bully Bottom, whose dedication to something deeper than fool — to the sheer delight of being unself-consciously and exuberantly what one is, and of asserting what one is with aplomb and complacence right in the face of the forces that are making a fool of one — offers once again a comic version of the experience of the tragic hero.

As if to make the pattern still more complicated, Shakespeare sometimes claps both voices into one man's speech. The obvious case is Falstaff. Falstaff ought to be an alazon. He has all the classic symptoms, apart from being fussed by language, and during most of the first two acts of *1 Henry IV* he is "engaged" with his fellow rascals in an enterprise which purposes to expose him. Poins and Hal plainly have the eiron's position at the puppet strings as they wait for Falstaff to reach the inn, and Hal etches this fact on our attention by his sly fooling at the expense of Francis. But the joke on Francis turns out to be inconclusive — in fact, falls flat and turns against its proposer; for while Francis is confused and says what Hal has predicted, his touching deference to the Prince and generosity in the matter of the pennyworth of sugar move our sympathy.

Mutatis mutandis, the process repeats itself in the jest that follows. The trap is sprung: Falstaff utters the lies that have been predicted, but again the result is inconclusive. Our usual way of acknowledging its inconclusiveness has been to take sides in the still unsettled argument as to whether or not Falstaff suspects the trick. An alternative way of acknowledging it would be to admit that, whatever the truth about Falstaff's consciousness, this is not what the scene shows Shakespeare to be interested in. Shakespeare is interested in the dramaturgical effect of thwarted expectancy, acted out in terms of a situation that derives ultimately from behind the tiring-house facade, like those we considered earlier: the actor who will not act the role set down for him, but insists on remaking it, to the ruin of the effect the author planned.

All begins well enough. Falstaff enters swaggering, as a good *miles gloriosus* should, and apparently, with his bluster about cowards and his appeal for confirmation to his confederates (for he too has a play outlined in his mind, in which, though he has rehearsed his company, he is to find their performance unsatisfactory), is about to make an easy prey. But then, as those stage-managers Hal and Poins do not at first understand, the play goes wrong. They make the comments called for in the script as they understand it:

What, fought you with them all?

Pray God you have not murd'red some of them.

What, four? Thou saidst but two even now.

Seven? Why, there were but four even now.

Prithee, let him alone. We shall have more anon.

So, two more already.

O monstrous! Eleven buckram men grown out of two! (2.4.174)

And if the alazon would only play his part, the effect on the theater audience would be a resounding discomfiture for him, like the discomfiture of Pistol or Parolles. But the part as Falstaff plays it has no such effect. On the contrary, Hal's and Poins's speeches seem prosy, lame, literalistic, like Hal's formerly with Francis; while Falstaff, with the con-

scious virtuosity of the great artists of mendacity ("Do so," he says at one
point in his story, "for it is worth the list'ning to") (2.4.200), soars off
into the world of pure comic romance so long as the lovely vision lasts —
where he will be joined by Don Quixote later.

It is as though Shakespeare were dramatizing Hal's frustrated sense of
what has happened to his triumph, when he makes him abruptly close his
intended toying with the victim in an explosion of abuse — comic abuse,
but still abuse:

> These lies are like their father that begets them — gross as a moun-
> tain, open, palpable. Why, thou clay-brained guts, thou knotty-
> pated fool, thou whoreson, obscene, greasy tallow-ketch. . . .
> (2.4.214)

The joke has recoiled on the joker — for of *course* the lies were open,
palpable: that was the cream of the jest; and to register it now so stri-
dently, without irony, in epithets of stupidity that are never relevant to
Falstaff and least of all right now, is to admit how completely he has
lost the comic initiative. Nothing that happens later, not even Falstaff's
shamefaced "Ah, no more of that, Hal, an thou lovest me!" (2.4.267), can
quite restore it to him either. The game is a draw, because the part that
was intended for the alazon in Falstaff was played by the eiron in him;
and the eiron in him goes on to take over the play *ex tempore*, makes
Henry appear as outrageous an ass as Bottom, and meets the comic
homiletics of the Old Order spoken by the "King" —

> Why dost thou converse with that trunk of humors, that bolting-
> hutch of beastliness, that swoll'n parcel of dropsies, that huge
> bombard of sack, that stuffed cloak-bag of guts? (2.4.426)

—with a handsome appeal to charity and forbearance spoken by the
champion of the New Order, the "Prince":

> If sack and sugar be a fault, God help the wicked! If to be old and
> merry be a sin, then many an old host that I know is damned. If to
> be fat be to be hated, then Pharaoh's lean kine are to be loved. No,
> my good lord, banish Peto, banish Bardolph, banish Poins; but for

33

sweet Jack Falstaff, kind Jack Falstaff, true Jack Falstaff, valiant Jack Falstaff, and therefore more valiant being, as he is, old Jack Falstaff, banish not him thy Harry's company. . . . (2.4.447)

It took Shakespeare all of 2 *Henry IV* to overcome the effects of this, and it is still questionable whether he succeeded.

1 Henry IV furnishes as good an illustration as can perhaps be found of the complex ways in which Shakespeare makes detachment and engagement evaluative factors in characterization throughout an entire play. In the largest design, we have the obsessively engaged Hotspur, an exceedingly refined and sympathetic redefinition of the alazon, who can trick himself just as effectively in the reading of *his* letter as Malvolio does, but more attractively. Over against him, Falstaff, whose status as *miles gloriosus* and engagement in the robbery mirror Hotspur's status as honor-seeker and engagement in the conspiracy; but whose escape from the role of others' dupe in the tavern scene, and whose detachment from the war — a detachment no more adequate, however, as total response than Hotspur's love of carnage — mark him as a more complicated type. Over against both of these, Hal, the inclusive man, as everyone has said, who can be detached from the Court yet engaged to its problems when the need arises, can exhibit both detachment and engagement on the field of battle, can praise his enemy as well as conquer him.

Such is apparently Shakespeare's general scheme. But the configurations of it alter repeatedly. Falstaff, as we have seen, is both alazon and eiron, boaster and ironist. Hal, an eiron in conception, sometimes plays alazon to Falstaff's eiron, not only in the tavern scene, but during the battle when it turns out that what "will sack a city" (5.3.52) in Falstaff's pistol-case is a bottle of sack. Hotspur, bickering with Glendower, becomes momentarily eiron to Glendower's alazon. When the King adds a new twist to the eiron's habitual linguistic dexterity by what amounts to a sartorial and coinage pun (he has many "counterfeit" Henries "marching in his coats"), Sir Walter Blunt, dead, gives a new dimension to engagement, like the tragic hero's ("Sir Walter Blunt. There's honor for you!") (5.3.32). Worcester and Vernon, deciding not to tell Hotspur of "the liberal and kind offer of the king" (5.2.2), make plain the quicksands that lie in an excess of detachment. And Falstaff, leaning over Blunt's corpse, as also later when taking on his back the body of Hotspur, further deepens the drama of ambiguity and pathos that the play is making with these terms by simplifying them to mean simply life versus death:

Counterfeit? I lie; I am no counterfeit. To die is to be a counterfeit, for he is but the counterfeit of a man who hath not the life of a man; but to counterfeit dying, when a man thereby liveth, is to be no counterfeit, but the true and perfect image of life indeed. (5.4.113)

It should not be overlooked that, like the lying after the robbery, this speech is an instance of Falstaff's departing from the role assigned him. Hal utters his epitaph for a dead Falstaff, and Falstaff promptly rises to wound the dead Hotspur in the thigh. But this time the audience's sympathy stays with Hal.

8

If I may turn for my conclusion to the optative mood, I should like to express a hope that interpretation may soon take more serious account than it recently has of Shakespeare's conventions for controlling engagement and detachment in the one area I have not mentioned here. I refer to the area of style. Shakespeare's dramatic style, as we all know, comprises a range of idioms and stage techniques whose poles are, on the one side, the decisively "emblematic" moment, illustrated in such scenes as the garden scene in *Richard II* and in such vocabularies as the Gentleman's description of Cordelia's tears in terms of holy water and pearls from diamonds dropped; and on the other side, the moment of decisively "psychological" truth, which occurs, for instance, when Lear exclaims, confusing the two persons he has loved most, "and my poor fool is hanged" (5.3.306), or when Othello's tortured mind turns on its tormentor with a demand that only underlines how far its corruption has gone: "Prove my love a whore!" (3.3.359). The actual writing of any given Shakespearean play moves back and forth along the line determined by these extremes, inclining, especially in the tragedies, toward the psychological end, yet rarely touching either pole.

The emblematic style is of course an instrument of detachment. Insisting on artifice, it increases our "distance" from the stage and makes us reflect on meaning, as Brecht desires. Conversely, the psychological style serves the ends of engagement, tends to draw us in and make us share the experiences we watch, become the person we behold. I can think of no better instance of the two styles in perfect congruence than Falstaff's speech on honor in *1 Henry IV.* It is a revealing expression of Falstaff's nature, or to put the matter the other way round as an audience must, we may read the speech straight back into the man, since there is nothing in it that the rest of the play does not confirm. At the same time, it is highly emblematic in that it accords with a scheme of definitions of honor which, lying quite outside Falstaff's individual awareness, permeates the play as a whole.

Not that the styles are always in such balance as this, nor need they be. In a speech like Hamlet's "O what a rogue and peasant slave am I" (2.2.534), we are swung sharply toward the psychological pole. The lines are *more* important for what they tell us about Hamlet's inner life since it was divulged to us last than for their relations to the play's larger patterns — though these should not be missed. On the other hand, with Hamlet's most famous speech, "To be or not to be," we are drawn back toward the emblematic pole. This speech too is profoundly expressive of Hamlet's inner life, but if we begin to read back from it as though it were exclusively a record of that life, we find ourselves entangled in such a pointless question as when Hamlet experienced "the law's delay" or "the spurns That patient merit of th' unworthy takes" (3.1.73), and so on. Clearly Shakespeare judged it more important at this juncture to expand our sense of Hamlet to that of universal figure, making us hear in his words the still sad music of humanity in all times and places, than to focus narrowly on the experience of young Hamlet the Dane.

These distinctions are obvious, embarrassingly hackneyed. Yet we seem unready to draw the necessary conclusion. By mistaking the emblematic mode for the psychological, scholars and critics of surprising repute have during the last four decades set out to prove Hamlet either a villain or a dramatized version of the death-wish, Othello a miserable egomaniac who spends his last moments cheering himself up, Edgar and

Cordelia a couple of nauseous prigs, and Prospero an irascible old tyrant, with — so it is asserted in some quarters — an unnatural interest in his daughter's chastity.

No one will deny that there are episodes and situations in Shakespeare where determination of the dominant mode has to be extraordinarily nice. Just how far, for instance, shall we read Hamlet's obscenities back into his character? Or how far regard them as expressions of a pervasive theme, of which he is one mouthpiece? Is Cordelia, at the opening of *Lear*, to be judged stubborn, even a trifle self-righteous, a true chip off the old block? Or is she already an emblematic figure of Patience under affliction and of Charity which "suffereth long and is kind"?

These are tricky questions, which will never be easy to resolve. But certainly our best chance of meeting them with the right weapons is to keep resolutely in view that whole arsenal of artifices and devices, so congenial to the Elizabethan stage, which have been touched on here and which now point our attention toward a further complex interrelation — that between play and history, between the families we see on Shakespeare's stage and the actual families of Elizabethan and Jacobean England.

CHAPTER THREE

PLAY AND HISTORY

I

THE reinterpretation of Shakespeare's plays, like Tennyson's brook, goes on forever. In a sense, they were first reinterpreted by his colleagues Heminges and Condell, who gave them a new context and status simply by juxtaposing them within the covers of a single large folio, a format usually reserved for theology and the classics of Greece and Rome. Subsequent interpretations have enabled them to survive the impertinence of neo-classical rules, the rationalism of the eighteenth-century textual editors, the *O altitudos* of Romantic criticism, and the sheer clutter of the Victorian proscenium stage.

In our own day, owing probably to the fact that much of the Shakespeare industry is now situated among academics, this process has accelerated. During a bare half-century we have seen the School of Character Analysis, very much in the ascendant when I went to university, ousted by the School of Imagery and New Criticism, and both of these, during especially the last two decades, steadily giving ground to what I will call the School of Performance, since its chief tenet seems to be that Shakespeare's plays are only to be known aright in actual productions. Meantime, ever more visible in the wings, eager for center-stage, the School of New Historicism comes on with Tarquin's ravishing strides; while just to its left and right, stretched out to the crack of doom like the race of Stuarts fated to descend from Banquo, marxism, feminism, structuralism, psychoanalysis, and many a shape as yet unnamed vie for position.

All this is doubtless as it should be, lest one good custom corrupt the world. Moreover, we do learn something from each vogue as it passes, if

39

only that it is not the direct "hot line" to the white radiance of eternity that it claims to be, but only a more or less cloudy prism that, if properly angled, may refract some shadow of it. We can profit greatly, for example, by accepting the notion that Shakespeare can be only or best known in performance if we recall simultaneously that, in *actual* performance, the plays have always reflected, and always will reflect, the theater, the technology, the acting and managerial styles, and the tastes, prejudices, and expectations of the audiences of a particular epoch. This is to say nothing of the added personal particularities that divide, say, a Burbage from a Betterton from an Olivier. Successful production of Shakespeare, as every drama critic will be happy to remind us, has always depended on the effort "to harness his power to the images and self-images of the times."[21]

In one respect the current emphasis on the performed play resembles the New-Critical and psychoanalytic approaches: all three in their pure forms eschew history. The New Critics, we all know, consciously scanted the historical dimensions of a literary work in order to establish more clearly its self-sufficiency as a work of art — on the whole, a worthwhile effort despite certain costs. The psychoanalysts also scant history, chiefly because it seems irrelevant to the world of timeless truth to which they believe their insights belong. The id, ego, and superego of the Freudians (not to mention the so-called Family Romance) and the anima/animus polarity of the Jungians (together with the collective unconscious) are presumed to stand outside or above history and to be unaffected by it, like the *primum mobile* in the old cosmology.

The performance approach, though emphatically and sometimes even excruciatingly historical in the sense that what emerges from it is the reflection of a specific time-bound epoch, is likely on that account to become all the more distanced from Shakespeare's own epoch and to undercut his habits of thought to indulge others more congenial. The point was once put forcibly by a reviewer of *The Taming of the Shrew*. The play staged straight, he noted, might well seem "annoyingly archaic and chauvinistic: Petruchio would be guillotined by today's sisters, and a tamed Kate would deserve her own equal rights amendment."[22] *Mutatis mutandis*, a contemporary of Dryden's or Johnson's might have spoken in this vein about Shakespeare's *King Lear* after seeing Nahum Tate's, which held audiences spellbound for a hundred and fifty years. (In Tate's adaptation of Shakespeare Cordelia lives on and marries Edgar.) As the death of Cordelia seemed unacceptable then because it jarred with conceptions of divine justice, so the submission of Kate seems unacceptable now because it jars with conceptions of sexual justice. In either case, Shakespeare is redirected out of his world into some other.

Let me say at once that in the theater it would be foolish to quarrel with this. Though even in the theater a boundary line is usefully drawn between interpretation and manipulation, the experience of several centuries testifies that a living secular theater cannot afford to pay overmuch attention to history, and will fail if it does. The average reader of Shakespeare, on the other hand, seems to me to have more complicated and perhaps more confusing goals. If it is wrong for him or her to view the plays as historical tracts, it is equally wrong to suppose that Shakespeare's greatness lies in his thinking like us. "The past," writes L. P. Hartley the novelist, "is a foreign country: they do things differently there."[23] Reading Shakespeare, I cannot but think, has among its chief rewards our encounter not simply with versions of ourselves but with the historical not-ourselves, the Other, the foreign country; where virginity, for instance, instead of being as with us a nuisance to be jettisoned at the nearest motel, turns out to be a prized possession; or where adultery, no longer regarded merely as a recipe for getting through the boredom of a longish weekend in Beverly Hills, can be described as an act

> That blurs the grace and blush of modesty,
> Calls virtue hypocrite, takes off the rose
> From the fair forehead of an innocent love
> And sets a blister there. (*Hamlet* 3.4.41)

Poor Hamlet — of course he must be mad! — or have incestuous thoughts about his mother: how else account for so much ado about nothing? As for Othello, *he* comes to think his wife has been slept with and makes such a dither about it you might think he'd lost his ticket to the World Series.

2

So my own effort in these pages is of another kind: an exploration, even if it must be shockingly superficial, of some of the relationships, or inter-faces, as a geologist might call them, between the fictional worlds that Shakespeare gives us in his plays and the historical "real" world of Eliz-abethan and early Jacobean England. The particular cluster of relation-ships I have in mind concerns the family: both as Shakespeare shapes it for his own structural and expressive purposes onstage and as it actually existed and functioned in the cities, towns, and villages of England, and in the manors and great houses of the squirearchy and aristocracy.[24] What, one wonders, were the vital interconnections of these two domes-ticities, historical and dramatic? At what points in which plays may one reasonably suppose that a contemporary spectator sensed cross-currents between the conflicts and configurations before him in the playhouse and those known from family life around him, or possibly from his own? Or to put these questions somewhat differently and in a form perhaps more manageable, what do we know about the family of history that might cast at least an oblique light on the Shakespearean family of art?

At first glance, the family of art looks to be entirely *sui generis*. If we imagine an English county populated only by the types represented in the plays, the purposeful artificiality of Shakespeare's family world be-comes strikingly apparent. A huge pyramidal base of affluent house-holds, each widening out from some center of authority such as king, prince, duke, rich merchant, or wealthy heiress, rests upside-down on an awesomely narrow apex of what a sober-minded modern historian would call economic support services. Servants and kept fools seem to be in reasonable supply; friars and priests likewise when needed to confirm a marriage or justify a bed-trick, though rarely for devotions; soldiers abound. But there are scandalously few burghers for the county town; still fewer lawyers, doctors, schoolmasters; no field or farmhouse la-borers whatever, at any rate none identified as such (unless we suppose that Audrey, Corin, or William from *As You Like It* qualify, or one or more of Falstaff's Gloucestershire draftees in 2 *Henry IV*), and only a handful of artisans, rather oddly assorted: a butcher and a bellows-mender, for instance, but no baker, and the only cobbler in the county one who learned his trade in Julius Caesar's Rome.

Such discrepancies divide Shakespeare's domestic worlds sharply from the one discovered to us by twentieth-century Tudor demographers. Yet in some sense, of course, Aristotle's claim for the higher truth of poetry holds even here. It was in these affluent great halls, after all, that the moral authority of English civilization was sustained, at least through Queen Elizabeth's time, as Shakespeare could not be unaware. And if in his *dramatis personae* the lower ranks seem to be mostly satellites of this authority, fringe for the kite's tail, this is in fact a true reflection of their historical situation — though with his customary acumen the playwright remembers what a kite's tail is for and gives to several of these hangers-on some shrewdly corrective counterthrusts against the follies, snobberies, and affectations of their betters.

Even more remarkably artificial at first glance is the constitution of the individual Shakespearean family. Putting aside the history plays, where family constituencies are determined in considerable part by factors outside the playwright's control, one may say that if you had been born into one of Shakespeare's imaginary households in the tragedies or comedies, you would have grown up, in a statistically startling number of instances, even allowing for sixteenth- and seventeenth-century death rates, with only one parent and that parent your father. Two figures tell all. Among the seventy young people of assorted ages and backgrounds that we meet with in these plays, Shakespeare allots a single parent to fifty-eight, a full complement to only twelve; and for fifty of the fifty-eight, the allotted parent is male.

About the female parent, furthermore, an extraordinary conspiracy of silence reigns. Should your father refer to your mother at all, it would doubtless be only to confirm his own paternity — as when Prospero reassures Miranda on this score by telling her "Thy mother was a piece of virtue, and She said thou wast my daughter" (*The Tempest*, 1.2.56) — and you, on your side, would show a corresponding disinclination to inquire further. There is, in truth, amazingly little interest in either mothers or mothering in most of Shakespeare, and the comparatively few mothers who are brought to our attention as mothers, though they include such exemplary figures as the Countess of Rossillion, Lady Macduff, Virgilia, and Hermione, include also Tamora, cruel Queen of the Goths in *Titus Andronicus*, Gertrude in *Hamlet*, Lady Macbeth (a mother at least by her own testimony), Volumnia in *Coriolanus*, and the poisoning Queen in *Cymbeline*, mother of the clod Cloten. Not — one may perhaps reasonably conclude — a puff for radiant Elizabethan motherhood. The fathers in these plays come off better.

If there is some personal bias underlying this treatment of mothers, we must leave it to be discovered by the psychobiographers; but the dramatic economies that Shakespeare achieves in this way are obvious enough, and one might argue, here again, that under these surface differences from historical reality there lurks a species of higher truth in the uncompromising image we are given of the actual disposition of power on the Elizabethan domestic scene. Fathers dominate Shakespeare's stage for the same reason and in the same ways that they dominated his society. The almost total authority granted them by law and custom meant that they inevitably became the initiators and prohibitors of action, the dispensers and withholders of wealth and privilege (including the privilege of marriage), and the meters-out of unappealable decrees both wise and unwise — all perquisites of power that in the real world as in fable precipitate drama. Mothers, lacking final authority altogether unless they were widows or queens, the playwright quite understandably shears away, either in the interest of dramatic clarity or possibly to convenience the boy-actors, who must always have found it less taxing to play Rosalind than Volumnia.

One other respect in which Shakespeare's families are statistically arbitrary is in the disposition of pairs of brothers into one good brother, one bad. Of the ten prominent brother-pairs in the comedies and tragedies, the two Antipholuses and the two Dromios in *The Comedy of Errors*, and the two sons of Duncan in *Macbeth*, constitute three. The other seven are Don John and Don Pedro in *Much Ado About Nothing*; Duke Ferdinand and Duke Senior, Oliver and Orlando in *As You Like It*; Claudius and Hamlet's father in *Hamlet*; Edmund and Edgar in *King*

Lear; and Antonio and Prospero, Alonso and Sebastian in *The Tempest* —
all seven divided in the same way as the archetypal brothers in Scripture,
Cain and Abel. Clearly, Shakespeare's preoccupation with this arche-
type, returned to so often in so many forms, far exceeds its incidence in
everyday experience, Elizabethan or our own. Yet as a way of dramatizing the mystery that this ancient story commemorates — registered, it
tells us, in our very genes — the fiction of the good and evil brother can
hardly be improved on.

It had, moreover, some plausibilities for Shakespeare's audience that
are now much attenuated. The primogenitural system, giving the estate
to the eldest son and requiring no necessary (indeed, tending to dis-
courage) provision for the other children, opened so many grounds for
selfishness in the heir and resentment in the disinherited that frater-
nal jealousies and intrigues were as common as quills on the fretful
porpentine. Younger brothers, comments one seventeenth-century observer, "are often the most unnatural enemies of their own house, upon
no stronger provocation than what nature and their own melancholy
thoughts present them."[25] This sounds almost like a real-life formula for
the fictional Don John in *Much Ado.* Had the observer gone on to de-
plore the frequent indifference and sometimes active hostility of the
elder brothers to the younger, as he might equally have done, he would
have sketched the real-life formula from which the Oliver of the early
scenes of *As You Like It* is drawn. For contemporary spectators, in other
words, an Oliver/Orlando or Don John/Don Pedro situation, though
not one likely to be met with seven times in every ten, could, and did,
provide an arresting image of a serious contemporary issue, even when
viewed through the highly tinted lenses of stage comedy and pastoral
romance.

3

In the foregoing examples, resemblances between Shakespeare's stage-
world and the world his audiences brought with them lie just beneath a
surface of apparent difference. Often the relation is more direct. To return to our earlier case in point, if you had been born into one of Shakespeare's stage families, it is just short of certain that you would not have

45

been nursed by your mother, but by a supposedly more vigorous woman of lower caste, in whose keeping you would have been placed, or who, alternatively, would have been brought into your household for the purpose. From the evidence of the plays this has been the fortune of (at the very least) Richard III (*Richard III*, 2.2.30), Juliet (*Romeo and Juliet*, 1.3.67), Marina (*Pericles*, 3.1.79), the two sons of Cymbeline (*Cymbeline*, 3.3.103), Mamillius (*The Winter's Tale*, 2.1.56), and the putative father of Jack Cade, who bases his claim to the crown on the circumstance that his allegedly Plantagenet father, having been put out to a wet nurse, was thus stolen and so kept from his rightful inheritance (*2 Henry VI*, 4.2.130). Here and there in the plays, it is true, a few characters speak as if mothers nursed their own children. Lavinia, in *Titus Andronicus*, for instance, chooses to assume that Tamora's sons have their cruelty direct from her breasts (2.3.144), and Aufidius tells the Volscians that Coriolanus has whined and roared away their victory "at his nurse's [meaning his mother's] tears" (*Coriolanus*, 5.6.96). Malvolio, too, getting in a thrust at women generally, says of the disguised Viola/Cesario waiting at Olivia's gate that "he speaks very shrewishly. One would think his mother's milk were scarce out of him" (*Twelfth Night*, 1.5.154). But these are put-downs, not facts. The only unmistakable testimonies in Shakespeare to a *well-born* woman's nursing her own child (the peasant Joan La Pucelle was of course nursed by hers: *1 Henry VI*, 5.4.27) are Rosalind's witty warning to Orlando ("O, that woman that cannot make her fault her husband's occasion, let her never nurse her child herself, for she will breed it like a fool," *As You Like It*, 4.1.159); Lady Macbeth's much-debated assertion that she has known "How tender 'tis to love the babe that milks me" (*Macbeth*, 1.7.55); Cleopatra's "Dost thou not see my baby at my breast, That sucks the nurse asleep" (*Antony and Cleopatra*, 5.2.308), and Hermione's complaint, at her trial, that her newborn child "is from my breast, The innocent milk in it most innocent mouth, Haled out to murder" (*The Winter's Tale*, 3.2.98).

The conflicting evidence on this matter in the plays mirrors with some accuracy the confused situation in the times. For though the Humanists, especially More and Erasmus, had advocated breast-feeding by the mother since early in the century (the Reformers all following suit), and though occasionally an aristocratic mother would have it recorded on her tombstone that she had nursed her children herself, the advice fell on deaf ears so far as most of the rich were concerned, and indeed many middle- and lower-class families as well; so the practice of "fostering out," as it was called, continued not much abated well into the eighteenth century — both Pope and Johnson, it is well known, having probably contracted their lifelong tubercular infections from this source.

After nursing, weaning. Shakespeare's evidence on this matter is somewhat surprising. Most Renaissance medical authorities favored weaning between eighteen and twenty-four months (Queen Elizabeth herself was weaned at a little over a year), but the only actual weaning referred to in the plays, Juliet's, comes at a full three years — a far higher upper limit than any recognized by the pediatric writers (with one Elizabethan exception) from Macrobius to Nicholas Culpepper in the eighteenth century.[26] What one suspects without being able to prove is that Shakespeare is in this matter a safer guide to actual practice than the doctors (whose aim is usually more normative than descriptive), and perhaps particularly to provincial practice in the country-side where he grew up.

His age for first walking tallies better with the authorities. Juliet, you will recall, at the time of her weaning at age 3 "could stand high-lone," could in fact run and waddle all about, and the day before had taken a fall and broken her brow. The nurse's emphasis on these attainments suggests that they were quite recent, and if so, they are not such as we would today single out for comment; by our expectations, in fact, they seem rather backward. But a recent study of the ages of children at first walking in the past indicates that at least well into the seventeenth century these dates ran late, James VI of Scotland, later to be James I of England, having walked first at about five years and a child of Anne Clifford's a half-century later at thirty-four months.[27] Hence Juliet at or somewhat under thirty-six months may again conform to the experience of the time.

By this age, in Shakespeare's day, whether you were male or female, you had long been wearing a costume very like your mother's. For boys, therefore, it was a great day when they could throw this off and go "breeched," like their fathers. Mamillius in *The Winter's Tale* appears to be on the brink of this *rite de passage* at the very moment when his father becomes mindlessly jealous:

> Looking on the lines
> Of my boy's face, methoughts I did recoil
> Twenty-three years, and saw myself unbreeched
> In my green velvet coat; my dagger muzzled . . . (1.2.153)

The historical interest of this passage is that it establishes the approximate age at which Leontes should be visualized by actor and director. The breeching of a boy child took place between five and seven—never, so far as I can discover, later than 7—which means that Mamillius cannot be ten here, as sometimes assumed (by 10, in any case, he would no longer be in the care of women), but must be reckoned an unbreeched 5, 6, or 7, and Leontes, therefore, probably not more than 28 to 30. Thus at the time of Perdita's recovery, he may be imagined to be somewhere between 44 and 46, approximately Shakespeare's own age at the time of writing the play.

At any age from seven on, if you were a child of well-bred or aristocratic parents, you would be sent off to school or to another household, preferably one sufficiently prestigious and influential to be advantageous to your parents and your own future, to learn the arts and manners of "gentilesse." The commonest age for this removal was around ten. Ten was also a common age for children of the lower ranks to be put out to domestic service and apprenticeships. The upshot of this displacement— which one present-day historian calls a scheme of "institutionalized abandonment"[28]—was that about three-quarters of the adolescent girl population and about two-thirds of the equivalent boy population lived away from home during the growing years of maximum psychic change and instability, when sexual and other appetites were keenest, under no other authority than that which their patrons or employers could establish over them, often by the whip. This, surely, is what the old shepherd in *The Winter's Tale* is grumbling about when he wishes there were "no age between ten and three-and-twenty, or that youth would sleep out the rest; for there is nothing in the between but getting wenches with child, wronging the ancientry, stealing, fighting" (3.3.58).

The old shepherd's upper limit appears to derive from contemporary work conditions as well. Twenty-three is the final year allotted to immaturity in a variety of Elizabethan regulatory statutes, including the Statute of Artificers (established in 1563, reaffirmed in 1573) which calls attention to "the licentiouse libertye of youthe before thei come to xxiiii yeares of aige," complains that some before reaching that age "have three or foure children, which often thei leave to the parish where thei dwelle to be kept," and then, still on the ground that till age twenty-four a man is for the most part "wilde, withoute judgment, & not of sufficyent experience to governe himselfe," prohibits any craftsman under twenty-four from taking an apprentice.[29] The aim of such statutes was to deny the entry of the young worker into the labor market as a full adult, but its side effect was to postpone marriage and settling down till after the dangerous period of which the old shepherd complains.

4

It may be apparent by this point that the historical family of Shakespeare's day was in several respects very different from ours. The "nuclear family," as sociologists call it, where the primary bonding is between father, mother, and children, had been shaking free for a century or more from the extended kinship family of earlier times, in which the first loyalty is to the clan. Not that this transition was as clear to the people going through it as it seems to students of family history today, or would have been viewed in the same terms in which we view it. Nevertheless, important changes in the character of family bonding were in the making, and new habits and expectations rubbed elbows with older ones.

Some interesting testimony to this effect appears in *3 Henry VI*. There (2.5.55) we are shown, in a famous allegorical moment much like the garden scene in *Richard II*, a father who has killed his son and a son

49

who has killed his father, their political allegiances having differed, one loyal to the house of Lancaster, the other to the house of York. Under the older kinship family of the period of the Wars of the Roses, when this action is supposed to have taken place, such divisions would not have been typical, as presented here, but exceptional, and in fact almost unthinkable. Shakespeare has given his material an anachronistic turn, consciously or otherwise, to stress the dread disorders brought about by faction, ruinous even to the (in Shakespeare's time) sacred patrilinear relationship of father and son — disorders soon to be repeated in the real world during the English Civil War, when one aristocratic family in seven was divided "father against child or brother against brother."[30] At the same time, however, whether or not the playwright grasped it intellectually, this confrontation of fathers and sons with opposing political loyalties illustrates the intensifying individualism requiring personal moral choice that was steadily eroding clan collectivism and replacing it with questions for the individual conscience like those soon to be scrutinized in *Hamlet*.

This does not mean, of course, that the patterns of feeling by which the extended kinship family had been supported became extinct. Far from it. Shakespeare's evidence is again interesting. For in the same play in which the autonomy of the individual conscience is imaged in the divided loyalties of fathers and sons who have killed each other, the boy Rutland pleads for his life to an angry Clifford, whose father has been killed by Rutland's father, only to hear his plea answered in the following terms:

Had I thy brethren here, their lives and thine
Were not revenge sufficient for me.
No, if I digged up thy forefathers' graves
And hung their rotten coffins up in chains,
It could not shake mine ire nor ease my heart.
The sight of any of the house of York
Is as a Fury to torment my soul;
And till I root out their accursèd line
And leave not one alive, I live in hell. (1.3.25)

Senecan and rhetorical as this is, it expresses vividly the law of vendetta by which clan and bloodline become responsible for the crime of any individual belonging to them—a law that had been observed as recently as the 1530s by Henry VIII himself in punishing the whole of the De la Pole family for the offense of a single member. It was still being observed by a succession of heads of aristocratic houses during Shakespeare's lifetime, even to muggings and murders in the streets of London, where because of that city's attractions, lineage quarrels often got transferred from their country origins. The feud in *Romeo and Juliet* with its street-fighting, like the questionings about revenge later raised in *Hamlet*, had applications for contemporaries much closer to home than Elsinore and Verona.

It will be apparent by now, too, that the early nuclear family was considerably less intimate and more austere than most of those we see today. It was bound together far more by external pressures from law, custom, tradition, and public opinion, combined with the immense interior pressure of patriarchal authority upheld by elaborate rituals of deference and respect. "Laugh not" with thy son, writes Thomas Becon in his Catechism of 1560, echoing the author of Ecclesiasticus:[31]

> lest thou weep with him also, and lest thy teeth be set on edge at the last. Give him no liberty in his youth and excuse not his folly. Bow down his neck while he is young: hit him on the sides while he is yet but a child, lest he wax stubborn and give no force of thee, and so thou shalt have heaviness of soul.

With minor changes of emphasis, this is approximately the burden of all domestic advice books down to Richard Baxter and beyond. Keep your distance from your children, never make companions of them, set them a good example. If you have to beat them, remind them that they have sinned against God as well as against you so that they will understand the beating to be for God's glory; and see to it that after punishment they kneel down and pray Him to "bless and sanctify" their stripes to their spiritual improvement. For in His infinite providence and wisdom—so one apologist insists in a particularly inspired passage—God has uniquely framed the human posteriors to support blows without risk of injury.[32]

Such nonsense is happily missing from Shakespeare's stage, but we do, of course, hear sometimes of whips and cudgels, and the rituals of obedience are well observed. "For what I will, I will, and there an end," says Proteus's father in *The Two Gentlemen of Verona* (1.3.65), referring to his intention to send his son to join Valentine at the Emperor's court; and this is likewise the expectation of old Capulet when he makes his "desperate tender" (*Romeo and Juliet*, 3.4.12) of Juliet's love to Paris, and earlier, when he compels Tybalt to simmer down with a rousing blow (1.5.84). Unlike Tybalt, however, most Shakespearean children obey without the need of violence, or else disobey by stealth, and when they know or fear they have offended, kneel for pardon.

They also kneel for blessing, and out of this custom, as we all remember, Shakespeare manufactures some wonderfully humorous scenes — like that in which old Gobbo blesses his upwardly mobile son in *The Merchant of Venice* (2.2.72) — along with some of the most touching incidents in dramatic literature, as when Cordelia kneels to Lear (*King Lear*, 4.7.58), Marina to Thaisa (*Pericles*, 5.3.45), and Perdita to Hermione (*The Winter's Tale*, 5.3.119). What one would like to know is whether those yet more poignant moments in which parent kneels to child, as happens with Volumnia (*Coriolanus*, 5.3.169) and Lear (*King Lear*, 4.7.59), were ever to be found in the actual lives of Elizabethan families, or are creations of the imagination solely: intimations of a world where the comic principle of misrule and topsy-turvy becomes transformed to tragic splendor by the needs and frailties we all share.

However this may be, the deference system as we find it in Shakespeare's family of art derives directly from its counterparts in history. Like the society around it, the Elizabethan family depended for the attainment of its goals on a structure of strict obedience; and this presupposed, in turn, as Henry Bolingbroke knew so well, the maintenance of a certain ritual space around the patriarchal head, be he king or father, to preserve his person "fresh and new," his presence "like to a robe pontifical, Ne'er seen but wondered at," and his state "Seldom, but sumptuous," like a feast (*1 Henry IV*, 3.2.55).

What, then, *were* an Elizabethan family's goals? If propertied, as all of Shakespeare's families are, its chief goals, not surprisingly, were self-perpetuation together with self-advancement in either wealth or influence or both. For a deeply religious family, on the other hand, especially one with Puritan leanings, the pursuit of goals like these was complicated by the conviction that its members were pilgrims en route to a celestial destination and must therefore consistently support and edify each other in the struggle to avoid sin.[33] Some coloration from this aspect of contemporary Puritanism may just conceivably have been borrowed by Shakespeare for his portraiture of certain siblings. Isabella's behavior with Claudio in *Measure for Measure* should probably be left out of account as a special case; but Luciana, to take a simpler example from *The Comedy of Errors,* has little to say to her sister Adriana during her troubles with her husband that is not morally admonitory: no expressions of sisterly tenderness break forth to comfort Adriana in her confusion and despair. A similar constraint, though touched with somewhat greater tenderness, seems to pervade the parting of Laertes and Ophelia (*Hamlet,* 1.3.5). Each lectures the other with a moralizing zeal reminiscent in tone, though not in language, of contemporary Puritan manuals, a tone that after another century of such influence will sour into the appalling self-complacencies of the novelist Samuel Richardson's model book of *Letters* and Defoe's *Religious Courtship.*

Still, even by a family with deep religious convictions, survival and advancement had to be kept firmly in mind, and the two main ways that the age left open for reaching these objectives were successful marriage and prudent transmission of family possessions at death. To these considerations let me now briefly turn.

5

Elizabethan marriages, as we all know and Shakespeare repeatedly tells us, were arranged marriages, unless they were elopements — the latter sometimes undertaken, as by Anne Page in *The Merry Wives of Windsor,* to avoid an undesirable partner. Marriage could be entered into easily, English custom and canon law demanding only espousals *de presenti* before witnesses, with no necessary mediation by the church till James I's time, and, once consummation had taken place, any contract became unbreachable. Shakespeare's marriages — rather interestingly, since so many of his plays were written before the requirement of clerical mediation by the canons of 1604 — are entered into without exception before a priest and in a church or friar's cell, and his opinion of marriages celebrated less formally *may* lurk in Jacques's counsel to Touchstone when the latter is about to let the ignorant Oliver Martext marry him to Audrey under the nearest tree.

> And will you, being a man of your breeding, be married under a bush like a beggar? Get you to church, and have a good priest that can tell you what marriage is. This fellow will but join you together as they join wainscot; then one of you will prove a shrunk panel, and like green timber, warp, warp. (*As You Like It*, 3.3.72)

Marriage being thus readily accessible, fathers had to look to their daughters or they would be snatched away from under their noses like the wench cited by Biondello in *The Taming of the Shrew*, who got herself "married in an afternoon as she went to the garden to fetch parsley to stuff a rabbit." The legal age of consent for girls was twelve, for boys fourteen, and though we know that very youthful marriages like Juliet's were statistically the exception, not the rule, they did occur.[34] Elizabeth Manners, for example, married the second Earl of Exeter in 1589, aged something more than thirteen, and bore him a child by the time she was $14\frac{1}{2}$ — very much the performance that Lady Capulet claims for herself. True, this sort of thing was roundly disapproved on the ground that parturition was dangerous for young mothers and would produce spindly offspring; nevertheless, as Touchstone was to put it, "wedlock would be nibbling" (*As You Like It*, 3.3.71). Among the rich, six percent of the children of peers married at 15 or under in the later sixteenth century, twenty-one percent at seventeen or under; and while these proportions are statistically negligible, they represent nearly forty individual unions. Among the middling and poor, likewise, despite the control exercised on some groups by the Statute of Artificers, early marriages remained com-

mon enough to impel Stubbes in his *Anatomie of Abuses*[35] to complain
that "every sawcie boy" can "catch up a woman and marie her" (Shakespeare himself, of course, fits into *this* category), and then, says Stubbes,
fill the land "with such store of poore people that in short time . . . it is
like to growe to great povertie. . . ."[36] Nor, apparently, was the problem
confined to saucy boys. "The forward Virgins of *our Age*," says the
author of a marriage manual of 1615, addressing, it would appear, chiefly
the middle classes, "are of Opinion" that, for marrying, "*Fourteen* is the
best Time of their Age, if *Thirteen* be not *better* than that; and they have
for the most Part the Example of their Mothers before them, to confirm
and approve their Ability."[37]

If, then, Shakespeare's disposition of the nuptial age question seems
ambiguous or inconsistent, it may be all the truer as a reflection of the
varying usage of the day. In the comedies, with the possible exception of
Hermia and her friend Helena, who are evidently quite young (Hermia's
wooing, we notice, has been with bracelets of hair and sweetmeats), and
also Anne Page, who is not yet seventeen, he parades before us an unexceptionable series of young women who give the distinct impression of
being comparatively adult: Kate, Bianca, Sylvia, Julia, Portia, Rosalind,
Celia, Beatrice, Hero, Viola, Olivia, and more. Yet in Juliet's case he has
gone out of his way to lower to fourteen the sixteen years she is allotted
in his source, and in the romances shows us a sixteen-year-old Perdita, a
fifteen-year-old Miranda, and a fourteen-year-old Marina, all married or
about to be at the end of the play.[38]

For the kinds of well-placed family that Shakespeare portrays, the
pressure to marry young came, as in old Capulet's case, from the oppor-
tunity to make a good match.[39] This meant, apart from the rough equiv-
alencies of blood and breeding that all Shakespeare's matches presup-
pose, a suitable jointure in the form of an annual income to be settled on
the bride by the groom's father, to take effect at the time of the groom's
death, and a suitable bridal portion to be paid outright in cash by the
bride's father. We do not know what immediate portion Juliet would
have brought Paris (in the long run she is heir to all that Capulet has) but
we are told that the shrew Kate is to bring immediately to the man who

marries her twenty thousand crowns, the equivalent approximately of £5,000. As this is an extraordinary figure in the 1590s, about two and a half times the going portion even among the highest peerage,[40] it seems clear that Baptista's announcement of this figure is part of the joke about Kate and may very possibly in the playwright's time have brought down the house.

Similar laughter no doubt attended the bidding between Tranio (playing Lucentio) and Gremio for the other daughter Bianca; but the cream of the jest in the original text is not that Baptista's computer blows up, as in one production I have seen, but much more probably that the enormous traffic in heiresses in the 1590s is being spoofed. This was a traffic highly competitive in two directions. On the man's side, marriage with an heiress was reckoned — throughout this whole period — to be the one widely available road to riches, and to travel it successfully seems to have had clinging to it, at any rate in Shakespeare's mind, the same romantic aura of high risks and fabulous rewards as hung about the great merchant venturers with their argosies abroad.

One may note the imaginative pairing of the two activities in Bassanio's quest for Portia as the Golden Fleece (*The Merchant of Venice*, 1.1.168) juxtaposed with Antonio's investments in similar expeditions elsewhere; or in Romeo's breathless exclamation at Juliet's beauty:

I am no pilot; yet, wert thou as far
As that vast shore washed with the farthest sea,
I should adventure for such merchandise;
(*Romeo and Juliet*, 2.2.82)

or in Troilus's imagination of Cressida as a fabulous Indian pearl, in pursuit of which he is the merchant-venturer and Pandarus his "bark" (1.1.96). Possibly a tinge of these associations lingers in *The Taming of the Shrew* when Gremio bids for Bianca with an argosy and Tranio/Lucentio replies with a whole merchant fleet plus its escort: "three great argosies, besides two galliasses And twelve tight galleys." But whether this is the case or not, an electricity from beyond the playhouse crackled about such bidding in Shakespeare's time that it is useful to be aware of.

56

What one also wants to be aware of is the electricity in the lines them-selves, which likewise sometimes gets lost in modern day productions. The device of the exploding computer in the performance just men-tioned seemed to me quite brilliant as a way of conveying the element of absurdity in the Bianca contest, but it misses altogether — in fact it tends to dissipate in farce — the great swell and billowing of the Renais-sance imagination to which the playwright gives free play in Gremio's inventory:

> Basins and ewers to lave her dainty hands;
> My hangings all of Tyrian tapestry;
> In ivory coffers I have stuffed my crowns;
> In cypress chests my arras counterpoints,
> Costly apparel, tents, and canopies,
> Fine linen, Turkey cushions bossed with pearl,
> Valence of Venice gold in needle work,
> Pewter and brass. . . .
> (*The Taming of the Shrew*, 2.1.350)

This is a kind of riches that computers do not compute.

The other side of this competitive traffic was the woman's. For her, too, if she were a gentlewoman, the occasion was momentous, for the age offered no alternative career. The nunneries — "convenient stowage for . . . withered daughters," as Milton would later put it with a Protes-tant contempt — were gone.[41] Gone too was the confessional, which in the older time could offer an oppressed wife both an outlet for her woes and the support of another authority figure against her husband's tyr-anny — and sometimes it offered yet more, as we know from the fabliaux. Equally gone were the theology and cult-practices that gave a virgin life its social and moral status. Meditations on the art not of keeping but of losing one's virginity now become the fashion, as in Parolles's conver-sation with Helena, and fall in snugly with Reformation propaganda against celibacy — for "your virginity, your old virginity, is like one of our French withered pears: it looks ill, it eats drily" (*All's Well That Ends Well*, 1.1.154). By an accompanying transvaluation, the dedicated virgin now becomes the "old maid," a drag upon her family[42] and hence condemned to lead apes in hell, as the adage had it, and as Kate and Beatrice remind themselves. And the figure of the shrew — who often enough in the real world was simply a woman cruelly trapped into an unpalatable arranged marriage (or else, like Beatrice, and possibly Kate, one whose apprehension of such a fate impelled her to keep up an ostensibly invincible front), held legally and denied all those freedoms sexual and other that the double standard allowed her husband to claim — this figure edges forward into the limelight as an interesting type, worthy now of more sympathetic examination, like Paulina in *The Winter's Tale*, or even, as in Beatrice's case, of becoming the true heroine of the play.

In short, the competition not simply for a husband but for a husband one could live with was on, intensified and complicated on the one hand by the emergent individualism we have seen elsewhere, which set a high value on personal choice, and on the other by an increase in population that enlarged the number of daughters in the race but not the fixed number of male heirs to estates — so that bridal portions had dramatically to increase. From 1530 to 1570 the average bridal portion among the well-to-do more than doubled, from about £400 to about £1,000. In the 1580s and 1590s it doubled again to about £2,000, the new figures being forced by the competition of the richer squirearchy. As a result the relation between the size of the portion (the cash-down settlement by the bride's father) and the size of the jointure (the annual income guaranteed the wife by the groom's father if the groom died) took a major shift from about five to one in the mid-sixteenth century, to about six and two-thirds to one in the mid-seventeenth.[43]

The interest of these figures for us is that in one case we seem to be able to compare information that Shakespeare lets slip with these historical norms. Anne Page in *The Merry Wives of Windsor* will have £700 from her grandfather's will at age 17 — so Hugh Evans informs Shallow and Slender — plus a substantial addition we are told her father is to make (1.1.52). The jointure that Shallow offers her on Slender's behalf is £150 a year (3.4.48). This is near enough to five to one, even without the expected paternal increment, to make us at least wonder whether Shakespeare's figures may not be fairly sophisticated. Certainly, at any rate, the £150 jointure would be bound to register on a contemporary audience in some degree and would provoke either a laugh for being too outrageously high or low, or else simply a flicker of recognition. Here again, it seems to me, the gap between a reading of Shakespeare's text and Shakespeare onstage shows clearly. There is no way that the significance of this £150 figure can be conveyed, artistically, to a twentieth-century theater audience, nor for that audience does it greatly matter. Yet for a student of the text, a little attention to history can help shape the response that the playwright expected. Shallow's offer is evidently a sound one, and Anne's father is right to be attracted by it — except for the one circumstance that his wife has spotted but he has not, or is willing to overlook. "That Slender," she says, in a passage which sketches more clearly than any other in Shakespeare the material context in which Elizabethan marriages were made: "That Slender, though well landed, is an idiot And him my husband best of all affects. The Doctor" — and now she turns to Caius, an idiot yet more egregious, though in this case she is the one oblivious — "is well-moneyed, and his friends Potent at court. He, none but he, shall have her" (4.4.84).

In the upshot, you will recall, neither has her. Master Fenton, who has blood and breeding but no money, wins her because he has her love, and the words with which at the play's end he excuses what he has done sum up a position whose validity was oftener and oftener being recognized by the marital advice books as the century turned:

> Hear the truth of it.
> You would have married her most shamefully,
> Where there was no proportion held in love.
> The truth is, she and I, long since contracted,
> Are now so sure that nothing can dissolve us.
> Th' offense is holy that she hath committed,
> And this deceit loses the name of craft,
> Of disobedience, or unduteous title,
> Since therein she doth evitate and shun
> A thousand irreligious cursèd hours

Which forcèd marriage would have brought upon her.
(*The Merry Wives of Windsor*, 5.5.207)

6

Shakespeare's role in these anatomies of mating was, one supposes, like the role of art for the Renaissance generally, *dulce et utile*, both entertaining and doctrinal. Viewed in one light, what he brought his audiences was escape into a golden world, where colliding aims could be adjusted amiably with respect for personal choice, as by Theseus in *A Midsummer Night's Dream*. Or where the stratagems of youth triumphed and were accepted by parents with a certain grace, as in *The Taming of the Shrew* and *The Merry Wives of Windsor*. Or where the father's will, quite literally in this case a will, bears the magical attribute of yielding only to the suitor who is also loved, as in *The Merchant of Venice*. Cheek by jowl with this, however, he brought a pervasive sanity of outlook and a humorous acceptance of human limitations such as intelligent participation in the personal relations of the *real* world also required. It would have been hard, surely, for a spectator to leave a performance of any of his comedies, even the earliest, without an exhilaratingly renewed consciousness of the illusions and enchantments of falling in love, the obscurity and complexity of the motives involved in giving oneself or being given to another, and the enormous risks and rewards of that commitment.

As much may be said of the tragedies, though in them the subject-matter shifts to husbands and wives, or parents and children, and the action darkens to include adultery, suicide, and murder. In both forms he holds up before his patrons some of their most cherished stereotypes and invites them, if they have eyes to see, to see. Women, urges the popular preacher Henry Smith in his *A Preparative to Marriage* of 1591, speaking for the vast majority of contemporary moralists, non-Puritan as well as Puritan, should be silent and obedient, and should stay at home.[44] Consciously or not, Shakespeare appears to be laughing this kind of stereotype out of court in *The Merry Wives of Windsor*. Mistress Page — with the full approval of her husband, says Mistress Quickly admiringly — is free to "Do what she will, say what she will, take all, pay all, go to bed when she list, rise when she list, all is as she will. And truly she deserves it; for if there be a kind woman in Windsor, she is one" (2.2.107). Mistress Ford has not the same degree of confidence from her husband, but goes her merry ways nonetheless, as great a talker and gadabout as her friend Mistress Page, and as great an offense to contemporary notions of what a good wife should be. In Coriolanus's wife Virgilia, on the other hand, we meet with a woman who is almost a paradigm of Elizabethan middle-class canons of wifely behavior, presented with great sympathy and obviously in somewhat favorable contrast to her witty but brittle and gossipy friend Valeria, in whose mouth "housekeepers" and "stitchery" seem to be primarily terms of disdain. In Shakespeare's book there are plainly as many ways of being a woman as there are women — an attitude that must have seemed to those who stopped to think about it a social revolution in itself.

Doctrinal, too, I am inclined to think, is the circumstance that the plays contain so few disloyal wives — the fear of cuckoldry being the great bogeyman that it was — and so many loyal ones. Loyal, moreover, like Mistress Ford, Desdemona, Hermione, and Imogen, in the most trying circumstances. The misguided outbursts of their husbands echo rather closely in substance, it is true, traditional indictments found in misogynistic literature from the Church Fathers down; and possibly, as one recent commentator argues, Shakespeare as a master showman was not above providing this kind of gratification for some parts of his audience. But the important point, of course, is precisely that the outbursts are misguided; the husbands are wrong.

Moreover, they are responding with what is essentially a stereotypical passion, however brilliantly expressed, to the most stereotypical of the anxieties to which the double standard gave rise. "Chastitie," Vives had urged in his *Instruction of a Christian Woman*,[45] "is the principall vertue of a woman, and counterpeyseth with al the reste: if shee have that, no man wyll loke for anie other: and if she lacke that, no man wyll regarde other."[46] Though Shakespeare knows this attitude well enough and sets as much store by sexual fidelity as he does by all the other loyalties, civilities, and restraints that differentiate men and women from animals, the form of fidelity he values most obviously transcends the physical and applies equally to men and women. What Portia expects from Brutus, by reason of "that great vow Which did incorporate and make us one" is his companionship and total trust, as if she were his second self:

> Am I your self
> But, as it were, in sort or limitation?
> To keep with you at meals, comfort your bed,
> And talk to you sometimes? Dwell I but in the suburbs
> Of your good pleasure? If it be no more,
> Portia is Brutus' harlot, not his wife.
> (*Julius Caesar,* 2.1.282)

That this same ideal should appear in Shakespeare's earliest play, *The Comedy of Errors*, gives it, I think, an added significance. If you play me false, Adriana says to Antipholus of Syracuse, thinking him her husband, I shall be as stained by your adultery as if I had committed the act myself:

> How comes it now, my husband, O, how comes it,
> That thou art then estrangèd from thyself?
> Thyself I call it, being strange to me,
> That, undividable, incorporate,
> Am better than thy dear self's better part.
> Ah, do not tear away thyself from me! . . .
> For if we two be one, and thou play false,
> I do digest the poison of thy flesh,
> Being strumpeted by thy contagion.
> (2.2.118, 141)

Yet this is also the playwright who could create in Cleopatra the *ultima Thule* of the strumpet and enchantress type, transforming it from a man-destroying Radigund or Circe figure to a vulnerable woman— "commanded By such poor passion as the maid that milks And does the meanest chares" (4.15.76)— and allowing it, up to a point, to declare and vindicate itself against the cool Octavia and the prurient gossips and the unforgiving self-righteousness of Puritan Rome. Whatever Shakespeare may have intended by this virtuoso performance, it could only have been achieved by a mind skeptical everywhere of cultural stereotypes and sensitive to, though not necessarily abstractly conscious of, the changes in outlook in his own time that would gradually make it possible for a play to be written called *All for Love: or, The World Well Lost*, and for an epic poem to be written about a "Paradise within thee, happier far."

7

In *The Taming of the Shrew*, after he has been outbid by Tranio impersonating Lucentio, Gremio turns to face him and expresses doubt that Lucentio's father will make good on the lavish promises just made to Baptista in his name.

> Sirrah young gamester, your father were a fool
> To give thee all and in his waning age
> Set foot under thy table. Tut, a toy!
> An old Italian fox is not so kind, my boy.
> (2.1.402)

Though Shakespeare cannot have been aware of it at the time, Gremio's "Your father were a fool To give thee all" points forward to another "old kind father, whose frank heart gave all." It also points outward. For if marriage was the next to commonest means by which property changed hands in Shakespeare's time, inheritance was the commonest, and the question of how best to pass on what one had, and when, was a live issue for all classes except the poorest and those among the rich whose estates were strictly entailed on the male heir. Then as now many a man longed like Lear to shake all cares and business from his age, conferring them on younger strengths, but for a variety of reasons found it impolitic to do so. Contemporary attitudes, as Keith Thomas has pointed out, show "an underlying hostility toward those who opted out of the economic process and a reluctance to devote much of society's limited resources to their maintenance":[47] a hostility that seems certain to reappear in the industrialized countries of our own day as aging populations on Social Security or other forms of national support become an increasing burden to the lessening populations still at work.

In Shakespeare's time, resentment against the old could spring from other causes as well. The work system was rigged, as we have seen already, to delay full participation in it by the young, and other age requirements advanced as the century wore on. The age of first communion rose from infancy to between twelve and fourteen. The legal age of majority moved upward from twelve and fourteen toward twenty-one. Even twenty-one came under strain from the civil lawyers who favored the Roman law majority of twenty-five. Moreover, it was the elderly — men in their forties, fifties, sixties — who were visibly entrenched in the seats of power, no less in the villages than in Parliament, the Courts, or Privy Council. To a youth looking about him with appraising eyes in the first decade of the new century, oppression by the elderly — who made up a very much smaller part of the total population then than now — must have seemed very real, a case of the tail wagging the dog, and the grumblings he had just heard in the new play at the Globe could easily have elicited a warm degree of understanding even if not approval.

> This policy and reverence of age makes the world bitter to the best of our times; keeps our fortunes from us till our oldness cannot relish them. I begin to find an idle and fond bondage in the oppression of aged tyranny, who sways, not as it hath power, but as it is suffered. (*King Lear*, 1.2.45)

There were other stresses of course. Many that exist always between youth and crabbed age were aggravated under Elizabeth by social and religious change. The natural scorn that vigor often feels for decay, particularly for the old "fuddy-duddy" (to whom a shorter term beginning with the same letter is now more usually applied) was sharpened during this period by wider dissemination and improvement of schooling to the point at which it was easy for a successful child on the make, like Launcelot Gobbo, to look down patronizingly on the ignorance of his parent and, as he says, "try confusions with him" (*The Merchant of Venice*, 2.2.33). It was evidently this sort of role-reversal that decided a schoolmaster of Henry Peacham's never to "teach any Scholler he had, further than his Father had learned before him," lest the sons should prove "saucy rogues" and "controule" their fathers.[48]

On similar intellectual grounds the early offspring of the English Reformation felt privileged to mock their parents: "My father," said one, "is an old doting foole and will fast upon the fryday, and my mother goeth alwayes mumbling on her beades. But you shall se me of another sorte, I warraunt you."[49] This catches the tone and almost the substance of Edmund's sneer at Gloucester's belief in "These late eclipses." As the dissenting sects multiplied, such attitudes multiplied with them: "If there were any good to be done in these days," Henry Smith assured his congregation, "it is the young men that must do it; for the old men are out of date, their courage stoops like their shoulders, their zeal is withered like their brows, their faith staggereth like their feet, and their religion is dead before them."[50]

As for some of the other defects that overtake the ancientry, these were found as disgusting, or at least as off-putting, as they have been in every period. "Their eyes purging thick amber and plumtree gum," complains Hamlet, out of Juvenal (*Hamlet*, 2.2.197). "Their spittings, coffings, froward dispositions, So irksome are," adds a poem of 1639.[51] "Has any man," asks a preacher in 1613,

> ever seene a poore aged man live at curtesie, in the house of his sonne with his daughter in law? doth not the good father in a short time, either by his coughing or spitting or teastiness or some sooneseene untowardnesse or other, become troublesome, either to his owne sonne or to his nice daughter in law with continuing so long chargeable & so much waited on, or to the children, with taking up their roome at the fire, or at the table, or to the servants, while his slow eating doth scant their reversions.[52]

The moral of such anecdotes, naturally enough, was, Be careful how you give away your property before death. The formal transfer of material resources by parents, advises a modern sociological handbook, "weakens their control over the junior generation, with the possible result of neglect or nonsupport";[53] or, as in the Renaissance any fool knew, "fathers that bear bags Shall see their children kind" (*King Lear*, 2.4.48). Any fool, but not necessarily every wise man. Sir Robert Plumpton, for instance, drew up in 1516 an indenture with his son and heir William Plumpton by which Will was to have "ordering and charge of all the houshold and goods therto longing, and his said father, and my lady his wife, to take their ease and rest at the proper costs and charges of the said Will." In addition, Will was to retain "al such servants as he thinks necessary or profitable for the wele of the said house except that the said Sir Robert his fader shall have three at his own pleasure, such as he will apointe."[54]

How the Plumpton experiment worked out we do not know, but it is recorded that Sir William Lisle in the mid-seventeenth century met his end in a single "nasty chamber, being all his son would allow him for his men, horses, dogs, provisions, and for the cooking of them."[55] Two stories, two centuries apart, will indicate how deeply ingrained in popular thought the apprehension of such an end at the hands of one's heir had become. One is an *exemplum* from a Middle English sermon, probably late fourteenth century, which tells of a rich man who married off his daughter and gave with her to his son-in-law his goods, his house, and all his land to provide for his support in future. The first year, his son-in-law

sett hym at is owne dische, and clothed hym in ys owne clothinge. And the second yere he sett hym at the ende of is borde, and suffred hym to fare sumwhat wers than he dud hym-selfe, both of mete and of clothe. And the thrid yere he sett hym with is children in the flore at the harthes ende; and the chambur that he leye in he seid that he muste nedes owt ther-of, for is wiff moste lie ther-in to that she were delyvered of hure child. And undur this coulour he put the old man owte of is chambur and in a lytill hows at the utmaste gate, ther he made hym for to lie.[56]

The other story is from *Pasquil's Jests*, published in 1604, only a year or two before *King Lear* was composed. This time it is to his own son that the old man gives all he has:

After the deed of gift was made, awhile the olde man sat at the upper end of the table; afterwards, they set him lower, about the middle of the table; next, at the tables end; and then, among the

66

servants; and, last of all, they made him a couch behind the doore
and covered him with olde sackcloth, where, with grief and sorrow,
the olde man dyed. When the olde man was buried, the young
man's eldest child sayd unto him: "I pray you, father, give me this
olde sackcloth." "What wouldst thou doe with it?" sayd his father.
"Forsooth," sayd the boy, "it shall serve to cover you, as it did my
old graundfather."[57]

My point is not, of course, that Shakespeare had all or any of these
episodes in mind when writing *King Lear*, though the gradualism of the
old man's humiliation in the two stories just recounted perhaps indicates
the existence of a formula that may have been influential in the framing
of Acts I and II. My point is simply that for an audience of contemporaries, much in the experience of the play was certain to come home with
the pang of familiar and homely truth, even though raised to the grandeur of a tragic parable. Thus what evidence we have suggests that,
beneath the elaborate rituals of respect, many of the young in Elizabeth's
and James's time were capable of entertaining such feelings of resentment as Edmund voices, even if not ordinarily accompanied by his homi-
cidal intentions; and that many of the old, for whatever psychological
reasons, behaved as tyrannically as Lear does — or Egeus in *A Midsummer Night's Dream* for that matter — when at last set free by seniority or
status from the yoke that they themselves had worn.

Thus, too, it need not have been impossible for a Jacobean spectator
to view the literal love-test from the source-play with which the tragedy
begins as a piece of dramatic shorthand, standing for all those efforts by
which, in his own family or in others, he had seen the very old seek
assurances of affection, longed for all the more, no doubt, when least
deserved. Perhaps he could also recognize in the old king's intuitions of a
world coming apart at the seams a similar fusion of the homely and
grand: on the one hand, an ancient father's querulous response to losses
of authority and power, including his own physical and mental power,
enlarged by vanity and terror to cosmic scope; on the other, a probing at
the profoundest level of those family and human-family bonds which,

while they hold, prevent humanity from preying on itself, like monsters of the deep.

I have often wondered, indeed, considering the prominence in this play of actions of ignoble obedience and servility set over against actions of noble disobedience and independence, whether it may not have seemed to a particularly thoughtful spectator that he was watching a critique of the entire contemporary structure of authority from the monarch to the patriarch — and moreover, as we see probably much more clearly than Shakespeare's audience could, of all authority as such: a tragic critique because the playwright knows that authority is not dispensable even in a world where parent has learned to kneel to child. There must always be someone who can "Rule in this realm, and the gored state sustain."

But these are speculations, nothing more. All that I would claim for certain is that here, as in his other plays, Shakespeare keeps up an elusive but fascinating traffic between the world of history and the world of art, the reality of the life around him and his re-visions of that life onstage. To the latter it is time to give some attention.

CHAPTER FOUR

THE AMBIGUITIES OF

Romeo and Juliet

I

Shakespeare's re-visioning of love in *Romeo and Juliet* owes much of its continuing popularity to variety. In mood and plot a tragic work, presenting with a rare sympathy the ecstatic passion of two very young lovers doomed by a combination of impetuousness, bad luck, and the total incomprehension of their families and friends, the play offers at the same time many of the attractions of high comedy. The characters are individualized, it is true, well beyond the usual comic types; but they show nonetheless some recognizable blood-ties with the kinds of people we expect to meet with in stage and film comedy: the Beautiful Ingenue, the Convention-Ridden Parents including the Irascible Father, the Parent-Approved Suitor, the Dashing Romantic Suitor, the Male Confidant and Female Confidante, the Bumbling Well-Meaning Counselor, and the rest.

In the great majority of its scenes, moreover, the play keeps firmly before us a detached comic perspective on events whose tragic intensities we are simultaneously being asked to share. This is the case for nearly all the lovers' scenes, where our sympathy for their rapture or peril is likely to be qualified by a certain amusement at their total self-absorption. It is also true of the two scenes, frequently misunderstood by critics though rarely by audiences, in which the lovers respond, successively, with embarrassingly exaggerated rhetoric, to the new circumstance of Tybalt's death and Romeo's banishment (3.2–3). No rhetoric that Shakespeare meant us to take seriously would have been accompanied, we may be sure, by (in Juliet's case) the hilarious obbligato of the

Nurse as she tries to escalate to the upper registers of romantic grief—
"Ah, weraday! he's dead, he's dead, he's dead!" (3.2.37) and (in Romeo's
case) by the irrelevant relevancies of the Friar. The Friar's fussy moral-
ism as he flutters about the prone body of his hysterical charge, trying
with wise saws and edifying examples to poultice a wound inaccessible to
any verbal comforts, let alone these, is as laughable in its way as the
adolescent antics that call it forth. Audiences sense this instinctively.
Though their hearts may go out to the lovers in their helplessness, they
laugh at everyone concerned—and they should. No one knew better
than the author of *A Midsummer Night's Dream* (written either just before or just after *Romeo and Juliet*) that young love, even in anguish, can
be extremely funny as well as, on occasion, breathtakingly beautiful.

Even more complicated feelings arise during the Capulets' mourning
for Juliet (4.5). On the one hand, our knowledge that they are not be-
reaved in fact makes for a detachment in our attitudes that is only in-
creased by the comic fluency, not to mention the imaginative barrenness,
of their grief: "But one, poor one, one poor and loving child" (4.5.46)—
"O day, O day, O day! O hateful day!" (4.5.52)—"O love! O life! Not
life, but love in death!" (4.5.58). On the other hand, we can hardly help
compassionating in some degree a sense of loss that we know is real for
them, and this compassion is inevitably deepened by what we sense or
know they have in store. Comic now, this grief ironically looks forward
to the tragic grief to come. Such episodes create a tragicomic texture for
the play in which fooling is almost as much at home as feeling, and in
which each way of looking at the world casts light upon the other.

Yet more important than these comic elements in the play's total
effect is its incorporation of romance—meaning by romance the conventions and value systems of popular romantic fiction. The very fact
that the tragedy depicted is a tragedy of lovers must have emphasized for
its first audiences that its deepest roots lay in romance, not tragedy; for
true tragedy, Elizabethan pundits never tired of declaring, should deal
with graver matters than love—with the fall of princes or the errors and
sufferings of actual historical men and women in high place. Shakespeare's venture in conceiving *Romeo and Juliet* as a tragedy was therefore

in some degree an innovation, possibly an experiment. Instead of personages on whom the fate of nations depended, it took for its hero and heroine a boy and girl in love; and instead of events accredited by history, its incidents were culled from the familiar props of the romantic tall tale: deadly feuds, masked balls, love-at-first-sight, meetings and partings by moonlight and dawn, surreptitious weddings, rope-ladders, sleeping potions, poison, reunions in the grave — an intoxicating mix!

Furthermore, having decided to make young love his theme, Shakespeare went all the way. His only source — a long narrative poem by Arthur Brooke called *The Tragicall Historye of Romeus and Juliet*[58] — had used its romantic yarn to carry a sober moral. "To this ende (good Reader)," Brooke tells us in his preface, "is this tragicall matter written":

> to describe unto thee a coople of unfortunate lovers, thralling themselves to unhonest desire, neglecting the authoritie and advise of parents and frendes, conferring [i.e. keeping] their principall counsels with dronken gossyppes [like the Nurse], and superstitious friers (the naturally fitte instrumentes of unchastitie) [Brooke shows marked hostility throughout his poem to the institutions of Roman Catholicism], attemptyng all adventures of peryll, for th' attaynyng of their wicked lust, usyng auricular [i.e. aural] confession (the key of whoredome, and treason) for furtherance of theyr purpose, abusyng the honorable name of lawefull mariage to cloke the shame of stolyn contracts, [and] finallye, by all means of unhonest lyfe, hastyng to most unhappye death.

In the poem itself, Brooke shows more sympathy with his young lovers than this prefatory warning would lead us to expect; but, for all that, their affair remains in his telling largely what it had been in several earlier tellings in Italian prose: a pathetic but commonplace attachment, memorable mainly for the sensational incidents and bizarre ironies of mischance with which it is entwined. Only in Shakespeare's hands did the love-story itself become the lyrical celebration of youthful passion that we all associate with the names of Romeo and Juliet today.

THE AMBIGUITIES OF *ROMEO AND JULIET*

2

Certainly, nowhere in literature has such passion been more winningly —
and more flatteringly — portrayed. Juliet is given by her creator, besides
beauty, a loving woman's selfless devotion together with a child's direct-
ness, and both qualities remain undimmed to the end:

> My bounty is as boundless as the sea,
> My love as deep. (2.2.133)

> O churl! drunk all, and left no friendly drop
> To help me after? (5.3.163)

Romeo, though much more self-conscious than she, is provided with an
energy of imagination that, once he has met Juliet, a genuine high passion kindles into bursts of adoration that no one who has been in love
easily forgets:

> O, she doth teach the torches to burn bright!
> It seems she hangs upon the cheek of night
> As a rich jewel in an Ethiop's ear — (1.5.44)

> Do thou but close our hands with holy words,
> Then love-devouring death do what he dare. (2.6.6)

> O my love! my wife!
> Death, that hath sucked the honey of thy breath,
> Hath had no power yet upon thy beauty.
> Thou art not conquered. Beauty's ensign yet
> Is crimson in thy lips and in thy cheeks,
> And death's pale flag is not advancèd there. (5.3.91)

The transforming effects of love are further evidenced in the fact that
it brings both lovers whatever personal maturity their short lives allow
them to attain. Under its strong direction, Juliet advances swiftly from
the little-girl naiveté of her first responses to the idea of marriage ("It is
an honor that I dream not of" 1.3.66), then through deceptions and
stratagems and thence to her cry of physical longing as she waits for the
horses of the sun to bring night and night to bring Romeo: "Gallop

apace, you fiery-footed steeds" (3.2.1). From there it is yet another giant step to the choice that her resolution to remain "an unstained wife to my sweet love" (4.1.88) requires of her, yet she makes it without an instant's hesitation or regret: "If all else fail, myself have power to die" (3.5.244).

Romeo, who has further to go than she, begins more derivatively. His love-melancholy at the play's opening is obviously in some part a pose. It evidently gives him pleasure to see himself in the role of Disappointed Suitor, Victim of a Cruel Cruel Maid, and he accordingly acts out for his friend Benvolio most of the attitudes that in his time were supposed to accompany that role—sleeplessness, avoidance of company, lassitude, despair—not forgetting the voguish language of antitheses, paradoxes, and strained metaphors that he voices in his first explosion about the feud and his frustrated love for Rosaline:

> Why then, O brawling love, O loving hate,
> O anything, of nothing first create!
> O heavy lightness, serious vanity,
> Misshapen chaos of well-seeming forms,
> Feather of lead, bright smoke, cold fire, sick health,
> Ever- Still-waking sleep, that is not what it is! (1.1.174)

What Shakespeare shows us in such speeches is a young man more interested in parading his symptoms than in the cure of his disease.

Thanks, however, to the feelings set aglow in him by Juliet, all this changes. From preoccupation with his symptoms, he rises to raptures that are real even if excessively self-conscious in the so-called first balcony scene ("How silver-sweet sound lovers' tongues by night" 2.2.166), and later to the tenderly insistent realism of his replies to Juliet during the second balcony scene:

> Night's candles are burnt out, and jocund day
> Stands tiptoe on the misty mountain-tops. (3.5.9)

Now it is she, not he, who longs to linger in the flattering dream: "Yond light is not daylight; I know it, I."

Then follows his lonely encounter with the apothecary: "I sell thee

poison; thou hast sold me none" (5.1.83). This, more than any other episode, seems to mark symbolically Romeo's coming of age. Its function in
the play is much like that of similar encounters in folktale and romance
where the hero shows his worthiness by attaching value to some unpre-
possessing gift or secret obtained from a sinister old man or woman.
Certainly Romeo's emphatic rejection here of gold — not only, as he puts
it, "poison to men's souls," but an appropriate emblem of all the mate-
rialists in the play who would make love serve their ends — constitutes
his ultimate accreditation as a romantic hero. This is only confirmed by
his recognition that poison is for him "cordial and not poison" since by
its means he will "lie . . . tonight" with Juliet in senses earlier unim-
agined.

   Though Shakespeare allows to neither of his protagonists in this play
the full tragic realization of what has happened to them that he will allow
such later figures as Hamlet and Othello, much less any anguished questionings about their own contribution to it, both do eventually reach a
maturity of feeling, if not of understanding, that was not theirs at the
play's beginning.

   Of climactic significance in this exaltation of romantic love is the fact
that the lovers are permitted to maintain, in the face of all the influences
that might corrupt or compromise it, an absolute integrity of devotion to
each other, and to express it with a lyricism untouched by the playful
cynicism or teasing sexual badinage so often indulged by Shakespeare's
lovers elsewhere. That the play has been unfailingly popular through so
many centuries onstage (as well as, nowadays, in several film versions)
may be traced in some part to this fact. Audiences respond to this love-
story as to an exemplum, a model, an ideal. And though the vision it
delineates has about as much resemblance to our ordinary human grop-
ings in these areas as the Aphrodite of Praxiteles to the efforts of a
pottery class, the effect is all the more ingratiating on that account.
"Here" — we can tell ourselves, knowing full well that we doubt as we tell
it — "is young love realized in its full delicacy, the slim bright edge of the
new moon: here is what the experience of first love ought to be, can be, at
rare moments perhaps has been — for others if not for us: *vivat Eros!*"

3

Around this idealized love-affair Shakespeare sets swirling a host of competing ideas, giving each its own idiom. Sampson and Gregory, for instance, with their crude talk of maidenheads, weapons, pretty pieces of flesh and the like, announce a cluster of attitudes in which love appears mainly as a form of male aggressiveness: "I will push Montague's men from the wall and thrust his maids to the wall" (1.1.15). Soon after this, when the noise of the street-brawl (verbal aggression having exploded into physical aggression) subsides, we hear Romeo and Benvolio discussing the inaccessibility of Rosaline. Here we have the other side of the coin — not male aggression but female coquetry carried to the point of tyranny and in its pride rejecting not simply Romeo's advances but all advances: "She hath forsworn to love" (1.1.221).

The idiom now is Petrarchan — drawn, that is to say, from a tradition of images and poetic conventions that goes back ultimately to poems addressed by the Italian poet Petrarch to a woman named Laura, whom (for what reasons is not clear) he was content to worship from afar. Over the centuries, it had become a standard literary love-language, used most often, as in Petrarch's case, to explore and express the emotions involved in a lover's longing for an unattainable beloved — whether unattainable because indifferent (like Rosaline in the play), or simply sequestered from the company of young men (as well-bred Elizabethan girls normally were till married), or already bespoke in marriage (as Juliet would have been had Romeo met her for the first time a week later). Longing being its chief subject-matter, much of the vocabulary of this tradition features love as a perpetual, forever unavailing amorous warfare, with Venus as patron of the battle, Cupid as archer, and the beloved as unconquerable stronghold or invulnerable foe. This is the imagery that Romeo and Benvolio resort to in describing Rosaline as one who goes "in strong proof of chastity well armed" and "will not stay the siege of loving terms" (1.1.208). It is also the imagery that Mercutio parodies whenever he and Romeo meet.

In this conversation, as noticed earlier, we are introduced to Romeo's own affectations, and then, as if to complete a sequence from "brutal"

(Sampson and Gregory) to "coquettish" (Rosaline) to "faddish" (Romeo) to "conventional," we turn to Paris and old Capulet. The young wooer, as Elizabethan protocol dictated, approaches the young lady's father with a proposition. The father predictably replies (with an apparent unconcern that soon fades): Why hurry? — Still, it's all right with *me* if you can obtain *her* consent (1.2.17). Predictably also, the mother visits the daughter and dwells upon the attractions of the suitor, especially on how fitting it will be for a Capulet to be the binding that locks in so much wealth:

That book in many's eyes doth share the glory,
That in gold clasps locks in the golden story.
(1.3.91)

No nonsense about love's embraces here: only gold clasps.

Meantime, to these materialist attitudes, the Nurse plays shrill echo. One of Shakespeare's most brilliant early character sketches, she is a shrewd but garrulous, warmhearted but naively vulgar soul, who finds it impossible to answer a simple question without dredging up with it all the seaweed that clings about it in her memory. The question is only about Juliet's age, but by the time the Nurse has settled it she has included her dead daughter Susan, an earthquake, Juliet's weaning, an absence of the elder Capulets in Mantua, and a vulgar witticism of her dead husband's about Juliet's falling and bumping her head. The unfading pleasure she takes in this little sexual joke (not to mention the kind of comparison that springs instantly to her mind when she describes the size of Juliet's bump) tells us most of what we need to know about *her* understanding of romantic love. After hearing her on the subject of "falling backward," we are not likely to be much surprised by her response to the proposal for Juliet's marriage: "Go, girl, seek happy nights to happy days" (1.3.105). Or by her later utilitarian response to Juliet's agony, when, being already married to Romeo, she faces a second forced marriage to Paris:

Beshrew my very heart,
I think you are happy in this second match,

76

For it excels your first; or if it did not,
Your first is dead — or 'twere as good he were
As living here and you no use of him. (3.5.223)

This contrast between the Nurse and Juliet is reinforced by Mercutio's contrast with Romeo. Mercutio knows all about the supposed pangs that love occasions and can speak that language as well as Romeo:

You are a lover. Borrow Cupid's wings
And soar with them above a common bound.
(1.4.17)

But he speaks it only to mock it. Knowing well that such feeling is often self-deceived — a disguise, in fact, for simple appetite — he appears to cherish the conviction that such it must always be: all that is real is sex. To every protest that Romeo makes about the preoccupations of his heart, Mercutio replies with a bawdy quip. He knows all about Queen Mab, too, and can describe her equipage with childlike wonder, enchantingly — until again he mocks her: he has no serious interest in what she represents. Our psychic inner-world of fancy, longing, mystery, and dream (on which Juliet will later confer a cosmic rhythm and splendor by associating it with the chariot of the sun god Apollo: 3.2.1), Mercutio here dismisses and shrinks to insignificance by associating it with the minuscule chariot of Mab, in whose Skinnerian world we are all reduced to programmed stimulus and response:

And in this state she gallops night by night
Through lovers' brains, and then they dream of love;
O'er courtiers' knees, that dream on curtsies straight;
O'er lawyers' fingers, that straight dream on fees;
O'er ladies' lips, who straight on kisses dream . . .
(1.4.70)

On the same "rational" grounds, Mercutio refuses credence to Romeo's dream and his consequent misgiving about going to the Capulet feast.

The play is to prove him wrong on several of these points, and the first instance occurs at once. For the "conjuration" of Rosaline that Shakespeare puts into his mouth as he and Benvolio look for their vanished companion after the ball (2.1.6) places this washroom chatter in immediate juxtaposition with the luminous beauty of Juliet and the exalted feelings she has stirred in Romeo — both of which we have just witnessed. Useful as an antidote to the maudlin worship of the Beautiful Cruel Lady (*La Belle Dame sans Merci*) whose caprices have enslaved Romeo, Mercutio's witty pruriencies are now seen to have come up against something to which they are irrelevant. Irrelevant, most obviously because directed at the wrong girl. But more deeply irrelevant, too, because so determinedly excluding the capability that men and women have of valuing each other as persons rather than sexual objects and of placing that value above all other imaginable values — exactly what we have just seen taking place a few moments earlier as Romeo and Juliet stand isolated from the rest of the world in the fourteen lines of a love-sonnet.

The rapt unanimity of feeling that they share within that sonnet unfolds, as the play proceeds, into the radiant experience that the coarser attitudes we have just been examining help to define and set apart. To earn our belief in that experience, or at the very least a suspension of our disbelief, Shakespeare undertakes to validate it for us by showing us that he is aware of crasser possibilities, even if his lovers are not. That he knows what he shows us in them is not within the reach of all — not, for instance, the County Parises of the world, however admirable they may be for other virtues. That he knows, even where it exists, such love as this is always under threat, not only from those whose values are determined by convention, like the Capulets, and no doubt equally the Montagues; but from those, like Mercutio, whose appraisal of human capabilities it considerably transcends, and from those, like the Nurse, with whose jovial but crude sensibility it is quite out of tune. And, moreover — a sufficiently tragic concession in itself — that he knows it must in the long run face defeat — if not by the world, then by our mortal nature, which allows nothing to remain in perpetuity, or even for very long, the thing it was. Everything that grows, he laments repeatedly in his Sonnets,

"Holds in perfection but a little moment" (1 5.2). In some part, *Romeo and Juliet* seems a poignant elaboration of that thought, in dramatic terms.

4

Just here, the play *may* intend to raise questions as well as paeans around the romantic experience it so much exalts. What, for instance, do the repeated hints that this love is as dangerous as it is beautiful — perhaps beautiful *because* dangerous — signify? Like the blaze of gunpowder, says Friar Laurence:

These violent delights have violent ends
And in their triumph die, like fire and powder,
Which, as they kiss, consume. (2.6.9)

To be sure, the friar is an old man, skeptical of youth's ways; yet can we help reflecting on this diagnosis when we recall at the play's end that five young people have died: Mercutio, Tybalt, Paris, Romeo, Juliet? Does it suffice to hold the feud alone accountable?

Then there is the repeated situation of enclosure. With the exception of their marriage scene at the exact center of the play, we see Romeo and Juliet together only in the interval between evening and dawn, and always in a kind of enclave or special space which is threatened from without. At the ball, they are framed by a sonnet and by a sudden quiet that is made the more striking and precarious by Tybalt's attempted intrusion. In the first balcony scene, their enclosure is the Capulets' walled garden, and the interview is twice on the point of interruption by the Nurse. In the second such scene, where the setting is Juliet's chamber, their leave-taking *is* interrupted, first by the Nurse's warning and then by Lady Capulet's appearance. Even in the tomb the social order intervenes, in the person of the Friar, between Romeo's suicide and Juliet's.

What goes on here, apart from the requirements of the plot, is a playwright's rendering of the feeling of intense but vulnerable privacy that all lovers know. So much the play clearly tells us. Does it also tell us that the unreconcilability of this love with the ordinary daylight world is a tragic consequence of its nature, a trait not separable from it without destroying the thing it is — and so more tragic on that account?

Similar ambiguities hover about the relationship established between the passion of Romeo and Juliet and the death that seems to be implicit in it. Significantly, the last scene takes place in a tomb. This is a remarkable dénouement, and we have been prepared for it by a succession of references, prophetic of the outcome even when dropped casually or in ignorance, in which love and death are identified or closely linked. First, by Juliet herself:

> Come, cords; come, nurse. I'll to my wedding bed;
> And death, not Romeo, take my maidenhead! (3.2.136)

Soon after, by her mother, angered at Juliet's disinclination to marry Paris: "I would the fool were married to her grave" (3.5.141). Next, by her father, supposing that his daughter's apparent death on the eve of her wedding is real: "Death is my son-in-law, Death is my heir" (4.5.38). Later, by Paris, acting on the same supposition at the tomb: "Sweet flower, with flowers thy bridal bed I strew" (5.3.12). And finally by Romeo:

> Shall I believe
> That unsubstantial Death is amorous,
> And that the lean abhorrèd monster keeps
> Thee here in dark to be his paramour?
> For fear of that I still will stay with thee. . . .
> (5.3.102)

The playwright's insistence throughout on pairing the bride-bed with the grave reaches a climax in the tomb-scene, where death and sexual consummation become indistinguishable as Romeo "dies" (a word often used in Renaissance literature to refer to the culmination of the sexual act) upon a kiss, and Juliet, plunging the dagger home, sighs: "there rust, and let me die" (5.3.120, 170).

We must recall, too, that from the moment they acknowledge their love these lovers have been made to sense that it spells or may spell doom:

Is she a Capulet?
O dear account! my life is my foe's debt. (1.5.117)

If he be marrièd,
My grave is like to be my wedding bed. (1.5.134)

Their apprehension can be attributed in part to the feud, but only in part. Juliet's lines above are spoken while she is yet in ignorance of Romeo's identity, and Romeo's premonitions of "Some consequence, yet hanging in the stars" (1.4.107) precede even his visit to the ball. We in the audience, moreover, have been assured from the very beginning that this love is "death-marked" (Prologue, 9).

What are we to make of such evidence? Does the play urge us to conclude that every high romantic passion, by its very finality and absoluteness, its inwardness and narcissism, is necessarily allied with death, even perhaps (however unconsciously) seeks death? being oblivious of all competing values to a degree that ordinary human lives cannot afford and determined to hold fast to a perfection that such lives cannot long sustain? and therefore tending irresistibly to a "love-death" because unable or unwilling to absorb the losses imposed by a "love-life"? Or is the implied connection at once simpler and more universal: that death is always the "other pole" required to generate love's meaning — the little negotiable domestic loves that most of us aspire to as much as the austerest romantic pang? that *our* loves, too, are "death-marked" and (in the senses that matter most) "star-crossed," because both marked and crossed by the general human fate, which is to die? and therefore that those audiences are right after all who, despite the play's concern with a particular pair of lovers in a particular situation, sense in it a universal parable that speaks eloquently to their own condition?

5

There are no certain answers to these questions, or even to the question whether the playwright intends them to be asked. What *is* certain is that when we see *Romeo and Juliet* in performance, or perform it alertly for ourselves in the theater of the mind, such problems tend to vanish in an experience that is altogether dramatic: an experience that owes more to gestures, groupings, movements onstage, stunning intensities and reversals of human feeling, breathtaking effects of color, light, and sound, than to theoretical considerations of the sort we have just been examining.

Consider, for instance, the first scene. Two swaggering boneheads in Capulet livery — the livery very probably a little frowsy like their manners and speech, their swagger only making more conspicuous the fear it is meant to hide — meet two similar figures wearing the contrasting colors of the Montagues. A scuffle follows. The stage resounds with cries, grunts, heavy-footed lunges, clumsy whacks and thwacks of short swords on small shields — the habitual armor of the lower classes. Though violent, the scene has at first a comic coloring, thanks to the ineptitude of the contestants, who show a marked disinclination to get hurt. Then, in almost instantaneous counterpoint, comes the encounter of the two young gentlemen. In dress, speech, and physical grace, they are "civilized" to a degree that the household servants are not; but once engaged they are far more deadly, for they fight with rapiers and are animated by a code of honor that stakes life itself on skills of hand and eye.

Thus comic violence draws in tragic violence — a foretaste of much to come — while around the two contending groups a general fracas grows. Some elderly citizens rush in carrying weapons as ancient as themselves and labor, farcically, to quell the fighting. On their heels come old Capulet and Montague, comic figures likewise, since neither their manifest years and frailty nor the supposed wisdom of old age has been able to abate their mindless commitment to the feud. Finally, his entry no doubt announced by a trumpet fanfare, the Prince arrives with his retinue. The authority of the state, expressed now in the regular declamatory rhythms of the Prince's "sentence" (1.1.79), prevails for the time being over individual passions, and the crowd drifts rapidly away.

What we have been shown is the susceptibility of a whole society to be cleft from top to bottom by an inherited vendetta (in our world it could as easily be some inflexibly racial frame of mind) in which, we soon discover, no one but Tybalt has more than a face-saving interest. Yet thanks to the atmosphere the feud has given rise to, even the peace-making Benvolio — the man of "good will," as his name implies — can be drawn into a street riot against his better judgment, and the security of the entire community can be put in jeopardy on the whim of a determined fool — a Malvolio, or man of "ill will," as Tybalt might equally have been called.

The entrance of Romeo is timed for this moment, following the outbreak rather than before it, to make the encumbrance of the feud, his blood-inheritance, crystal clear. Over the conversation that Benvolio holds with the elder Montagues, which prepares us for Romeo's appearance (alone, distracted, his clothing very possibly disheveled as the clothing of those subject to love-melancholy was popularly supposed to be), and also over the conversation that Benvolio holds with him, the shadow of the violence we have just seen hangs heavily. The condition of "death-marked love," to which the Prologue has called attention (line 9), is thus acted out in a half-comic form that will quickly become tragic. Like Hamlet, who in some ways resembles him, Romeo has inherited a time which is "out of joint" and which nothing short of his own and several other "misadventured piteous overthrows" (Prologue, 7) can redeem. Still comparatively detached from the feud as we encounter him now (though already "in love" with a Capulet), he will be drawn moment by moment further into quicksands, each apparent escape — e.g. the marriage with Juliet, which should *unite* the two families — becoming an additional step in the progress of events that sweeps both lovers to their doom.

Here, then, is one way in which *Romeo and Juliet* comes powerfully home to us in performance: as a fast-moving succession of situations, each gripping in itself but also making part of a headlong race to ruin, even though that race does not lack for the little ironical postponements and detours that allow an audience teasing hopes of a happier issue. But the play registers in other emphatic ways as well. As an experience of vivid contrasts, for instance, in a world that is tense with polarities of every sort. Extreme youth — Juliet is only fourteen, Romeo (we may guess) in late adolescence — tugs at extreme age, for despite Lady Capulet's odd comment (1.3.71) all four parents give the impression of being somewhat along in years, as are obviously the Friar and Nurse. Passionate love grapples with passionate hate, and eventually, at great cost enjoys an ambiguous triumph. The brightness of the lovers, in their images of each other, dazzles against the darkness of their situation, while at the same time, paradoxically, the night world becomes more and more their sole resource and the daylight world more and more the possession of forces inimical to them. Then there are the sharply conflicting attitudes toward love and sex, already touched on; the extremes of haste and deliberation; the great joys giving way to overwhelming griefs; the noise, bustle, and uproar of public affairs juxtaposed against the hushed inward-turning ecstasies of lovers' longing and lovers' meeting.

All these opposites and many more make part of our experience in this play, but again not as theoretical contraries — only as vivid impressions of eye and ear. To take one more example, worldliness and innocence — an innocence not yet broken by the world — are among the polarities on which *Romeo and Juliet* is founded, but they take shape onstage only in the particularized form of Juliet, sitting (in 1.3) a little apart from her elders, perhaps wearing some white garment in keeping with the impression she seems intended by her words to make on us; while her nurse and mother, each with characteristic motives and preoccupations, preside over what we recognize as a coming of age, a tribal rite of passage, a "debut," in short, into what both older women take to be her appropriate next phase in the human life-cycle of birth, copulation, and death. Eventually, her innocence outwits their wisdom, but the price exacted is appalling.

6

In conclusion, something must be said about what for many of today's readers and spectators is the most striking single feature of *Romeo and Juliet:* its formalism. The pronounced general symmetries that have gone into its configuration are obvious enough. Three confrontations of the warring houses, each followed by a pronouncement from the Prince, mirror each other successively at 1.1, 3.1, and 5.3 — except that the consequences crescendo in seriousness: no one dies during the first, two are dead after the second, and three, including the protagonists, after the third. Equally visible at a glance are the variations played on balancing personalities: a bawdy Nurse flanks Juliet in 1.3 and a bawdy Mercutio flanks Romeo in 1.4; or, again, a sober Benvolio, trying to cool a hot Tybalt in 1.1, parallels a sober Benvolio trying to cool a hot Mercutio in 3.1. Yet curiously enough this stress on "forms" only evokes more keenly, when the play is seen and heard, our sense of its immense reserves of dramatic and linguistic power. As a highbred horse shows his truest fire when curbed, so the artifices of the play's style and structure create a condition of containment from which its energies break out with double force. Energies that explode on the slightest provocation into horse-play, sword-play, wordplay, love-play. Energies that smolder in Tybalt's and Lady Capulet's hatred of the Montagues and bubble over in Mercutio's witty scorn of everything that looks like posturing or fakery, whether Romeo's premonitions and dreams (1.4), Tybalt's dancing-masterish fencing style (2.4.20), or the Nurse's affectation of being a *grande dame*, all got up in her best fineries with a man-servant to go before (2.4.95). Energies, furthermore, that flow like a high-voltage current through the love scenes, idealizing everything they touch, and in the potion and tomb scenes so overpower all other considerations that Juliet can drink off the Friar's potion despite her terror, and Romeo can unhesitatingly storm the Capulet tomb in order to be reunited with his wife on their mutual death-and-marriage-bed.

Behind all these energies, of course, releasing but at the same time shaping them, stands the energy of Shakespeare's own imagination, in sheer exuberance of creation melting down old forms to make them new. The ancient conceit comparing the beloved lady's beauty to various kinds of dazzling light becomes in his hands Juliet hanging upon the cheek of night like a rich jewel in an Ethiop's ear (1.5.46), Juliet showing at her window like a sunrise in the East (2.2.2), Juliet making even the grave "a feasting presence full of light" (5.3.86). Similarly the time-worn conception of the lover as a ship tossed by storms of passion or misfortune in the attempt to reach safe harbor in his lady's favor takes on in Shakespeare's reinterpretation of it a passionate urgency:

I am no pilot; yet, wert thou as far
As that vast shore washed with the farthest sea,
I should adventure for such merchandise. (2.2.82)

Later, when Romeo swallows the apothecary's drug, this time-worn metaphor is strikingly reinterpreted:

Come, bitter conduct; come, unsavory guide!
Thou desperate pilot, now at once run on
The dashing rocks thy seasick weary bark!
Here's to my love! [*Drinks.*] O true apothecary!
Thy drugs are quick. Thus with a kiss I die.
(5.3.116)

So too with the lover's "blazon." Properly speaking, the blazon in Renaissance love-poetry is a descriptive inventory of the beloved's charms, moving lingeringly and luxuriously, item by item, from her golden hair to her shapely foot. In *Romeo and Juliet*, the convention reappears, but is significantly displaced from the true beloved (Juliet) to the imagined beloved (Rosaline), is subordinated to a formula of conjuration derived from demonology (possibly a further insult), and is spoken not by the lover in praise of the beloved but by the scoffer, who throws doubt on the whole spectrum of high romantic feeling by indicating very clearly what he believes to be its crass sources:

I conjure thee by Rosaline's bright eyes,
By her high forehead and her scarlet lip,
By her fine foot, straight leg, and quivering thigh,
And the demesnes that there adjacent lie,
That in thy likeness thou appear to us! (2.1.17)

But these verbal transformations are only the surface outcroppings of Shakespeare's originality in *Romeo and Juliet*. What many in his audiences must have responded to at a deeper level, unanalyzed but felt, is the presence of certain psychological experiences familiar to all who have ever loved, for which he has managed to find in his story of two hapless lovers unobtrusive but unforgettable dramatic forms. One such experience is the mysterious mix in every sexual passion of attraction and repulsion, love and hate. *Odi et amo:* "I hate and I love," wrote the Roman poet Catullus, and Shakespeare has captured the phenomenon memorably in his play, not simply in dramatizing a quite literal mixture of attraction and repulsion in Juliet when her husband kills her kinsman, but in keeping at all times clear the psychological interface between the love story itself and its environment of hate. The very phrases in which contemporary and earlier poets had summed up the latent antagonism of the sexes as well as the power of a particular beloved woman to hurt her lover by disdain — woman seen as "dearest enemy," an unconquerable "fortress," a warrior with "killing" eyes — become charged with new meaning in *Romeo and Juliet* through their radical implication in the plot itself:

> My only love sprung from my only hate! . . .
> ? — Prodigious birth of love it is to me
> That I must love a loathèd enemy. (1.5.138)

> Alack, there lies more peril in thine eye
> Than twenty of their swords! (2.2.71)

> Thou are not conquered — Beauty's ensign yet
> Is crimson in thy lips and in thy cheeks,
> And death's pale flag is not advancèd there.
> (5.3.94)

Similarly with the masculine sense of woman as a mysterious being withheld — a being to be wooed, not conquered, and only to be fully known when given by her own free choice. This sense — a constant theme of Elizabethan love-poetry — pervades the play, and again the favorite images and phrases of the literary tradition take on a new and glowing life through being reinterpreted in action. In his chatter about Rosaline, Romeo had invoked idly the Petrarchan image of woman as unyielding fortress, but when this image returns at the play's end, in the last passage quoted above, the unyielding fortress is plain to be seen on the stage in Juliet's yet living form, and it is only to the paramour death, not Romeo, that she lies unyielding. When Romeo reclaims her for his own by freely choosing to be her husband in death as well as life, she gives herself in turn to be again his wife by her free choice in falling upon his dagger. What is also to be observed is that this same sequence of events has already been acted out in the happier setting of the Capulet garden. To that garden — which is itself partly a dramatic realization of the parallel that from Biblical times had been drawn between a virgin and a *hortus conclusus* or closed garden — Romeo is attracted by desire. The girl he meets there, however, though virgin, is so far from being an Unconquerable Fortress or a *Belle Dame sans Merci*, that she can show her love for him more freely and less self-consciously than he can show his for her:

> My bounty is as boundless as the sea,
> My love as deep; the more I give to thee
> The more I have, for both are infinite.
> (2.2.133)

It is no more than appropriate, therefore, that when he ascends to her chamber for their wedding night, it is by means of a rope-ladder that he has supplied and she has lowered to him. The Petrarchan image of woman as fortress, unyielding and therefore to be taken only by assault (as in the *macho* language of the servants in the first scene), yields, like his own experience of Rosaline, to a truer definition in which love is a gift to be freely given and received.

The most remarkable among the ancient phrases that Shakespeare regenerates by causing them to be acted out in front of us is every lover's conviction that love must conquer death: *Amor vincit omnia*. Around this phrase and the corresponding psychological urgencies, the play's last scene is plainly built. Romeo, as has already been pointed out, asserts his claim to Juliet against death's claim; in the person of the Lover he breaks open the Tomb, which by the power of his passion and her beauty is transformed to a presence-chamber filled with light; and though he dies beside her, he manages to carve out through his idealizing imagination an enigmatic space — last of the many enclaves in which we see them — in which death and sexual consummation coincide — "Thus with a kiss I die" (5.3.120). "There rust, and let me die" (5.3.170).

7

An awesome close to a lavish pageant of romantic feeling. Yet we must not suppose that Shakespeare intends us to let it go entirely unchallenged. Against its idealized shape, complete with operatic deaths and high-flown lyric utterances, he has already set for our contemplation a far messier, prosier, less predictable death-scene — one much more like those we meet with in our own world: Mercutio's. Mercutio's death is anything but a consummation and far from being lyrical in either content or form. Like his parody of the lover's blazon earlier, his last words seem calculated to puncture and shrivel up yet another body of posturing and pretense: that a man's death is to be reckoned some sort of special or heroic occasion — that it comes about, as in romantic literature generally, only after great deeds, great wounds, or meeting with a great adversary (in fact, even a scratch will do it) — and that it must not be accompanied by expressed resentments or ironies, but only by such noble expressions of magnanimity and acceptance of one's fate as accord with the idea of making a good end.

ROMEO: Courage, man. The hurt cannot be much.
MERCUTIO: No, 'tis not so deep as a well, nor so wide as a church door; but 'tis enough, 'twill serve. Ask for me tomorrow and you shall find me a grave man. I am peppered, I warrant, for this world. A plague a both your houses! Zounds, a dog, a rat, a mouse, a cat, to scratch a man to death! a braggart, a rogue, a villain, that fights by the book of arithmetic! Why the devil came you between us? I was hurt under your arm. (3.1.93)

No pithy "last words" here: only scorn and anger at the sheer contingency and arbitrariness of what was quite unnecessary but has nevertheless taken place.

This death and these speeches — indeed all of Mercutio's speeches — suggest a possible other scale in which the lovers' devotion to each other and their "victory" at the close may be weighed. Looked at through *his* perspective, the lovers' ideal experience of each other, the exalted images they feed on, the absolute fidelity to which they sacrifice their lives may be reckoned among the fictions by which men and women deceive themselves about their true natures and the nature of their world. On the other hand, looked at through *their* perspective, his reading of reality must appear near-sighted and reductive, for the fictions men and women live by are often their best throw at truth, whether about themselves or about the world.

In *Romeo and Juliet* Shakespeare has juxtaposed these two divergent value systems — the last and climactic pair of contraries in that scheme of contrasts at which we earlier glanced — without allowing them to touch. Mercutio never learns of Romeo's mature love for Juliet, and his death is well behind us when we encounter theirs. Perhaps the playwright feared that either view, if brought too close to its opposite, would shatter. Later, he will be more venturesome. His tragic heroes from Hamlet on are required to know the world in both perspectives simultaneously and the experience tears them apart, as it still does some today.

CHAPTER FIVE

THE MODERNITY OF

Julius Caesar

I

I N a tribute composed to introduce the collection of plays that we now call the *First Folio*, Shakespeare's fellow playwright Ben Jonson spoke of his colleague's works as not of an age but for all time. Though the compliment was something of a commonplace in Renaissance funerary rhetoric, it has proved to be remarkably clairvoyant, at least up to the present hour. And of no play, perhaps, has the continuing relevance been more striking than that of *Julius Caesar*, which again and again twentieth-century directors and producers have successfully presented as a parable for our days.

Among the many aspects of the play that contribute to its modernity, one in particular, to my mind, stands out, and it is to this exclusively, leaving out much, that I want to call attention here. The place to begin is the second scene.

We have just learned from scene I of Caesar's return in triumph from warring on Pompey's sons. We have seen the warm though fickle adulation of the crowd and the apprehension of the tribunes. Now we are to see the great man himself. The procession enters to triumphal music; with hubbub of a great press of people; with young men stripped for the ceremonial races, among them Antony; with statesmen in their togas: Decius, Cicero, Brutus, Cassius, Casca; with the two wives Calphurnia and Portia; and, in the lead, for not even Calphurnia is permitted at his side, the great man. As he starts to speak, an expectant hush settles over the gathering. What does the great man have on his mind?

CAESAR:
Calphurnia.

CASCA: Peace, ho! Caesar speaks.

CAESAR: Calphurnia.

CALPHURNIA:
Here, my lord.

CAESAR:
Stand you directly in Antonius' way
When he doth run his course. Antonius.

ANTONY:
Caesar, my lord?

CAESAR:
Forget not in your speed, Antonius,
To touch Calphurnia; for our elders say,
The barren, touched in this holy chase,
Shake off their sterile curse.

ANTONY: I shall remember.
When Caesar says, "Do this," it is performed.

(1.2.1)

What the great man had on his mind, it appears, was to remind his wife, in this public place, that she is sterile; that there is an old tradition about how sterility can be removed; and that while of course he is much too sophisticated to accept such a superstition himself — it is "our elders" who say it — still, Calphurnia had jolly well better get out there and get tagged!

Then the procession takes up again. The hubbub is resumed, but once more an expectant silence settles as a voice is heard.

SOOTHSAYER: Caesar!

CAESAR: Ha! Who calls?

CASCA:
Bid every noise be still. Peace yet again!

CAESAR:
Who is it in the press that calls on me?

I hear a tongue shriller than all the music
Cry "Caesar!" Speak. Caesar is turned to hear.

SOOTHSAYER:
Beware the ides of March.

CAESAR: What man is that?

BRUTUS:
A soothsayer bids you beware the ides of March.

CAESAR:
Set him before me; let me see his face.

CASSIUS:
Fellow, come from the throng; look upon Caesar.

CAESAR:
What say'st thou to me now? Speak once again.

SOOTHSAYER:
Beware the ides of March.

CAESAR:
He is a dreamer. Let us leave him. Pass. (1.2.13)

It is easy to see from even these small instances, I think, how a first-rate dramatic imagination works. There is no hint of any procession in Plutarch, Shakespeare's source. "Caesar," says Plutarch, "*sat* to behold."[59] There is no mention of Calphurnia in Plutarch's account of the Lupercalian race, and there is no mention anywhere of her sterility. Shakespeare, in nine lines, has given us an unforgettable picture of a man who would like to be emperor, pathetically concerned that he lacks an heir, and determined, even at the cost of making his wife a public spectacle, to establish that this is owing to no lack of virility in him. The first episode thus dramatizes instantaneously what I take to be the oncoming theme of the play: that a man's will is not enough; that there are other matters to be reckoned with, like the infertility of one's wife, or one's own affliction of the falling sickness that spoils everything one hoped for just at the instant when one had it almost in one's hand. Brutus will be obliged to learn this lesson too.

In the second episode the theme develops. We see again the uneasy rationalism that everybody in this play affects; we hear it reverberate in the faint contempt — almost a challenge — of Brutus's words as he turns to Caesar: "A soothsayer bids you beware the ides of March." Yet underneath, in the soothsayer's quiet defiance as he refuses to quail under Caesar's imperious gaze, and in his soberly reiterated warning, Shakespeare allows us to catch a hint of something else, something far more primitive and mysterious, from which rationalism in this play keeps trying vainly to cut itself away: "He is a dreamer. Let us leave him. Pass." Only we in the audience are in a position to see that the dreamer has foretold the path down which all these reasoners will go to their fatal encounter at the Capitol.

Meantime, in these same two episodes, we have learned something about the character of Caesar. In the first, it was the Caesar of human frailties who spoke to us, the husband with his hopeful superstition. In the second, it was the marble superman of state, impassive, impervious, speaking of himself in the third person: "Speak! Caesar is turned to hear." He even has the soothsayer brought before his face to repeat the message, as if the thought that somehow, in awe of the marble presence, the message would falter and dissolve: how can a superman need to beware the ides of March?

We hardly have time to do more than glimpse here a man of divided selves, then he is gone. But in his absence, the words of Cassius confirm our glimpse. Cassius's description of him exhibits the same duality that we had noticed earlier. On the one hand, an extremely ordinary man whose stamina in the swimming match was soon exhausted; who, when he had a fever once in Spain, shook and groaned like a sick girl; who even now, as we soon learn, is falling down with epilepsy in the market place. On the other hand, a being who has somehow become a god, who "bears the palm alone," who "bestrides the narrow world Like a colossus" (1.2.135). When the procession returns, no longer festive but angry, tense, there is the same effect once more. Our one Caesar shows a normal man's suspicion of his enemies, voices some shrewd human observations about Cassius, says to Antony, "Come on my right hand, for this ear is deaf" (1.2.213). Our other Caesar says, as if he were suddenly reminded of something he had forgotten, "I rather tell thee what is to be feared Than what I fear, for always I am Caesar" (1.2.211).

Wherever Caesar appears hereafter, we shall find this distinctive division in him, and nowhere more so than in the scene in which he receives the conspirators at his house. Some aspects of this scene seem calculated for nothing other than to fix upon our minds the superman conception, the Big Brother of Orwell's *1984*, the great resonant name echoing down the halls of time. Thus at the beginning of the scene:

> The things that threatened me
> Ne'er looked but on my back. When they shall see
> The face of Caesar, they are vanishèd. (2.2.10)

And again later:

> Danger knows full well
> That Caesar is more dangerous than he.
> We are two lions littered in one day,
> And I the elder and more terrible. (2.2.44)

And again still later: "Shall Caesar send a lie?" (2.2.65). And again: "The cause is in my will: I will not come." (2.2.71)

Other aspects of this scene, including his concern about Calphurnia's dream, his vacillation about going to the senate house, his anxiety about the portents of the night, plainly mark out his human weaknesses. Finally, as is the habit in this Rome, he puts the irrational from him that his wife's intuitions and her dream embody; he accepts the rationalization of the irrational that Decius skillfully manufactures, and, as earlier at the Lupercalia, hides from himself his own vivid sense of forces that lie beyond the will's control by attributing it to her:

> How foolish do your fears seem now, Calphurnia!
> I am ashamèd I did yield to them.
> Give me my robe, for I will go. (2.2.105)

2

So far we have looked at Caesar, the title personage of the play and its historical center. It is time now to consider Brutus, the play's tragic center, whom we also find to be a divided man — "poor Brutus," to use

95

his own phrase, "with himself at war" (1.2.46). That war, we realize as the scene progresses, is a conflict between a quiet, essentially domestic and loving nature, and a powerful integrity expressing itself in a sense of honorable duty to the commonweal. This duality is what Cassius probes in his long disquisition about the mirror. The Brutus looking into the glass that Cassius figuratively holds up to him, the Brutus of this moment, now, in Rome, is a grave studious private man, of a wonderfully gentle temper as we shall see again and again later on; very slow to passion, as Cassius's ill-concealed disappointment in having failed to kindle him to an immediate response reveals; a man whose sensitive nature recoils at the hint of violence lurking in some of Cassius's speeches, just as he has already recoiled at going with Caesar to the market place, to witness the mass hysteria of clapping hands, sweaty nightcaps, and stinking breath. This is the present self that looks into Cassius's mirror.

The image that looks back out, that Cassius wants him to see, the potential other Brutus, is the man of public spirit, worried already by his uncertainty about Caesar's intentions, lineal descendant of an earlier Brutus who drove a would-be monarch from the city, a republican whose body is visibly stiffening in our sight at each huzza from the Forum, and whose anxiety, though he makes no reply to Cassius's inflammatory language, keeps bursting to the surface: "What means this shouting? I do fear the people Choose Caesar for their king" (1.2.79). The problem at the tragic center of the play, we begin to sense, is the tug of private versus public, the individual versus a world he never made, any citizen anywhere versus the selective service greetings that history is always mailing out to each of us. And this problem is to be traversed by the other tug this scene presents, between the irrational and the rational, the destiny we imagine we can control and the destiny that sweeps all before it.

Through 1.2, Brutus's patriotic self, the self that responds to these selective service greetings, is no more than a reflection in a mirror, a mere anxiety in his own brain, about which he refuses to confide, even to Cassius. In 2.1, we see the public self making further headway. First, there is Brutus's argument with himself about the threat of Caesar, and in his conclusion that Caesar must be killed we note how far his private self—he is, after all, one of Caesar's closest friends—has been invaded by the self of public spirit. From here on, the course of the invasion accelerates. A letter comes, tossed from the public world into the private world, into Brutus's garden, addressing, as Cassius had, the patriot image reflected in the mirror: "Brutus, thou sleep'st. Awake, and see thyself!" (2.1.46). Then follows the well-known brief soliloquy (which Shakespeare was to expand into the whole play of *Macbeth*), showing us that Brutus's mind has moved on from the phase of decision to the inquietudes that follow decision:

> Between the acting of a dreadful thing
> And the first motion, all the interim is
> Like a phantasma, or a hideous dream.
> (2.1.63)

Brutus anticipates here the dreamlike mood and motion with which Macbeth moves to the murder of Duncan. What is important to observe, however, is that these lines again stress the gulf that separates motive from action, that which is interior in man and controllable by his will from that which, once acted, becomes independent of him and moves with a life of its own. This gulf is a no man's land, a phantasma, a hideous dream.

Finally, there arrives in such a form that no audience can miss it the actual visible invasion itself, as this peaceful garden-quiet is intruded on by knocking, like the knocking of fate in Beethoven's Fifth Symphony, and by men with faces hidden in their cloaks. Following this, a lovely interlude with Portia serves to emphasize how much the private self, the private world, has been shattered. There is something close to discord here—as much of a discord as these gentle people are capable of—and though there is a reconciliation at the end and Brutus's promise to confide in her soon, this division in the family is an omen. So is the knock of the latecomer, Caius Ligarius, which reminds us once again of the exactions of the public life. And when Ligarius throws off his sick man's kerchief on learning that there is an honorable exploit afoot, we may see in it an epitome of the whole scene, a graphic visible renunciation, like

97

Brutus's (or like Prince Hal's at about the same time in Shakespeare's career) of the private good to the public; and we may see this also in Brutus's own exit a few lines later, not into the inner house where Portia waits for him, but out into the thunder and lightning of the public life of Rome. It is not without significance that at our final glimpse of Portia, two scenes later, she too stands outside the privacy of the house, her mind wholly occupied with thoughts of what is happening at the Capitol, trying to put on a public self for Brutus's sake: "Run, Lucius, and commend me to my lord; Say I am merry . . ." (2.4.44).

3

Meantime, at the Capitol, the tragic center and the historical center meet. The suspense is very great as Caesar, seeing the Soothsayer in the throng, reminds him that the ides of March are come, and receives in answer, "Ay, Caesar, but not gone" (3.1.2). More suspense is generated as Artemidorus presses forward with the paper that we know contains a full discovery of the plot. Decius, apprehensive, steps quickly into the breach with another paper, a petition from Trebonius. More suspense still as Popilius sidles past Cassius with the whisper, "I wish your enterprise today may thrive" (3.1.13), and then moves on to Caesar's side, where he engages him in animated talk. But they detect no tell-tale change in Caesar's countenance; Trebonius steps into his assignment and takes Antony aside; Metellus Cimber throws himself at Caesar's feet; Brutus gives the signal to "Press near and second him" (3.1.29), and Caesar's "Are we all ready?" (3.1.31) draws every eye to Caesar's chair. One by one they all kneel before this demigod — an effective tableau which gives a coloring of priest-like ritual to what they are about to do. Caesar is to bleed, but, as Brutus has said, they will sublimate the act into a sacrifice:

> Let's kill him boldly but not wrathfully;
> Let's carve him as a dish fit for the gods,
> Not hew him as a carcass fit for hounds.
> (2.1.172)

In performance, everything in the scene will reflect this ceremonial attitude to emphasize the almost fatuous cleavage between the spirit of the enterprise and its bloody result.

The Caesar we are permitted to see as all this ceremony is preparing will be almost entirely the superman, for obvious reasons. To give a color of justice to Brutus's act, even if we happen to think the assassination a mistake as many members of an Elizabethan audience emphatically would, Caesar must be seen in a mood of super-humanity at least as fatuous as the conspirators' mood of sacrifice. Hence Shakespeare makes him first of all insult Metellus Cimber: "If thou dost bend and pray and fawn for him, I spurn thee like a cur" (3.1.45), and then comment with intolerable pomposity — in fact, blasphemy — on his own iron resolution, which he alleges to be immovable even by prayer and thus superior to the very gods. Finally, Shakespeare puts into his mouth one of those supreme arrogances that can hardly fail to remind us of the ancient adage "Whom the gods would destroy they first make mad." "Hence!" Caesar cries, "Wilt thou lift up Olympus?" (3.1.74). It is at just this point, when the colossus Caesar drunk with self-importance is before us, that Casca strikes. Then they all strike, with a last blow that brings out for the final time the other, human side of this double Caesar: "*Et tu, Brute?*" (3.1.77).

And now this little group of men has altered history. The representative of the evil direction it was taking toward autocratic power lies dead before them. The direction to which it must be restored becomes emphatic in Cassius's cry of "Liberty, freedom, and enfranchisement!" (3.1.81). Solemnly, and again like priests who have just sacrificed a victim, they kneel together and bathe their hands and swords in Caesar's blood. Brutus exclaims:

Then walk we forth, even to the market place,
And waving our red weapons o'er our heads,
Let's all cry, "Peace, freedom, and liberty!"
(3.1.108)

If the conjunction of those red hands and weapons with this slogan is not enough to give an audience a start, the next passage will; for now the conspirators explicitly invoke the judgment of history on their deed. On the stages of theaters the world over, so they anticipate, this lofty incident will be re-enacted, and

> So oft as that shall be,
> So often shall the knot of us be called
> The men that gave their country liberty.
> (3.1.116)

We in the audience, recalling what actually did result in Rome — the civil wars, the long line of despotic emperors — cannot miss the irony of their prediction, an irony that insists on our recognizing that this effort to control the consequences of an act is doomed to fail. (It is a theme that Shakespeare will touch again in *Macbeth* and *Lear*.) Why does it fail?

One reason why is shown us in the next few moments. The leader of this assault on history, like many another reformer, is a man of high idealism, who devoutly believes that the rest of the world is like himself. It was just to kill Caesar — so he persuades himself — because he was a threat to freedom. It would not have been just to kill Antony, and he vetoes the idea. Even now, when the consequence of that decision has come back to face him in the shape of Antony's servant kneeling before him, he sees no reason to reconsider it. There are good grounds for what they have done, he says; Antony will hear them, and be satisfied. With Antony, who shortly arrives in person, he takes this line again:

> Our reasons are so full of good regard
> That were you, Antony, the son of Caesar
> You should be satisfied. (3.1.224)

With equal confidence in the reasonableness of human nature, he puts by Cassius's fears of what Antony will do if allowed to address the people: "By your pardon; I will myself into the pulpit first And show the reason of our Caesar's death" (3.1.236). Here is a man so much a friend of Caesar's that he is still speaking of him as "our Caesar," so capable of rising to what he takes to be his duty that he has taken on the leadership of those who killed him, so trusting of common decency that he expects the populace will respond to reason, and Antony to honor the obligation laid on him by their permitting him to speak. At such a man, one hardly knows whether to laugh or cry.

The same mixture of feelings is likely to be stirring in us as Brutus speaks to the people in 3.2. As everybody knows, this is a speech in what used to be called the great liberal tradition, which assumes that men in the mass are reasonable. It has therefore been made a prose oration, spare and terse in diction, tightly patterned in syntax so that it requires close attention, and founded, with respect to its argument, on three elements: the abstract sentiment of duty to the state (because he endangered Rome, Caesar had to be slain); the abstract sentiment of political justice (because he had delusions of grandeur, Caesar deserved his fall); and the moral authority of the man Brutus.

As long as that moral authority is concretely before them in Brutus's presence, the populace is impressed. But since even trained minds do not always respond well to abstractions, they quite misunderstand the content of his argument, as one of them indicates by shouting, "Let him be Caesar!" (3.2.41). What moves them is the obvious sincerity and the known integrity of the speaker; and when he finishes, they are ready to carry him off on their shoulders on that account alone, leaving Antony a vacant Forum. The fair-mindedness of Brutus is thrilling but painful to behold as he calms this triumphal surge in his favor, urges them to stay and hear Antony, and then, in a moment very impressive dramatically as well as symbolically, walks off the stage, alone. We see then, if we have not seen before, a possible first answer to the question why the effort to take control of history failed as it so often does, blinkered by its own idealism.

4

When Antony takes the rostrum, we sense a possible second answer. It has been remarked that in a school for demagogues this speech should be the whole curriculum. Antony himself describes its method when he observes in the preceding scene, apropos of the effect of Caesar's dead body on the messenger from Octavius, "Passion, I see, is catching" (3.1.283). A statement that cannot be made about reason, as many of us learn to our cost.

Antony's speech differs from Brutus's as night from day. Brutus formulates from the outset positive propositions about Caesar and about his own motives on no other authority than his own. Because of his known integrity, Brutus can do this. Antony takes the safer alternative of concealing propositions in questions, by which the audience's mind is then guided to conclusions which seem its own:

> He hath brought many captives home to Rome,
> Whose ransoms did the general coffers fill.
> Did this in Caesar seem ambitious?
> (3.2.88)

> You all did see that on the Lupercal
> I thrice presented him a kingly crown,
> Which he did thrice refuse: Was this ambition?
> (3.2.95)

How well Shakespeare knew crowds becomes clear in the replies to Antony. Brutus, appealing to reason, is greeted with wild outbursts of emotion: "Let him be Caesar!" Antony appeals only to emotion and pocketbooks, but now they say, "Methinks there is much reason in his sayings," and chew upon it seriously.

With equal skill, Antony stirs up impulses only to thwart them. He appeals to curiosity and greed in the matter of the will, but then withholds it teasingly. In the same manner, he stirs up rage against the conspirators while pretending to dampen it (3.2.151): "I fear I wrong the honorable men Whose daggers have stabbed Caesar; I do fear it." Finally, he rests his case, not, like Brutus, on abstractions centering in the state and political justice, but on emotions centering in the individual listener. The first great crescendo of the speech, which culminates in the passage on Caesar's wounds, appeals first to pity and then to indignation. The second, culminating in the reading of Caesar's will, appeals first to curiosity and greed, then to gratitude.

His management of the will is particularly cunning: it is an item more concrete than words, an actual tantalizing document that can be flashed before the eye, as in many a modern political TV sound byte. He describes it at first vaguely, as being of such a sort that they would honor Caesar for it. Then, closer home, as something which would show "how Caesar loved you" (3.2.141). Then, with an undisguised appeal to self-interest, as a testament that will make them his "heirs." The emotions aroused by this news enable him to make a final test of his ironical refrain about "honorable men," and finding the results all that he had hoped, he can come down now among the crowd as one of them, and appeal directly to their feelings by appealing to his own: "If you have tears, prepare to shed them now" (3.2.169).

The power of this direct appeal to passion can be seen at its close. Where formerly we had a populace, now we have a mob. As a mob, its mind can be sealed against later recoveries of rationality by the insinuation that all reasoning is simply a surface covering up private grudges, like the "reason" they have heard from Brutus; whereas from Antony himself, the plain, blunt friend of Caesar, they are getting the plain, blunt truth and (a favorite trick) only what they already know.

So they are called back to hear the will. Antony no longer needs this as an incentive to riot; the mingled rage and pity he has aroused will take care of that. But, after the lynching when the hangover comes, and you are remembering how that fellow looked, swaying a little on the rope's end, with his eyes bugging out and the veins knotted at his temples, then it is good to have something really reasonable to cling to, like seventy-five drachmas (or thirty pieces of silver) and some orchards along a river.

By this point, we can fully understand that a further ground for the failure of the effort to control history is what has been left out of account — what all these Romans from the beginning, except Antony, have been trying to leave out of account: the phenomenon of feeling, one of many nonrational factors in the life of men, in the life of the world, in the processes of history itself — of which this blind infuriated mob is one kind of exemplification. Too secure in his own fancied suppression of this influence, Brutus has failed altogether to reckon with its power. Thus he could seriously say to Antony in the passage quoted earlier: Antony, even if you were "the son of Caesar You should be satisfied," as if the feeling of a son for a murdered father could ever be "satisfied" by reasons. And thus, too, urging the crowd to hear Antony, he could walk off the stage alone, the very figure of embodied "reason," unaware that only the irrational is catching.

Meantime, the scene of the mob tearing Cinna the Poet to pieces simply for having the same name as one of the conspirators (3.3) confirms the victory of unreason and gives us our first taste of the chaos invoked by Antony when he stood alone over Caesar's corpse. Now, reconsidering that prediction and this mob, we recognize a third reason why attempts to direct the course of history have usually failed. We have seen already that history is only minimally responsive to noble motives, only minimally responsive to rationality. Now we see clearly what was hinted in the beginning by those two episodes with Calphurnia and the soothsayer — that it is only minimally responsive to conscious human influence of any sort. With all their reasons, the conspirators and Caesar only carried out what the soothsayer foreknew. There is, in short — at least as this play sees it — a degree of determinism in history, whether we call it cultural, fatal, or providential, which *helps* to shape our ends, "Roughhew them how we will" (*Hamlet*, 5.2.11). One of the alternative names of that factor in this play is Caesarism, cult of the ever regenerating Will to Power. Brutus puts the point, all unconsciously, when the conspirators are gathered at his house:

> We all stand up against the spirit of Caesar,
> And in the spirit of men there is no blood.
> O that we then could come by Caesar's spirit,
> And not dismember Caesar! But, alas,
> Caesar must bleed for it. (2.1.167)

Then Caesar does bleed for it; but his spirit, as Brutus's own remark might have told him, proves invulnerable. It is simply set free by his assassination, and now, as Antony says, "ranging for revenge, . . . Shall in these confines with a monarch's voice Cry 'Havoc' and let slip the dogs of war" (3.1.270).

5

The rest of the play is self-explanatory. It is clear all through Acts 4 and 5 that Brutus and Cassius are defeated before they begin to fight. Antony knows it and says so at 5.1. Cassius knows it too. Cassius, an Epicurean in philosophy and therefore one who has never heretofore believed in omens, now mistrusts his former rationalism: he suspects there may be something after all in those ravens, crows, and kites that wheel overhead. Brutus too mistrusts *his* rationalism. As a Stoic, his philosophy requires him to repudiate suicide, but he admits to Cassius that if the need comes he will repudiate philosophy instead. This, like Cassius' statement, is an unconscious admission of the force of the non-rational in human affairs, a non-rational influence that makes its presence felt again and again during the great battle. Cassius, for instance, fails to learn in time that Octavius "Is overthrown by noble Brutus' power" (5.3.52), becomes the victim of a mistaken report of Titinius's death, runs on his sword crying, "Caesar, thou art revenged" (5.3.45), and is greeted, dead, by Brutus, in words that make still clearer their defeat by a power unforeseen: "O Julius Caesar, thou art mighty yet! Thy spirit walks abroad and turns our swords In our own proper entrails" (5.3.94). In the same vein, when it is Brutus's turn to die, we learn that the ghost of Caesar has reappeared, and he thrusts the sword home, saying, "Caesar, now be still" (5.5.50).

Among the many topics on which Shakespeare casts a cold eye in this short play — among them the nature of heroism, the toll that public life exacts, the legitimacy of power, the danger of violent change (this last especially relevant in 1599 because of the growing concern for the succession after the aging Queen should die) — the aspect that seems to me to account best for its hold on audiences in our totalitarian century of putsches, coups, and assassinations is its stress on the always ambiguous relation between humankind and history. During the first half of the play, what we are chiefly conscious of is the human will as a force in history — men making choices, controlling events. Our typical scenes are 1.2, where a man is trying to make up his mind; or 2.1, where a man first reaches a decision and then, with his fellows, lays plans to implement it; or 2.2, where we have Decius Brutus persuading Caesar to decide to go to the senate house; or 3.1 and 3.2, where up through the assassination, and even up through Antony's speech, men are still, so to speak, imping-ing on history, moulding it to their conscious will.

But then comes a change. Though we still have men in action trying to mould their world (or else we would have no play at all), one senses a real shift in the direction of the impact. We begin to feel the insufficiency of noble aims, for history is also consequences; the insufficiency of reason and rational expectation, for the ultimate consequences of an act in history are unpredictable, and usually, by all human standards, illogical as well; and finally, the insufficiency of the human will itself, for there is always something to be reckoned with that is nonhuman and inscrutable — Nemesis, Moira, Fortuna, the Parcae, Providence, Determinism: men have had many names for it, but it is always there. Accordingly, in the second half of the play, our typical scenes are those like 3.3, where Antony has raised something that is no longer under his control or anyone's. Or like 4.1, where we see men acting as if, under the thumb of expediency or necessity or call it what you will, they no longer had wills of their own but prick down the names of nephews and brothers indiscriminately for slaughter. Or like 4.3 and all the scenes thereafter, where we are constantly made to feel that Cassius and Brutus are in the hands of something bigger than they know.

In this light, we can see readily enough why it is that Shakespeare gives Julius Caesar a double character. The dilemma in all violence is that the human Caesar who has human ailments and is a human friend is the Caesar who can be killed. Whereas the marmoreal Caesar, the everlasting Big Brother, must repeatedly be killed but never dies because he lurks in each of us and all together. Any political system is a potential Rome, and there is no reason for the citizen of any country, when he reads or watches a production of *Julius Caesar*, to imagine that this is ancient history.

CHAPTER SIX

"THE READINESS IS ALL"

Hamlet

I

Great plays, we know, each present us with something that can be called a world. A world like our own in being made of people, actions, situations, thoughts, feelings, and much more, but unlike our own in being perfectly, or almost perfectly, significant and coherent. In a play's world, each part implies the other parts, and each lives, means, with the life and meaning of the rest.

This is the reason, as we also know, why the worlds of great plays so greatly differ. Othello in Hamlet's position, we sometimes say, would have no problem; what we are really saying is that Othello in Hamlet's position would not exist. The conception we have of Othello is a function of the characters who help define him, Desdemona, honest Iago, Cassio, and the rest; of his history of travel and war; of a great storm that divides his ship from Cassio's, and a handkerchief; of a quiet night in Venice broken by cries about an old black ram; of a quiet night in Cyprus broken by sword-play; of a quiet bedroom where a woman goes to bed in her wedding sheets and a man comes in with a light to put out the light; and above all, of a language, a language with many voices in it, gentle, rasping, querulous, or foul, but all counterpointing the one great voice:

Keep up your bright swords, for the dew will rust them. (1.2.59)

O thou weed
Who art so lovely fair and smell'st so sweet
That the sense aches at thee. . . . (4.2.67)

107

> Yet I'll not shed her blood
> Nor scar that whiter skin of hers than snow,
> And smooth as monumental alabaster. (5.2.3)

Without this particular world of voices, persons, events, the world that both expresses and contains him, Othello is unimaginable. And so, I think, are Brutus, Antony, King Lear, Macbeth — and Hamlet. We come back then to Hamlet's world, of all the tragic worlds that Shakespeare made, easily the most various and brilliant, the most elusive. It is with no thought of doing justice to it that I single out three of its attributes for comment. I know well that no one is likely to accept another's reading of *Hamlet*, that anyone who tries to throw light on one part of the play usually throws the rest into deeper shadow, and that what I have to say leaves out many problems — to mention only one, the knotty problem of the text. All I would say in defense of the materials I have chosen is that they seem to me interesting, close to the root of the matter even if we continue to differ about what the root of the matter is, and explanatory, in a modest way, of this play's peculiar hold on everyone's imagination, its almost mythic status, one might say, as a paradigm of the process of "growing up."

2

The first attribute that impresses us, I think, is the play's mysteriousness. We often hear it said, perhaps with truth, that every great work of art has a mystery at the heart; but the mystery of *Hamlet* is something else. We feel its presence in the numberless explanations that have been brought forward for Hamlet's delay, his madness, his ghost, his treatment of Polonius, or Ophelia, or his mother; and in the controversies that still go on about whether the play is "undoubtedly a failure" (T. S. Eliot's phrase) or one of the greatest artistic triumphs; whether, if it is a triumph, it belongs to the highest order of tragedy; whether, if it is such a tragedy, its hero is to be taken as a man of exquisite moral sensibility (Bradley's view) or an egomaniac (Madariaga's view).

Doubtless there have been more of these controversies and explanations than the play requires; for in Hamlet, to paraphrase a remark of Falstaff's quoted earlier, we have a character who is not only mad in himself but a cause that madness can seize on the rest of us. Still, the very existence of so many theories and counter-theories, many of them formulated by sober heads, gives food for thought. *Hamlet* seems to lie closer to the illogical logic of life than Shakespeare's other tragedies. And while the causes of this situation may be sought by saying that Shakespeare revised the play so often that eventually the motivations were smudged over, or that the original old play has been here or there imperfectly digested, or that the problems of Hamlet lay so close to Shakespeare's heart that he could not quite distance them in the formal terms of art, we have still as critics to deal with effects, not causes. As others have noted, the play's very lack of a rigorous type of causal logic seems to be a part of its point.

Moreover, the matter goes deeper than this. Hamlet's world is preeminently in the interrogative mood. It reverberates with questions, anguished, meditative, alarmed. There are questions that in this play, to an extent I think unparalleled in any other, mark the phases and even the nuances of the action, helping to establish its peculiar baffled tone. There are other questions whose interrogations, innocent at first glance, are subsequently seen to have reached beyond their contexts and to point toward some pervasive inscrutability in Hamlet's world as a whole. Such is that tense series of challenges with which the tragedy begins: Bernardo's of Francisco, "Who's there?" Francisco's of Horatio and Marcellus, "Who is there?" Horatio's of the ghost, "What art thou . . . ?"

And then there are the famous questions. In them the interrogations seem to point not only beyond the context but beyond the play, out of Hamlet's predicaments into everyone's: "What a piece of work is a man! . . . And yet to me what is this quintessence of dust?" (2.2.300). "To be, or not to be—that is the question" (3.1.56). "Get thee to a nunnery. Why wouldst thou be a breeder of sinners?" (3.1.121). "I am very proud, revengeful, ambitious, with more offenses at my beck than I have thoughts to put them in, imagination to give them shape, or time to act them in. What should such fellows as I do crawling between earth and heaven?" (3.1.124). "Dost thou think Alexander looked o' this fashion i' th' earth? . . . And smelt so?" (5.1.185).

Further, Hamlet's world is a world of riddles. The hero's own language is often riddling, as the critics have pointed out. When he puns, his puns have receding depths in them, like the one which constitutes his first speech: "A little more than kin, and less than kind!" (1.2.65). His utterances in madness, even if wild and whirling, are simultaneously, as Polonius discovers, pregnant: "Do you know me, my lord?" "Excellent well. You are a fishmonger" (2.2.173). Even the madness itself is riddling: How much is real? How much is feigned? What does it mean?

Sane or mad, Hamlet's mind plays restlessly about his world, turning up one riddle upon another. The riddle of character, for example, and how it is that in a man whose virtues else are "pure as grace," some vicious mole of nature, some "dram of evil," can "all the noble substance [oft adulter]" (1.4.36). Or the riddle of the player's art, and how a man can so project himself into a fiction, a dream of passion, that he can weep for Hecuba (2.2.535). Or the riddle of action: how we may think too little — "What to ourselves in passion we propose," says the player-king. "The passion ending, doth the purpose lose" (3.2.186); and again, how we may think too much: "Thus conscience does make cowards of us all, And thus the native hue of resolution Is sicklied o'er with the pale cast of thought" (3.1.83).

There are also more immediate riddles. His mother — how could she "on this fair mountain leave to feed, And batten on this moor" (3.4.67)? The ghost — which may be a devil, for "the devil hath power T' assume a pleasing shape" (2.2.585). Ophelia — what does her behavior to him mean? Surprising her in her closet, he falls to such perusal of her face as he would draw it (2.1.90). Even the king at his prayers is a riddle. Will a revenge that takes him in the purging of his soul be vengeance, or hire and salary (3.3.79)? As for himself, Hamlet realizes, he is the greatest riddle of all — a mystery, he warns Rosencrantz and Guildenstern, from which he will not have the heart plucked out. He cannot tell why he has of late lost all his mirth, forgone all custom of exercises. Still less can he tell why he delays: "I do not know Why yet I live to say, 'This thing's to do,' Sith I have cause, and will, and strength, and means To do 't" (4.4.43).

Thus the mysteriousness of Hamlet's world is of a piece. It is not simply a matter of missing motivations, to be expunged if only we could find the perfect clue. It is built in. It is evidently an important part of what the play wishes to say to us. And it is certainly an element that the play thrusts upon us from the opening word. Everyone, I think, recalls the mysteriousness of that first scene. The cold middle of the night on the castle platform, the muffled sentries, the uneasy atmosphere of apprehension, the challenges leaping out of the dark, the questions that follow the challenges, feeling out the darkness, searching for identities, for relations, for assurance. "Bernardo?" "Have you had quiet guard?" "Who hath relieved you?" "What, is Horatio there?" "What, has this thing appeared again tonight?" "Looks 'a not like the king?" "How now, Horatio! . . . Is not this something more than fantasy? What think you on 't?" "Is it not like the King?" "Why this same strict and most observant watch . . . ?" "Shall I strike at it with my partisan?" "Do you consent we shall acquaint [young Hamlet] with it?"

We need not be surprised that critics and playgoers alike have been tempted to see in this an evocation not simply of Hamlet's world but of their own. Human beings in their aspect of bafflement, moving in darkness on a rampart between two worlds, unable to reject, or quite accept, the one that, when they face it, "to-shakes" their dispositions with thoughts beyond the reaches of their souls — comforting themselves with hints and guesses. We hear these hints and guesses whispering through the darkness as the several watchers speak. "At least, the whisper goes so" (1.1.80), says one. "I think it be no other but e'en so," says another. "I have heard" that on the crowing of the cock "Th' extravagant and erring spirit hies To his confine," says a third. "Some say" at Christmas time "This bird of dawning" sings all night, "And then, they say, no spirit dare stir abroad." "So have I heard," says the first, "and do in part believe it." However we choose to take the scene, it is clear that it creates a world where uncertainties are of the essence.

3

Meantime, such is Shakespeare's economy, a second attribute of Hamlet's world has been put before us. This is the problematic nature of reality and the relation of reality to appearance. The play begins with an appearance, an "apparition," to use Marcellus's term — the ghost. And the ghost is somehow real, indeed the vehicle of realities. Through its revelation, the glittering surface of Claudius's court is pierced, and Hamlet comes to know, and we do, that the king is not only hateful to him but the murderer of his father, that his mother is guilty of adultery as well as incest. Yet there is a dilemma in the revelation. For possibly the apparition *is* an apparition, a devil who has assumed his father's shape.

This dilemma, once established, recurs on every hand. From the court's point of view, there is Hamlet's madness. Polonius investigates and gets some strange advice about his daughter: "Conception is a blessing, but as your daughter may conceive, friend, look to 't" (2.2.184). Rosencrantz and Guildenstern investigate and get the strange confidence that "Man delights not me — nor woman neither" (2.2.305). Ophelia is "loosed" to Hamlet (Polonius's vulgar word), while Polonius and the king hide behind the arras; and what they hear is a strange indictment of human nature, and a riddling threat: "Those that are married already — all but one — shall live" (3.1.147).

On the other hand, from Hamlet's point of view, there is Ophelia. Kneeling here at her prayers, she seems the image of innocence and devotion. Yet she is of the sex for whom he has already found the name Frailty, and she is also, as he seems either madly or sanely to divine, a decoy in a trick. The famous cry — "Get thee to a nunnery" — shows the anguish of his uncertainty. If Ophelia is what she seems, this dirty-minded world of murder, incest, lust, adultery, is no place for her. Were she "as chaste as ice, as pure as snow" (3.1.136), she could not escape its calumny. And if she is not what she seems, then a nunnery in its other sense of brothel is relevant to her. In the scene that follows he treats her as if she were indeed an inmate of a brothel.

Likewise, from Hamlet's point of view, there is the enigma of the king. If the ghost is *only* an appearance, then possibly the king's appearance is reality. He must try it further. By means of a second and different kind of "apparition," the play within the play, he does so. But then, immediately after, he stumbles on the king at prayer (3.3). This appearance has a relish of salvation in it. If the king dies now, his soul may yet be saved. Yet actually, as we know, the king's efforts to come to terms with heaven have been unavailing; his words fly up, his thoughts remain below. If Hamlet means the conventional revenger's reasons that he gives for sparing Claudius, it was the perfect moment not to spare him — when the sinner was acknowledging his guilt, yet unrepentant. The perfect moment, but it was hidden, like so much else in the play, behind an arras.

There are two arrases in his mother's room (3.4). Hamlet thrusts his sword through one of them. Now at last he has got to the heart of the evil, or so he thinks. But now it is the wrong man; now he himself is a murderer. The other arras he stabs through with his words — like daggers, says the queen. He makes her shrink under the contrast he points between her present husband and his father. But as the play now stands (matters are somewhat clearer in the bad Quarto), it is hard to be sure how far the queen grasps the fact that her second husband is the murderer of her first. And it is hard to say what may be signified by her inability to see the ghost, who now for the last time appears. In one sense at least, the ghost is the supreme reality, representative of the hidden ultimate power, in Bradley's terms — witnessing from beyond the grave against this hollow world. Yet the man who is capable of seeing through to this reality, the queen thinks is mad. "To whom do you speak this?" she cries to her son. "Do you see nothing there?" (3.4.132) he asks, incredulous. And she replies: "Nothing at all; yet all that is I see." Here certainly we have the imperturbable self-confidence of the worldly world, its layers on layers of habituation, so that when the reality is before its very eyes it cannot detect is presence.

Like mystery, this problem of reality is central to the play and written deep into its idiom. Shakespeare's favorite terms in *Hamlet* are words of ordinary usage that pose the question of appearances in a fundamental form. "Apparition" I have already mentioned. Another term is "seems." When we say, as Ophelia says of Hamlet leaving her closet, "He seemed to find his way without his eyes" (2.1.98), we mean one thing. When we say, as Hamlet says to his mother in the first court-scene, "Seems,

Madam! . . . I know not 'seems' " (1.2.76), we mean another. And when we say, as Hamlet says to Horatio before the play within the play, "And after, we will both our judgments join In censure of his seeming" (3.2.83), we mean both at once. The ambiguities of "seem" coil and uncoil throughout this play, and over against them is set the idea of "seeing." So Hamlet challenges the king in his triumphant letter announcing his return to Denmark: "To-morrow shall I beg leave to see your kingly eyes" (4.7.44). Yet "seeing" itself can be ambiguous, as we recognize from Hamlet's uncertainty about the ghost; or from that statement of his mother's already quoted: "Nothing at all; yet all that is I see."

Another term of like importance is "assume." What we assume may be what we are not: "The devil hath power T' assume a pleasing shape" (2.2.585). But it may be what we are: "If it assume my noble father's person, I'll speak to it" (1.2.244). And it may be what we are not yet, but would become; thus Hamlet advises his mother, "Assume a virtue, if you have it not." The perplexity in the word points to a real perplexity in Hamlet's and our own experience. We assume our habits—and habits are like costumes, as the word implies: "My father, in his habit as he lived!" (3.4.136). Yet these habits become ourselves in time: "That monster custom, who all sense doth eat, Of habits devil, is angel yet in this, That to the use of actions fair and good He likewise gives a frock or livery That aptly is put on" (3.4.162).

Two other terms I wish to instance are "put on" and "shape." The shape of something is the form under which we are accustomed to apprehend it: "Do you see yonder cloud that's almost in shape of a camel?" But a shape may also be a disguise—even, in Shakespeare's time, an actor's costume or an actor's role. This is the meaning when the king says to Laertes as they lay the plot against Hamlet's life: "Weigh what convenience both of time and means May fit us to our shape" (4.7.148). "Put on" supplies an analogous ambiguity. Shakespeare's mind seems to worry this phrase in the play much as Hamlet's mind worries the problem of acting in a world of surfaces, or the king's mind worries the meaning of Hamlet's transformation. Hamlet has put an antic disposition on, that the king knows. But what does "put on" mean? A mask, or a frock or livery—our "habit"? The king is left guessing, and so are we.

4

What is found in the play's key terms is also found in its imagery. Miss Spurgeon has called attention to a pattern of disease images in *Hamlet*, to which I shall return. But the play has other patterns equally striking. One of these, as my earlier quotations hint, is based on clothes. In the world of surfaces to which Shakespeare exposes us in *Hamlet*, clothes are naturally a factor of importance. "The apparel oft proclaims the man," Polonius assures Laertes, cataloguing maxims in the young man's ear as he is about to leave for Paris (1.3.72). Oft, but not always. And so he sends his man Reynaldo to look into Laertes's life there — even, if need be, to put a false dress of accusation upon his son ("What forgeries you please"), the better by indirections to find directions out (2.1.66). On the same grounds, he takes Hamlet's vows to Ophelia as false apparel. They are bawds, he tells her — or if we do not like Theobald's emendation, they are bonds — in masquerade, "Not of that dye which their invest-ments show, But mere implorators of unholy suits" (1.3.128).

This breach between the outer and the inner stirs no special emotion in Polonius, because he is always either behind an arras or prying into one, but it shakes Hamlet to the core. Here so recently was his mother in her widow's weeds, the tears still flushing in her gallèd eyes; yet now within a month, a little month, before even her funeral shoes are old, she has married with his uncle. Her mourning was all clothes. Not so his own, he bitterly replies, when she asks him to cast his "nighted color off." " 'Tis not alone my inky cloak, good mother" — and not alone, he adds, the sighs, the tears, the dejected havior of the visage — "That can denote me truly." These indeed seem,

For they are actions that a man might play,
But I have that within which passeth show —
These but the trappings and the suits of woe.

What we must not overlook here is Hamlet's visible attire, giving the verbal imagery a theatrical extension. Hamlet's apparel now is his inky cloak, mark of his grief for his father, mark also of his character as a man of melancholy, mark possibly too of his being one in whom appearance

115

and reality are attuned. Later, in madness, with his mind disordered, he will wear his costume in a corresponding disarray, the disarray that Ophelia describes so vividly to Polonius and that producers of the play rarely give sufficient heed to: "Lord Hamlet with his doublet all unbraced, No hat upon his head, his stockings fouled, Ungartered, and down-gyvèd to his ankle" (2.1.78). Here the only question will be, as with the madness itself, how much is studied, how much is real. Still later, by a third costume, the simple traveler's garb in which we find him new come from shipboard, Shakespeare will show us that we have a third aspect of the man.

A second pattern of imagery springs from terms of painting: the paints, the colorings, the varnishes that may either conceal, or, as the painter's art, reveal. Art in Claudius conceals. "The harlot's cheek," he tells us in his one aside, "beautied with plast'ring art, Is not more ugly to the thing that helps it Than is my deed to my most painted word" (3.1.50). Art in Ophelia, loosed to Hamlet in the episode already noticed to which this speech of the king's is prelude, is more complex. She looks so beautiful — "the celestial, and my soul's idol, the most beautified Ophelia," Hamlet has called her in his love letter (2.2.109). But now, what does beautified mean? Perfected with all the innocent beauties of a lovely woman? Or "beautified" like the harlot's cheek? "I have heard of your paintings too, well enough. God hath given you one face, and you make yourselves another" (3.1.142).

Yet art, differently used, may serve the truth. By using an "image" (his own word) of a murder done in Vienna, Hamlet cuts through to the king's guilt; holds "as 'twere, the mirror up to nature," shows "virtue her own feature, scorn her own image, and the very age and body of the time" — which is out of joint — "his form and pressure" (3.2.20). Something similar he does again in his mother's bedroom, painting for her in words "the rank sweat of an enseamèd bed," making her recoil in horror from his "counterfeit presentment of two brothers," and holding, if we may trust a stage tradition, his father's picture beside his uncle's. Here again the verbal imagery is realized visually on the stage.

The most pervasive of Shakespeare's image patterns in this play, however, is the pattern evolved around the three words, show, act, play. "Show" seems to be Shakespeare's unifying image in *Hamlet*. Through it he pulls together and exhibits in a single focus much of the diverse material in his play. The ideas of seeming, assuming, and putting on; the images of clothing, painting, mirroring; the episode of the dumb show and the play within the play; the characters of Polonius, Laertes, Ophelia, Claudius, Gertrude, Rosencrantz and Guildenstern, Hamlet himself—all these at one time or another, and usually more than once, are drawn into the range of implications flung around the play by "show."

"Act," on the other hand, I take to be the play's radical metaphor. It distills the various perplexities about the character of reality into a residual perplexity about the character of an act. What, this play asks again and again, is an act? What is its relation to the inner act, the intent? "If I drown myself wittingly," says the clown in the graveyard, "it argues an act, and an act hath three branches—it is to act, to do, and to perform" (5.1.9). Or again, the play asks, how does action relate to passion, that "lapsed in time and passion" I can let "go by Th' important acting of your dread command" (3.4.108); and to thought, which can so sickly o'er the native hue of resolution that "enterprises of great pitch and moment With this regard their currents turn awry, And lose the name of action" (3.1.86); and to words, which are not acts, and so we dare not be content to unpack our hearts with them, and yet are acts of a sort, for we may speak daggers though we use none. Or still again, how does an act (a deed) relate to an act (a pretense)? For an action may be nothing but pretense. So Polonius readying Ophelia for the interview with Hamlet, with "pious action," as he phrases it, "sugar[s] o'er The devil himself" (3.1.48). Or it may not be a pretense, yet not what it appears. So Hamlet spares the king, finding him in an act that has some "relish of salvation in 't." Or it may be a pretense that is also the first foothold of a new reality, as when we assume a virtue though we have it not. Or it may be a pretense that is actually a mirroring of reality, like the play within the play, or the tragedy of *Hamlet*.

To this network of implications, the third term, "play," adds an additional dimension. "Play" is a more precise word, in Elizabethan parlance at least, for all the elements in *Hamlet* that pertain to the art of the theatre; and it extends their field of reference till we see that every major personage in the tragedy is a player in some sense, and every major episode a play. The court plays, Hamlet plays, the players play, Rosencrantz and Guildenstern try to play on Hamlet, though they cannot play on his recorders — here we have an extension to a musical sense. And the final duel, by a further extension, becomes itself a play, in which everyone but Claudius and Laertes plays his role in ignorance: "The queen desires you to use some gentle entertainment to Laertes before you fall to play" (5.2.195). "I . . . will this brother's wager frankly play." "Give him the cup." — "I'll play this bout first."

The full extension of this theme is best evidenced in the play within the play itself. Here, in the bodily presence of these traveling players, bringing with them the latest playhouse gossip out of London, we have suddenly a situation that tends to dissolve the normal barriers between the fictive and the real. For here on the stage before us is a play of false appearances in which an actor called the player-king is playing. But there is also on the stage, Claudius, another player-king, who is a spectator of this player. And there is on the stage, besides, a prince who is a spectator of both these player-kings and who plays with great intensity a player's role himself. And around these kings and that prince is a group of courtly spectators — Gertrude, Rosencrantz, Guildenstern, Polonius, and the rest — and they, as we have come to know, are players too. And lastly there are ourselves, an audience watching all these audiences who are also players. Where, it may suddenly occur to us to ask, does the playing end? Which *are* the guilty creatures sitting at a play? When is an act not an "act"?

5

The mysteriousness of Hamlet's world, while it pervades the tragedy, finds its point of greatest dramatic concentration in the first act, and its symbol in the first scene. The problems of appearance and reality also pervade the play as a whole, but come to a climax in Acts 2 and 3, and possibly their best symbol is the play-within-the-play. Our third attribute, though again it is one that crops out everywhere, reaches its full development in Acts 4 and 5. It is not easy to find an appropriate name for this attribute, but perhaps "mortality" will serve, if we remember to mean by mortality the heartache and the thousand natural shocks that flesh is heir to, not simply death.

The powerful sense of mortality in *Hamlet* is conveyed to us, I think, in three ways. First, there is the play's emphasis on human weakness, the instability of human purpose, the subjection of humanity to fortune — all that we might call the aspect of failure in human nature. Hamlet opens this theme in Act 1, when he describes how from that single blemish, perhaps not even the victim's fault, a man's whole character may take corruption. Claudius dwells on it again, to an extent that goes far beyond the needs of the occasion, while engaged in seducing Laertes to step behind the arras of a seemer's world and dispose of Hamlet by a trick. Time qualifies everything, Claudius says, including love, including purpose. As for love — it has a "plurisy" in it and dies of its own too much. As for purpose — "That we would do, We should do when we would, for this 'would' changes, And hath abatements and delays as many As there are tongues, are hands, are accidents, And then this 'should' is like a spendthrift sigh, That hurts by easing" (4.7.116). The player-king, in his long speeches to his queen in the play within the play, sets the matter in a still darker light. She means these protestations of undying love, he knows, but our purposes depend on our memory, and our memory fades fast. Or else, he suggests, we propose something to ourselves in a condition of strong feeling, but then the feeling goes, and with it the resolve. Or else our fortunes change, he adds, and with these our loves: "The great man down, you mark his favorite flies" (3.2.180). The subjection of human aims to fortune is a reiterated theme in *Hamlet*, as earlier in *Julius Caesar* and subsequently in *Lear*. Fortune is the harlot goddess in whose secret parts men like Rosencrantz and Guildenstern live and thrive; the strumpet who threw down Troy and Hecuba and Priam; the outrageous foe whose slings and arrows a man of principle must suffer or seek release in suicide. Horatio suffers them with composure: he is one of the blessed few "Whose blood and judgment are so well commeddled That they are not a pipe for Fortune's finger To sound what stop she please" (3.2.66). For Hamlet the task is of a greater difficulty.

Next, and intimately related to this matter of infirmity, is the emphasis on infection — the ulcer, the hidden abscess, "th' imposthume of much wealth and peace That inward breaks, and shows no cause without Why the man dies" (4.4.27). Miss Spurgeon, who was the first to call attention to this aspect of the play, has well remarked that so far as Shakespeare's pictorial imagination is concerned, the problem in *Hamlet* is not a problem of the will and reason, "of a mind too philosophical or a nature temperamentally unfitted to act quickly," or even a problem of the individual at all. Rather, it is a condition — "a condition for which the individual himself is apparently not responsible, any more than the sick man is to blame for the infection which strikes and devours him, but which, nevertheless, in its course and development, impartially and relentlessly, annihilates him and others, innocent and guilty alike."[60] "That," she adds, "is the tragedy of *Hamlet*, as it is perhaps the chief tragic mystery of life." This is a perceptive comment, for it reminds us that Hamlet's situation is mainly not of his own manufacture, as are the situations of Shakespeare's other tragic heroes. He has inherited it; he is "born to set it right."

We must not, however, neglect to add to this what another student of Shakespeare's imagery has noticed — that the infection in Denmark is presented alternatively as poison. Here, of course, responsibility is implied, for the poisoner of the play is Claudius. The juice he pours into the ear of the elder Hamlet is a combined poison and disease, a "leperous distilment" that curds "The thin and wholesome blood" (1.5.64). From this fatal center, unwholesomeness spreads out till there is something rotten in all Denmark. Hamlet tells us that his "wit's diseased" (3.2.308), the queen speaks of her "sick soul" (4.5.17), the king is troubled by "the hectic" (4.3.65) in his blood, Laertes meditates revenge to warm "the sickness in [his] heart" (4.7.54), the people of the kingdom grow "muddied, Thick and unwholesome in their thoughts" (4.5.81); and even Ophelia's madness is said to be "the poison of deep grief" (4.5.75). In the end, all save Ophelia die of that poison in a literal as well as figurative sense.

But the chief form in which the theme of mortality reaches us, it seems to me, is as a profound consciousness of loss. Hamlet's father expresses something of the kind when he tells Hamlet how his "seeming-virtuous queen," betraying a love which "was of that dignity That it went hand in hand even with the vow I made to her in marriage," had chosen to "decline Upon a wretch whose natural gifts were poor To those of mine." "O Hamlet, what a falling off was there!" (1.5.46). Ophelia expresses it again, on hearing Hamlet's denunciation of love and woman in the nunnery scene, which she takes to be the product of a disordered brain:

O what a noble mind is here o'erthrown!
The courtier's, soldier's, scholar's, eye, tongue, sword;
Th' expectancy and rose of the fair state,
The glass of fashion and the mould of form,
Th' observed of all observers, quite, quite, down! (3.1.150)

The passage invites us to remember that we have never actually seen such a Hamlet — that his mother's marriage has brought a falling off in him before we meet him. And then there is that further falling off, if I may call it so, when Ophelia too goes mad — "Divided from herself and her fair judgment, Without the which we are pictures, or mere beasts" (4.5.85).

Time was, the play keeps reminding us, when Denmark was a different place. That was before Hamlet's mother took off "the rose From the fair forehead of an innocent love" (3.4.43) and set a blister there. Hamlet then was still "Th' expectancy and rose of the fair state" (3.1.152); Ophelia, the "rose of May" (4.5.157). For Denmark was a garden then, when his father ruled. There had been something heroic about his father — a king who met the threats to Denmark in open battle, fought with Norway, smote the sledded Polacks on the ice, slew the elder Fortinbras in an honorable trial of strength. There had been something godlike about his father too: "Hyperion's curls, the front of Jove himself, An eye like Mars . . . , A station like the herald Mercury" (3.4.57). But, the ghost reveals, a serpent was in the garden, and "The serpent that did sting thy father's life Now wears his crown" (1.5.39). The martial virtues

121

are put by now. The threats to Denmark are attended to by policy, by agents working deviously for and through an uncle. The moral virtues are put by too. Hyperion's throne is occupied by "a vice of kings" (3.4.99), "a king of shreds and patches" (3.4.103); Hyperion's bed, by a satyr, a paddock, a bat, a gib, a bloat king with reechy kisses. The garden is unweeded now, and "grows to seed. Things rank and gross in nature Possess it merely" (1.2.136). Even in himself he feels the taint, the taint of being his mother's son; and that other taint, from an earlier garden, of which he admonishes Ophelia: "For virtue cannot so inoculate our old stock but we shall relish of it." "Why wouldst thou be a breeder of sinners?" "What should such fellows as I do crawling between earth and heaven?" (3.1.117).

"Hamlet is painfully aware," says E. M. W. Tillyard, "of the baffling human predicament between the angels and the beasts, between the glory of having been made in God's image and the incrimination of being descended from fallen Adam."[61] To this we may add, I think, that Hamlet is more than aware of it; he exemplifies it; and it is for this reason that his problem appeals to us so powerfully as an image of our own.

6

Hamlet's problem, in its crudest form, is simply the problem of the avenger: he must carry out the injunction of the ghost and kill the king. But this problem, as I ventured to suggest at the outset, is presented in terms of a certain kind of world. The ghost's injunction to act becomes so inextricably bound up for Hamlet with the character of the world in which the action must be taken—its mysteriousness, its baffling appearances, its deep consciousness of infection, frailty, and loss—that he cannot come to terms with either without coming to terms with both.

When we first see him in the play, he is clearly a very young man, sensitive and idealistic, suffering the first shock of growing up. He has taken the garden at face value, we might say, supposing mankind to be only a little lower than the angels. Now in his mother's hasty and incestuous marriage, he discovers evidence of something else, something bestial—though even a beast, he thinks, would have mourned longer. Then comes the revelation of the ghost, bringing a second shock. Not so much because he now knows that his serpent-uncle killed his father; his prophetic soul had almost suspected this. Not entirely, even, because he knows now how far below the angels humanity has fallen in his mother, and how lust — these were the ghost's words — "though to a radiant angel linked Will sate itself in a celestial bed, And prey on garbage" (1.5.55). Rather, because he now sees everywhere, but especially in his own nature, the general taint, taking from life its meaning, from woman her integrity, from the will its strength, turning reason into madness. Hamlet is not the first young man to have felt the heavy and the weary weight of all this unintelligible world; and, like the others, he must come to terms with it.

The ghost's injunction of revenge unfolds a different facet of his problem. The young man growing up is not to be allowed simply to endure a rotten world, he must also act in it. Yet how to begin, among so many enigmatic surfaces? Even Claudius, whom he now knows to be the core of the ulcer, has a plausible exterior. And around Claudius, swathing the evil out of sight, he encounters all those other exteriors, as we have seen. Some of them already deeply infected beneath, like his mother. Some noble, but marked for infection, like Laertes. Some not particularly corrupt but infinitely corruptible, like Rosencrantz and Guildenstern; some mostly weak and foolish like Polonius and Osric. Some, like Ophelia, innocent, yet in their innocence still serving to "skin and film the ulcerous place" (3.4.148).

And this is not all. The act required of him, though retributive justice, is one that necessarily involves the doer in the general guilt. Not only because it involves a killing; but because to get at the world of seeming one is impelled to use its weapons. He himself, before he finishes, has become a player, has put an antic disposition on, has killed a man — the wrong man — has helped drive Ophelia mad, and has sent two friends of his youth to death, mining below their mines, and hoisting the engineer with his own petard. He had never meant to dirty himself with these things, but from the moment of the ghost's challenge to act, this dirtying was inevitable. It is the condition of living at all in such a world. To quote

Polonius, who knew that world so well, men become "a little soiled i' th' working" (2.1.40). Here is another matter with which Hamlet has to come to terms.

Human infirmity — all that I have discussed with reference to instability, infection, loss — supplies the problem with its third phase. Hamlet has not only to accept the mystery of man's condition between the angels and the brutes, and not only to act in a perplexing and soiling world. He has also to act within the human limits — "with shabby equipment always deteriorating," if I may adapt some phrases from T. S. Eliot's *East Coker*, "In the general mess of imprecision of feeling, Undisciplined squads of emotion." Hamlet is aware of that fine poise of body and mind, feeling and thought, that suits the action to the word, the word to the action; that acquires and begets a temperance in the very torrent, tempest, and whirlwind of passion; but he cannot at first achieve it in himself. He vacillates between undisciplined squads of emotion and thinking too precisely on the event. He learns to his cost how easily action can be lost in "acting," and loses it there for a time himself. But these again are only the terms of every man's life. As Anatole France reminds us in a famous apostrophe to Hamlet: "What one of us thinks without contradiction and acts without incoherence? What one of us is not mad? What one of us does not say with a mixture of pity, comradeship, admiration, and horror, Goodnight, sweet Prince!"

7

In the last act of the play (or so it seems to me, for I know there can be differences on this point), Hamlet accepts his world and we discover a different man. Shakespeare does not outline for us the process of acceptance any more than he had done with Romeo or was to do with Othello. But he leads us strongly to expect an altered Hamlet, and then, in my opinion, provides him. We must recall that at this point Hamlet has been absent from the stage during several scenes, and that such absences in Shakespearean tragedy usually warn us to be on the watch for a new phase in the development of the character. It is so when we leave King Lear in Gloucester's farmhouse and find him again in Dover fields. It is so when we leave Macbeth at the witches' cave and rejoin him at Dunsinane, hearing of the armies that beset it. Furthermore, and this is an important matter in the theater — especially important in a play in which the symbolism of clothing has figured largely — Hamlet now looks different. He is wearing a different dress — probably, as Granville-Barker thinks, his "seagown scarfed" about him, but in any case no longer the disordered costume of his antic disposition. The effect is not entirely dissimilar to that in *Lear*, when the old king wakes out of his madness to find fresh garments on him.

Still more important, Hamlet displays a considerable change of mood. This is not a matter of the way we take the passage about defying augury. It is a matter of Hamlet's whole deportment, in which I feel we may legitimately see the deportment of a man who has undergone some form of insight or self-discovery in the tragic sense. Bradley's term for it is fatalism, but if this is what we wish to call it, we must at least acknowledge that it is fatalism of a very distinctive kind — a kind that Shakespeare has been willing to touch with the associations of the saying in St. Matthew about the fall of a sparrow, and with Hamlet's recognition that a divinity shapes our ends. The point is not that Hamlet has suddenly become religious; he has been religious all through the play. The point is that he has now learned, and accepted, the boundaries in which human action, human judgment, are enclosed.

Till his return from the voyage he had been trying to act beyond these, had been encroaching on the role of Providence, if I may exaggerate to make a vital point. He had been too quick to take the burden of the whole world and its condition upon his limited and finite self. Faced with a task of sufficient difficulty in its own right, he had dilated it into a cosmic problem — as indeed every task is, but if we think about this too precisely we cannot act at all. The whole time is out of joint, he feels, and in his young man's egocentricity, he will set it right. Hence he misjudges Ophelia, seeing in her only a breeder of sinners. Hence he misjudges himself, seeing himself a vermin crawling between earth and heaven. Hence he takes it upon himself to be his mother's conscience, though the ghost has warned that this is no fit task for him, and returns to repeat the warning: "Leave her to heaven, And to those thorns that in her bosom lodge" (1.5.86). Even with the king, Hamlet has sought to play at God. *He* it must be who decides the issue of Claudius's salvation, saving him for a more damnable occasion.

Now, he has learned that there are limits to the before and after that human reason can comprehend. Rashness, even, is sometimes good. Through rashness he has saved his life from the commission for his death, "and praised be rashness for it" (5.2.7). This happy circumstance and the unexpected arrival of the pirate ship make it plain that the roles of life are not entirely self-assigned. "There's a divinity that shapes our ends. Rough-hew them how we will" (5.2.10). Hamlet is ready now for what may happen, seeking neither to foreknow it nor avoid it. "If it be now, 'tis not to come; if it be not to come, it will be now; if it be not now, yet it will come. The readiness is all" (5.2.209).

The crucial evidence of Hamlet's new frame of mind, as I understand it, is the graveyard scene. Here, in its ultimate symbol, he confronts, recognizes, and accepts the condition of being human. It is not simply that he now accepts death, though Shakespeare shows him accepting it in ever more poignant forms: first, in the imagined persons of the politician, the courtier, and the lawyer, who laid their little schemes "to circumvent God" (5.1.75), as Hamlet puts it, but now lie here; then in Yorick, whom he knew and played with as a child; and then in Ophelia. This last death tears from him a final cry of passion, but the striking contrast between his behavior and Laertes's reveals how deeply he has changed.

Still, it is not the fact of death that invests this scene with its peculiar power. It is instead the haunting mystery of life itself that Hamlet's speeches point to, holding in its inscrutable folds those other mysteries that he has wrestled with so long. These he now knows for what they are, and lays them by. The mystery of evil is present here — for this is after all the universal graveyard, where, as the clown says humorously, he holds up Adam's profession; where the scheming politician, the hollow courtier, the tricky lawyer, the emperor and the clown and the beautiful young maiden, all come together in an emblem of the world; where even,

Hamlet murmurs, one might expect to stumble on "Cain's jawbone, that did the first murder" (5.1.73).

The mystery of reality is here too—for death puts the question "What is real?" in its irreducible form, and in the end uncovers all appearances: "Is this the fine of his fines and the recovery of his recoveries, to have his fine pate full of fine dirt?" (5.1.98). "Now get you to my lady's chamber, and tell her, let her paint an inch thick, to this favor she must come" (5.1.180). Or if we need more evidence of this mystery, there is the anger of Laertes at the lack of ceremonial trappings, and the ambiguous character of Ophelia's own death. "Is she to be buried in Christian burial when she wilfully seeks her own salvation?" (5.1.1) asks the gravedigger.

And last of all, but most pervasive of all, there is the mystery of human limitation. The grotesque nature of man's little joys, his big ambitions. The fact that the man who used to bear us on his back is now a skull that smells; that the noble dust of Alexander somewhere plugs a bunghole; that "Imperious Caesar, dead and turned to clay, Might stop a hole to keep the wind away" (5.1.200). Above all, the fact that a pit of clay is "meet" for such a guest as man, as the gravedigger tells us in his song, and yet that, despite all frailties and limitations, "That skull had a tongue in it, and could sing once" (5.1.71).

After the graveyard and what it indicates has come to pass in him, we know that Hamlet is ready for the final contest of mighty opposites. He accepts the world as it is, the world as a duel, in which, whether we know it or not, evil holds the poisoned rapier and the poisoned chalice waits; and in which, if we win at all, it costs not less than everything. I think we understand by the close of Shakespeare's *Hamlet* why it is that unlike the other tragic heroes he is given a soldier's rites upon the stage. For as William Butler Yeats once said, "Why should we honor those who die on the field of battle? A man may show as reckless a courage in entering into the abyss of himself."[62]

CHAPTER SEVEN

"SPEAK OF ME AS I AM"

Othello

I

T HERE is probably no play of Shakespeare's about which at the present time the interpretations of critics differ so radically and at so many points as about *Othello*.[63]
This is partly owing to extraneous factors that have nothing to do with the play. One such, of course, is the nature of criticism, colored as it always is and must be by the pressures of a particular culture and time as well as the biases, experiences, and values of the individual practitioner. A notably perplexing addition to this traditional fountain of discrepancy has emerged in recent years with the formation of group ideologies of the sort mentioned in the preface to this volume, which annex the distortions of a program to the already myopic character of the personal lens. And further, at least in the United States, there is the circumstance that most literary criticism including Shakespeare criticism is carried on in college and university faculties, where, for advancement if one is young and notoriety if one is not, it has become more expedient to voice new opinions than to improve on old ones — "And give to dust that is a little gilt More laud than gilt o'er-dusted" (*Troilus and Cressida*, 3.3.177).

This having been said, it remains true that over the years much in *Othello* itself has invited and continues to invite disagreement. Historically, the critical record shows that playgoers and readers alike have been troubled, when not shocked or outraged, by the union of a black man with a white woman. That a beautiful Venetian girl should fall in love with "a veritable negro"[64] seemed to many implausible, in fact "monstrous." The words are Coleridge's, but the sentiment was widely shared and, on the nineteenth-century stage, was increasingly taken into account by "orientalizing" the hero, making him appear to be what one of that century's best-known actor-directors declared he emphatically was: "not a negro" but "a stately Arab."[65] Perhaps nothing manifests more clearly the dependence of critical opinion on more general climates of opinion than the realization that an Arab Othello in the 1990s would be fully as likely to meet with audience condescension as any African chief.

Today, haunted as we are by our unfinished history of racial and ethnic intolerance, and possibly to a far greater extent than the conscious mind understands by ancient taboos against sexual unions outside the bounds of cult, caste, tribe, or race (each of which, after all, is only xenophobia writ large), it becomes difficult to find an angle of vision that does not appropriate *Othello* to some sociological or political cause. Add to this the vast ranges of untrammeled speculation that open when one applies twentieth-century psychosexual lore to fictitious personages in an early seventeenth-century play, and the opportunities for dissension, not to say confusion, proliferate like rabbits.

No assumption should be made that the interpretation of *Othello* attempted in the ensuing pages is imagined by its author to be the "right" one or the "best." Like all the views advanced in this book, it carries its own existentially personal baggage. What it undertakes merely is to look at the play without invoking either the older inhibitions about miscegenation that have exercised so many in the past and still exercise too many, or the newer psychoanalytic suppositions (questionable enough when applied to living persons, as the quarrels among the several schools show), whose tendency when superimposed on the contrived creations of dramatic artifice is to dissolve necessary distinctions between reality and stage. My aim, in short, is to bear in mind, first, that the currents of thought and feeling swirling through the play are fed by a *Renaissance* sensibility and, second, that the play unfolds itself for audiences in the theater and readers in the study not by topics but speech by speech and scene by scene — far less an occasion for consulting-room theories of repression and psychoses than a vehicle of situations, movements, gestures, colors, sounds, and acts and words that break the heart.

2

A striking feature of Hamlet's world, it may be recalled, is mystery. Not only his own, which he is not about to have plucked out either by himself or others, but the larger mysteries on which he broods and among which, like the rest of us, he has to learn to live and act.

It is obvious that Othello's world differs sharply. Mystery may be operative in the motivation of Iago — "Will you, I pray, demand that demi-devil Why he hath thus ensnared my soul and body?" (5.2.301) — though one suspects he refuses to reply because his creator has no answer (on these matters, who has?) and certainly does not wish to remove from him the implication so carefully nurtured throughout the play and in the impassioned question just cited that he connects with something beyond understanding, like the witches in *Macbeth*.

In any event, what comes to us most forcefully from the stage in *Othello* is not mystery but the agony of loss, loss all the more tragic, in some instances, for not being inevitable. Brabantio loses (in every sense) his much-loved only child and eventually dies of grief. Cassio in a drunken moment loses his soldier's discipline, then his lieutenancy and his cherished comradeship with Othello. Othello, in turn, losing under Iago's tuition his ability to distinguish the individual woman he married from the standard cynical stereotype, abandons with it all pride in his profession together with the self-command that made him the man he was. And Desdemona, through no real fault of her own, loses the magical handkerchief.

Magical in *my* view, though I know how far opinions differ on this point, as a way of asking us to recognize that the love these lovers share before Iago's corruption sets in does indeed have magic in its web, contains a "work" (3.3.296) that a relationship like Cassio's and Bianca's can never match or "take out," commands a power that sets it as far above the commonplace as Desdemona is in the radiant generosity and innocence that makes her vulnerable, as Othello is in the "free and open nature" (1.3.393) that makes *him* vulnerable, and in the courage and determination to do justice on himself that earns the closing accolade: "For he was great of heart" (5.2.361).

To my mind, it is precisely the loss of a love as rare and magical as the fabled handkerchief by a pair of lovers whose vulnerabilities are insepa-rable from their beauties that tears at the feelings throughout this play and brings to any audience listening to Othello's comparison of himself to "the base Indian"[66] (5.2.347) who threw a pearl away richer than all his tribe — not knowing what he had or what it was worth — a shock of self-recognition.

Supporting and extending the sense of irretrievable loss that the play conveys is a succession of poignant retrospectives opening on what we realize, though the speakers may not, was a securer or freer or happier or at least less perplexing condition than the one now being experienced. Othello, recounting before the Senate the toils and hazards of his past life to refute charges of witchcraft in his wooing that could cost his life, evokes for us, if not for himself, the "unhousèd free condition" (1.2.26) he has put behind him for the love of Desdemona. Even Iago is allowed his brief memory of a stay in "sweet England" (2.3.83), where the natives were "most potent in potting" (2.3.72), and he no doubt held his own with the best.

The most moving retrospectives come later. Desdemona, preparing for bed on the night that will be her last, remembers her mother's maid "called Barbary":

She was in love, and he she loved proved mad
And did forsake her. She had a song of "Willow;"
An old thing 'twas; but it expressed her fortune,
And she died singing it. That song to-night
Will not go from my mind. (4.3.25)

Here time present, in which Desdemona speaks and sings, and time future, in which we know she (like Barbary) is to die from an absolute fidelity to her intuition of what love is and means, recede even as we watch into a lost time past, when Desdemona had a mother and all love's agonies and complexities could be comprehended in a song. A song, moreover, bringing to her consciousness the sheltered world in which she grew up, now balanced beside the world she chose. In that other world, her husband might have been a Venetian gentleman, someone like Lodovico perhaps — "a proper man," she confides to Emilia — such a man as surely would never strike his wife in public or humiliate her in private as a common prostitute? But the song itself refuses to take sides. And as she sings, she seems to be understanding that there is no world worth living in without love, and no love worth having that is immune to pain — if not from the particular wounds she has met with, then by others. Surely one of the key epiphanic moments in all drama, the song serves to remind us that Shakespeare's own song of "Willow," about the tragedies and treacheries of love, is the play before our eyes.

The last remembrance of things past belongs to Othello. As he stabs himself, he recalls a moment "in Aleppo once" (5.2.352), when at the risk of his life (for the fate of any Christian who assaulted a native in Aleppo was immediate death) he struck down a Turk who had struck a Venetian and traduced the state. He has been that Turk in his treatment of Desdemona, and he now punishes his deed by executing himself. But he also knows that on that occasion as on so many others he has put his life on the line for Venice. Let the record then stand as it really is, tragically mixed: "Speak of me as I am" (5.2.342). It is a caveat not to be ignored as we turn to the first scenes.

3

Scene 1, we all remember, takes place on a dark street in Venice. So dark in most modern stagings that at first we are only conscious of clashing voices, one saying impatiently, "Tush, never tell me!," the other replying, "'Sblood, but you'll not hear me!" Though we will perhaps not notice at the time, it may occur to us later that this "'Sblood" (for "God's Blood"), like the "Zounds" (for "God's Wounds") that explodes twice from these lips in the next few minutes, is calculated to tell us something about this speaker, whose first word initiates a program of profaning, trivializing, and vulgarizing that will end only when the play ends.

Meantime, this same speaker, whose name it now develops is Iago, has been assuring his companion of his hatred for someone he calls "the Moor" (1.1.40). The Moor, it seems, ignoring Iago's rightful claim, has appointed as his lieutenant a West-Point type named Cassio, whose soldiership is "Mere prattle without practice" (1.3.26). If we are inclined for a moment to feel some sympathy for Iago's resentment, it is soon qualified by the *non sequitur* of his argument. He craves the profit of what he calls the "old gradation, where each second Stood heir to the first" (1.1.37) Yet he has only scorn for the kind of investment that made the old gradation feasible. Not for him the loyalties that bind Kent to Lear, Enobarbus to Antony, or, in this play, Emilia to Desdemona and Cassio to Othello. No. "Whip me such honest knaves." "For, sir, It is as sure as you are Roderigo, . . . not I for love and duty But seeming so for my peculiar end" (1.1.55). Here again, an alacrity in defaming, not only the particular trust that in the soldier's trade is as indispensable as armor but the very bonds that make civil society possible, should later give us pause.

But only later. For suddenly the two voices get down to business and we learn what that matter is for which Roderigo has been reproaching his companion. The Moor, it seems, has run off with the daughter of a Venetian senator, Brabantio, at whose house they are about to raise an outcry. Once convinced by what they say, Brabantio and his household swarm into the street with torches. The scene is visually unforgettable. And is meant to be, for it will be many times repeated: one torch, or many torches, or perhaps only a single taper, moving in the darkness of our ignorance of each other. A darkness, we increasingly understand, not confined to the stage. What do we know, really (no matter how intimately we live with them), about that man or woman sitting beside us in the next chair?

Just now, however, as we listen to his plans evolve, the darkness seems chiefly to be Iago's element. In the darkness of this Venetian street, he moves to disrupt Othello's marriage if he can. Later, in the darkness of a street in Cyprus, he will close his trap on Cassio, involving him in a scuffle that will cost him his lieutenancy. Still later, in that dark island outpost, he will set Roderigo to ambush Cassio, and so (he hopes) be rid of both. Simultaneously, in a darkness that he has insinuated into Othello's mind, Desdemona will be strangled. So when we see Othello make that fateful entry into their bedroom bearing a pitifully small light, we are to bear in mind this opening moment when, for all his torches, Brabantio quite misunderstands what has long been before his eyes. It is not Othello only who proves vulnerable to Iago's darkness, but, in some degree, everyone in the play.

4

Scene 2 brings us further evidence about Iago. If the manuscript of the play, it has often been remarked, had been lost except for the first scene, the only Othello we would know would be the stereotypical white man's version of the black man that Iago and Roderigo contemptuously describe: "the thick-lips" (1.1.66), "an old black ram" (1.1.88), "a Barbary horse" (1.1.111), "the gross clasps of a lascivious Moor" (1.1.125). This Othello is a Muslim, for that was a primary meaning of Moor in Shakespeare's time. He is also "an extravagant and wheeling stranger" (1.1.135), meaning a rootless alien with no settled home. He is as well a typical blowhard soldier, a *miles gloriosus*, "Horribly stuffed" says Iago, "with epithets of war" (1.1.14). And he is apparently some sort of sexual satyr, since that is what Iago's grosser insults imply. His black skin, moreover, links him with lechery and especially with the devil. "A Moor, Of all that bears man's shape, likest a divell," writes Shakespeare's contemporary Thomas Heywood.[67] If you don't stop this elopement, Iago advises Brabantio, "the devil will make a grandsire of you" (1.1.91).

To all this, you will recall, the second scene brings a startling change. Our satyr, it turns out, has eloped with Desdemona not because (as in Iago's book and many since) a black man is always in rut, but because he loves her and, as we are soon to learn, she loves him. Our braggart soldier and rootless alien, we now discover, is a prince, who when he knows "that boasting is an honor" (1.2.20) will let it be told that he descends from "men of royal siege" (1.2.22). As for our Muslim, he is in point of fact a Christian, one of Christendom's champions in the defense of Europe against "the general enemy Ottoman" (1.3.49). Cyprus, every Elizabethan knew, had long been a bastion in that defense. It was only thirty-odd years since the sultan's armies had been thrown back from the walls of Vienna.

Here is an about-face indeed. And we may reasonably guess that such an entire reversal of perspective, not found in the other tragedies, is purposeful. One requirement, clearly, was to prepare *Othello's* first audiences for a figure as unassimilable as Othello is to many of the stereotypes of Moorishness present in the culture and regularly purveyed on the contemporary stage — by Shakespeare's own Aaron, for instance, in *Titus Andronicus.* As all rhetoricians know, and all debate teams, to show complete familiarity with a popular opinion and even what at first may be taken for a degree of sympathy with it is the most politic way to gain a hearing for another view. It is also the likeliest way to give that other view maximum dramatic impact when disclosed, as we have just seen happening in Scene 2.

But perhaps the greatest single gain from the reversal was that it required an audience to discover how easily it could be led into mistaken judgments, especially judgments that had been found congenial, and especially when packaged by a skilled manipulator of lies and truths. For a few moments, we in the theater are placed in a situation interestingly parallel to that in which Othello will soon find himself. As we are invited (with alarming success, theater history shows) to buy into the stereotype of the brutal Moor, Othello will be invited to buy into the stereotype of the promiscuous Venetian wife who lets only God see the pranks she dare not show her husband. The crucial difference is that the play immediately sets us right, while not till its end will Othello's knowledge equal ours. When it does, he will respond to Iago as we do.

Or at least, as the play asks us to do. Hazlitt gets it right, it seems to me, when he says that Iago's fascination for us combines equal parts of admiration and horror.[68] Admiration for his cunning, his resourceful opportunism, his street-smart confidences, his public charm. Horror at the envious fury raging inside that cool exterior which drives him to shrivel with his caustic cynicism and destroy with his murderous indifference anyone and anything with qualities beyond his grasp. His reaction to Cassio — "He hath a daily beauty in his life That makes me ugly" (5.1.19) — says it all.

Yet our disposition recently on both stage and page has been to downplay the horror, ignore the implication of his many references to one whom Macbeth calls "the common enemy of man" (3.1.69), and present an ingratiating stage manager comically engaged in exploding an "exsufflicate" or stuffed-shirt Othello. Possibly this distortion reflects the uneasiness, not to say downright discomfort, that in the age of Freud we tend to bring to the contemplation of whatever looks to be heroic or magnificent or grand.[69] Or possibly it springs from the current fashionable conviction in academic circles that all relationships are power relationships and the customary fidelities of the married state merely masks to hide a greedy capitalist enclosure of private property. Whatever its source, it has diminished our empathy with the play's hero and made more acceptable to us than they should be all those hard-bitten "truths," as it flatters us to call them, all those faint-hearted scepticisms and incredulities, by which like Iago we cut what makes us ugly down to an unthreatening size.

What should be noticed in particular is that, essentially, Shakespeare invented Iago;[70] set him down in his *dramatis personae* with the single epithet "a villain"; and devoted most of the play's lines and scenes to showing in detail the cunning, malignancy, and cruelty of his nature, including the cowardice of his murder of his wife. It seems to me therefore impossible to believe, as some recent critics would have us do, that the root causes of Othello's ruin are to be sought in some profound moral or psychological deficiency peculiar to *him*. He shows, to be sure, the degree of inexperience that follows naturally from his being a new husband, a soldier who has spent his entire previous life in the field, an outsider unacquainted with Venetian ways, and a man whose straightforward nature assumes the like in others. These are failings that a skilled manipulator can exploit, and their exploitation is precisely what we watch with sinking hearts. But once we go beyond this to postulate a deep and deadly fault in Othello's inmost being we come up against the implausible conclusion that one of the most experienced of dramatists has badly bungled his play. For what he has created in Iago, in that case, is a master intriguer and corrupter with no function proportionate to his stature, if what he exists to do has already been done for him by a self-doomed victim. A master intriguer, moreover, whose repeated assertion of diabolical power may well remind his theater audience of an earlier occasion when envy and a plausible exterior destroyed a pair of innocents.

5

This same scene has much to say about Othello, the nature of whose tragedy it begins to define. Fresh from alarming Brabantio, Iago now seeks to alarm his master by recounting Brabantio's abuse. Othello remains composed: " 'Tis better as it is" (1.2.6). Then an armed group appears with torches. Iago urges Othello to withdraw, claiming it is "the raisèd father and his friends" (1.2.29), and no doubt hoping that withdrawal will be taken as a sign of guilt. Othello remains composed: "Not I; I must be found" (1.2.30). A second armed group appears. This time it *is* Brabantio and his party, and there is the flash of drawn steel. Othello remains composed: "Keep up your bright swords," (1.2.59) he says, with the professional soldier's amusement at the department-store glitter of civilian weapons, "for the dew will rust them." Brabantio then assails Othello with every insult in the white man's book. What girl, he asks, least of all my daughter, would "Run from her guardage to the sooty bosom Of such a thing as thou?" (1.2.70). Othello remains composed: "Hold your hands, Both you of my inclining and the rest. Were it my cue to fight, I should have known it Without a prompter" (1.2.81).

These repeated upsurgings of violence against calm establish what I take to be the play's fundamental dramatic rhythm. Calm—sleep, in fact—invaded by uproar and violent language at Brabantio's house. Calm resisting and quelling violence in the three encounters just described. Calm unruffled before the Senate, easily blowing away Brabantio's violent charges. Calm of fulfilled happiness in the central scenes, attacked and gradually possessed by forms of violence it has no art to cope with. Finally at the play's close, calm retrieved and reasserted at great cost. All these confrontations are vivid in our experience when we see *Othello* in the theater and should, I think, warn us that the core of tragedy is to be looked for here where it is found in Shakespeare's other tragedies of this period. Compressed to six words, the inmost shape of tragedy in all these plays—its common denominator—is the shape that Hamlet gives it unwittingly in his first soliloquy: "That it should come to this" (1.2.137).

That, in other words, a young idealistic student should become, even against his will, an intriguer and killer, as Hamlet does. Or that a great king should be reduced to beggary and madness, and by his own daughters, as Lear is. Or that a man gifted with a moral imagination so intense that even the anticipation of murder can make his hair stand on end should reach a condition so benumbed, so supped full with horrors, that to go back is as tedious as "go o'er," as happens to Macbeth. Or that the greatest soldier of the ancient world, once the king of courtesy, should be reduced to having his rival's emissary whipped, as in the case of Antony. Or that an earlier famous soldier should be so mastered by self-will and pride as to defect to the national enemy and war against his kin—the story of Coriolanus.

Here is where tragedy normally resides in Shakespeare's mature work, and I see no evidence that it resides elsewhere in *Othello*. There would be nothing tragic, in the senses of tragic that apply to drama, in the commission of a murder by one who was in fact a barbarian—that is melodrama. Or about the anguish of a lover naturally inclined to jealousy—that is one of the oldest of comic themes, touched on already in *The Merry Wives*. What seems to me tragic in *Othello* is precisely that its hero is not a barbarian and, as he himself tells us, not *easily* jealous—in short, that it is possible for a human being who is what Othello is repeatedly shown to be at the play's beginning to become what he has become by its end: his command of himself and others shattered, his mind fouled, his occupation gone, his embrace of love changed to the embrace of murder. Or, as Lodovico the Venetian ambassador puts it, in words that only an ideologue could ignore, "Oh thou Othello, that wert once so good, Fall'n in the practice of a damnèd slave. What shall be said to thee?" (5.2.291).

If tragedy, as Aristotle thought, has to do with terror, Othello's being brought to kill the thing he loves *is* terror, for it can happen to us, and does, as many a newspaper headline will remind us. And if pity too is part of the tragic experience, here is pity in its intensest form, for we know it to be a law of life in our world that what is beautiful is always vulnerable and what is precious can cause the greatest pain.

6

I have dwelt considerably on these opening scenes, since in the theater we cannot ignore them any more than we can ignore the climax to which they point: the great moment on the sea-wall when Othello and Desdemona are reunited.

By this time, there has been considerable suspense as we watch Othello escorted to the Senate House under guard, his personal fate uncertain till the story of his wooing wins the Senators as securely as the story of his life won Desdemona. More suspense as we wait for Desdemona to appear, followed by a shock of surprise as we learn how mature and spirited she is and how little her father knew her: "A maiden never bold; Of spirit so still and quiet that her motion Blushed at herself" (1.3.94). Or should we say perhaps instead that what she discovered when she "saw Othello's visage in his mind" released something in her own that was waiting to be released, as when the sleeping princess wakes to the kiss of the wandering prince?

Then falls the first of many hardships. The Duke declares Othello must away tonight. "Tonight, my lord?" says Desdemona, with what feelings we can guess.[71] "This night," comes the firm reply. After which Othello has four words: "With all my heart" (1.3.278).

Much has been made of these words. And if we believe that Othello is a sexual cripple, or has a narcissistic incapacity to love any but himself, or is emotionally underdeveloped because of some problem in achieving separation from his mother during infancy, or, conversely, is a man so passionate he dreads his powerful sexuality (four popular theories of recent years), we will expect the actor to speak the four words briskly and on the upbeat, as if his martial ego were straining like a sled-dog to release him from this pickle.

But if we believe otherwise and see in Othello one version of the warrior-lover figure so congenial to the Renaissance imagination, the occasion will be treated very differently. After the Duke's ultimatum, several seconds of painful silence ensue while Othello gazes longingly, even despairingly, at his new wife, as she at him, and then says with a sigh in his voice and a tone that conveys his disappointment along with his recognition that in the soldier's trade orders are orders: "With all my heart." It is one of the most telling moments in the play and, performed as suggested here, only confirms the depth of their affection, together with the persistent theme of loss.

When next we see the lovers, they come like mythic figures from the sea. The great storm is winding down, having first destroyed the Turkish fleet; and the perils of the Cyprus voyage (seas, winds, "guttered rocks, and congregated sands" [2.1.69]) — moved by beauty — so Cassio's courtly gallantries would persuade us — have let "go safely by The divine Desdemona" (2.1.72). This is tall talk. Tall talk that like so much else in this tragic play (as earlier in *Romeo and Juliet*, later in *Antony and Cleopatra*) weaves into it some of the colorings of romance: that genre of writing, as Henry James once pointed out, in which experience is "liberated, . . . disengaged, disembroiled, disencumbered, exempt from the conditions that we usually know to attach to it . . . and drag upon it."[72] Romance colorings leap out again as Cassio utters his prayer for the lovers' safety, enfolding their reunion in the ancient myth that human sexual consummation brings fruition to all other things:

> Great Jove, Othello guard,
> And swell his sail with thine own pow'rful breath,
> That he may bless this bay with his tall ship,
> Make love's quick pants in Desdemona's arms,
> Give renewed fire to our extincted spirits,
> And bring all Cyprus comfort! (2.1.77)

As he speaks, Desdemona enters, wearing a traveling gown of purest white (or so it was in one production I recall), high on the crest of the abutment that defends the city from the sea. For a thrilling instant, her radiance transforms all that lies about her. Then she descends, Cassio painting her once again in great brush strokes of legend, as if it were the homecoming of some divinity. (Should we perhaps remember here that Cyprus is the ancient home of Aphrodite?) "O behold!" he cries,

The riches of the ship is come on shore!
You men of Cyprus, let her have your knees.
Hail to thee, lady! and the grace of heaven,
Before, behind thee, and on every hand,
Enwheel thee round! (2.1.82)

And then, quite suddenly, another voice is heard, sharp and mocking. "Sir," says this voice to Cassio, who has saluted Emilia with a kiss, "Would she give you so much of her lips As of her tongue she oft bestows on me, You'ld have enough" (2.1.100). Romance may disencumber all it pleases from those conditions "that we usually know to attach to it," but in tragic life their "drag" will still be felt.

At Othello's entry, the pattern recurs. He stands at the top of the sea-wall where Desdemona stood before, and she goes up to his side. His robe of state is red, and with it folded about them both she is visibly his "fair warrior" (2.1.180) — so he calls her — and for that moment they command the scene, lost in a joy that those below (significantly) look up to. "If it were now to die" (2.1.187), Othello says, voicing the Renaissance lover's sense of an achieved perfection already containing all that life can offer, but fused with the tragic hero's intimation of some doom possibly yet hanging in the stars:

If it were now to die,
'Twere now to be most happy; for I fear
My soul hath her content so absolute
That not another comfort like to this
Succeeds in unknown fate. (2.1.187)

May "this, and this," he adds, kissing her, "the greatest discords be That e'er our hearts shall make." But then, from down below, reserved this time for our ears alone, comes the interrupting challenge of a man in black: "O you are well tuned now! But I'll set down the pegs that make this music, As honest as I am" (2.1.197).

7

Iago's untuning of their "music" — plainly a glancing allusion on Shakespeare's part to the belief that when the universe sprang from Chaos to become a Harmony in which the compelling force was Eros (the same belief that underlies Othello's exclamation at Desdemona's beauty, "Perdition catch my soul, But I do love thee, and when I love thee not, Chaos is come again" (3.3.90) — occupies the so-called "temptation scene" of the third act. We come to this from two earlier temptations. In the first, Roderigo's tentative resistance to the maxim that love is "merely a lust of the blood and a permission of the will" (1.3.333) succumbs so completely to Iago's corrosive references to the wedding night of Othello and Desdemona — "when she is sated with his body, she will find the error of her choice" (1.3.347) — that he revises his ambitions from a not very seriously intended suicide to "enjoying" her (1.3.354). In the second, having been tested along this same fault-line and found impregnable (2.3.15), Cassio incautiously accepts Iago's invitation to a night of good fellowship and drink, and so becomes an easy mark for the street brawl that loses him his lieutenancy.

Othello's temptation is the culmination of these. The brilliance of its adaptation of complex psychological materials to the conditions of theater deserves a monograph. One can only say here that the scene *plays* best when the director establishes a distinctive area or symbolic object at either end of the stage. One is to be suggestive of Desdemona — perhaps a pair of virginals or a lute, since we know she "sings, plays, and dances" (3.3.185) (A lute will have the advantage of making more explicit the image of strings "well tuned.") The other area or object should be a reminder of Cassio — a chair, say, or couch, on which still lies (preferably) an offering of flowers, but possibly a hat or cloak or some other possession easily identified as his, left behind in his hasty retreat. During the course of the scene, Iago will drive Othello, with many rebounds, from the area of the lute to the area of the hat or nosegay. At this spot, having roared out his wish that Cassio had "forty thousand lives" (3.3.442), Othello kneels with Iago in their mutual oath of revenge.

All this has to do with the scene onstage, where few audiences have ever been in doubt about its power and persuasiveness. On the other hand, the scene *reads* better if we bear in mind Santayana's remark about poetry in general. "Poetry is not at its best," he writes, "when it depicts a

143

further possible experience, but when it initiates us, by feigning something that as an experience is impossible, into the meaning of the experience we have actually had."[73] So we are asked here to let clock time fade into emotional time (the play's much-discussed "double-time scheme" facilitates this), in order that the playwright may crowd into one intense theatrical experience the mysterious evolution of states of feeling that can, and do if spread over days or weeks in the real world, lead human beings from confidence to perplexity to doubt to surrender to breakdown.

"Mysterious" is the crucial term; for though Shakespeare gives us here on the side of realism a notable succession of psychological advances and retreats, he seems to have known as well as we do that these are all finally "signals" alerting us to psychological events, not the events themselves, which even in our therapies today remain graspable only by metaphor. And he knew also as a practicing playwright that creatures sitting at a play in his time did not expect (nor probably could he have provided) elaborate verisimilitudes of intellection at work. Often he is content to signal psychic change simply by absenting his hero from the stage, as with Hamlet and Lear, and as with Othello in mid-scene here. But elsewhere in this scene he goes all out to give his indicators of mental process the maximum illusion of reality. Edmund in *King Lear* deceives Gloucester into thinking Edgar is about to kill him in something less than ninety seconds of playing time. Here, by contrast, Iago's silences, evasions, and insinuations prior to Othello's first exit make up a plausible quarter-hour sequence establishing just those conditions of perplexity and doubt that the street brawl has already shown us Othello's forthright nature cannot endure.[74]

8

Soon after this, we witness the heart-breaking consequences of Iago's triumph. Othello — "the nature Whom passion could not shake, whose solid virtue The shot of accident, nor dart of chance, Could neither graze nor pierce" (4.1.257) — erupts in anger at Desdemona for having mislaid the handkerchief that in some occult way represents love's "magic." In full view of the embassy just arrived from Venice, he strikes her in the face; and, his mind having been turned into a brothel, proceeds to turn his home into one, greeting Emilia as a procuress and Desdemona as a woman for sale.

When next we see him for any length of time, he is in their bedroom contemplating her beauty by the candle in his hand. We have reached this scene after another street brawl, with the usual outcries, the usual flash of steel, the usual torches pitted vainly against the several sorts of darkness that surround all action in this play. But now for a moment we have calm, this time judicial calm — "It is the cause, it is the cause, my soul" — until Desdemona in her innocence insists on not playing the role of guilty wife that Othello's perverted script demands. What rouses him again to anger is noteworthy. When at the news of Cassio's death she bursts into tears and cries out, "Alas, he is betrayed and I undone!" (5.2.76), she looks and speaks like the guilty woman he believes her to be. She means only that Cassio has been falsely accused, and now there is no witness left to confirm her innocence. But to Othello she seems to be saying, "Cassio is exposed, and now I am done for." Taking her tears as further confirmation, he kills her.

Much of the rest of the play is devoted to exposing the details of Iago's plot (5.2.181), Othello's role becoming largely that of suffering auditor. But when Lodovico says at last, "Bring [him] away," Othello interposes. "Soft you! a word or two before you go" (5.2.338). He draws from the bed the great red robe of state in which he entered Cyprus as commander and in which he entered Desdemona's bedroom as officer of state to carry out an execution, flinging it now across his shoulders as if he were preparing for another of his life's journeys, this one his last. But he knows he will not be going. If the scene in their bedroom was, as he now understands, a blind miscarriage of truth and justice, this is to be his reaffirmation of both. He will have nothing extenuated, but nothing set down in malice either: "Speak of me as I am." Much of the preceding tragic action, we have by now come to realize, consists in a losing contest between those six words and six others that were burned on our attention in the first scene: "I am not what I am."

Here, as elsewhere, Shakespeare conveys a vivid sense of Othello's personality in his speech. Nothing could be simpler or more direct than "Speak of me as I am," or "'Tis better as it is," or "Not I. I must be found," or "Soft you, a word or two before you go." This is the Othello whose language has been shaped and seasoned by a life in action, whose forthright idiom expresses nobly the "free and open nature" — acknowledged so scornfully by Iago — "That thinks men honest that but seem to be so" (1.3.394). But there is another stratum in Othello's language, as in his person. He is an outsider and speaks as one; a traveler with a haunting past; a Mauretanian prince whose every gesture in the early scenes has the dignity of Saladin; and (as always) he is the larger-than-life Shakespearean hero, brushed in this instance with the glamor that Africa's rumored kingdoms once held for Western eyes. The natural language of this stratum, as in African and Middle Eastern poetry generally, is opulent and grand; and in this farewell, as at other moments earlier, his imagination roams freely through time and space to give his pain of loss the widest possible definition:

> Then must you speak
> Of one that loved not wisely, but too well;
> Of one not easily jealous, but, being wrought,
> Perplexed in the extreme; of one whose hand,
> Like the base Indian, threw a pearl away
> Richer than all his tribe; of one whose subdued eyes,
> Albeit unusèd to the melting mood,
> Drop tears as fast as the Arabian trees
> Their med'cinable gum. Set you down this.
> And say besides that in Aleppo once,
> Where a malignant and a turbaned Turk
> Beat a Venetian, and traduced the state,
> I took by th' throat the circumcisèd dog,
> And smote him thus. (5.2.343)

Driving the dagger home, he moves painfully to the bed where Desdemona lies and, as his last words tell us, dies "upon a kiss."

9

"A tragedy without meaning," says Granville-Barker of this close; and others have echoed him since.[75] Certainly, as in *Hamlet*, there is much of death before us on the stage. Moreover — what is uniquely painful in this play — these dead have higher claims on our sympathy than Claudius, Gertrude, and Laertes. Whatever their frailties, these were essentially good people of great integrity (Roderigo would be the exception but his body is not on the stage) brought down in considerable part by the envious ego of "some eternal villain," as Emilia calls him before she knows his name, "Some busy and insinuating rogue, Some cogging, cozening slave" (4.2.131).

Still, one wonders. Is there not more to it than Granville-Barker allows? The Orson Welles film of *Othello*, despite many faults, caught in its opening frames, it seemed to me, a poignant question rather than a verdict. These showed the upturned dead faces of Othello and Desdemona lying side by side on their funeral cortege as it moved slowly down the Cyprian fortifications, silhouetted against the sky and sea.[76] They were beautiful faces, at peace now, the black skin glowing beside the white, the white radiant beside the black, together here in death as in the play we saw them first, when Desdemona stepped to Othello's side to assure the Senators of her love.

The dazzling contrast of those still faces conveyed superbly (when one paused to reflect) the leap of faith that all love is — "And when I love thee not, Chaos is come again" — together with a thrilling sense that what was about to be put at risk in the play to follow was the immemorial human dream of creating a world in which (as in Renaissance cosmologies) polar opposites are held in harmony by love: black and white, male and female, warrior and "moth of peace," together with all those other contraries that it was believed perfection called for. "As with the bow and the lyre," Heraclitus had said, "so with the world: it is the tension of opposing forces that makes the structure one."[77]

The very idea of such a dream is laughable to Iago, as it is to all of us in our Iago moods, and for a time is made to seem so to Othello. Yet we see it forming again from the ruins of his life as he learns the truth about

147

Desdemona and crawls to her side to die "upon a kiss." The words by this time are charged. They have in them the accents of the Elizabethan love poets in their struggle to affirm love's authority over death. And they bring with them — unavoidably, I believe, in a play so studded with patterns of iteration — the two earlier moments when we have seen these lovers kiss. One was on the sea-wall, where he greeted her with words that show unmistakably with what values Shakespeare is associating them: "O my fair warrior," an all but exact translation, as Rosalie Colie long ago pointed out, of Petrarch's address to Laura: "O dolce mia guerriera;"[78] and where Shakespeare also gives him, to describe his joy, the traditional sonnet figure of the laboring bark come home to harbor and heaven in the beloved's arms:

> O my soul's joy!
> If after every tempest come such calms,
> May the winds blow till they have wakened death!
> And let the laboring bark climb hills of seas
> Olympus-high, and duck again as low
> As hell's from heaven. (2.1.182)

The other moment occurs in their bedroom when he kisses her before he kills her. The scene is bitterly ironic when set against the earlier scene, and the irony is only deepened by his entering (as we have seen so many in this play do, quite unaware how dark the surrounding darkness is) "with a light" — says the quarto stage direction — which he then compares to the light that shines in Desdemona as she sleeps. (Can it be an accident that from this moment on she is always seen by him as having an inner radiance: the rose, the alabaster, the one entire and perfect chyrsolite, the pearl richer than all his tribe?) "Put out the light," he says, referring to the taper in his hand,

> and then put out the light:
> If I quench thee, thou flaming minister,
> I can again thy former light restore,
> Should I repent me; but once put out thy light,
> Thou cunning'st pattern of excelling nature,

I know not where is that Promethean heat
That can thy light relume. (5.2.7)

And then he quenches both. The taper first, for even by its flickering fire the figure before him can never be other than Desdemona, the lovely individual woman he married and of whom he once exclaimed, "If she be false, O, then heaven mocks itself! I'll not believe't" (3.3.278). But now, given over to Iago's darker outlook on sexuality, he can abstract her into the generalized category of disloyal wife and commit her to a generalized fate.

Much of the horror of this scene for spectators in the theater lies in its seeming to mark the irreparable defeat of something greatly precious that Desdemona's whole being has asserted and Iago's whole being has denied. Yet it is against our sense of defeat at this point that we are invited to witness at the play's end Othello's reinstatement of the commitment he had made at the beginning. "My life upon her faith!" (1.3.294), he had told Brabantio then. Now he makes that promise good.

I kissed thee ere I killed thee; no way but this,
Killing myself, to die upon a kiss.

I believe these lines ask us to understand that though he now does justice on himself to punish his injustice to Desdemona, it is love, not justice, that he declares for at the last. What Iago's philosophy seeks throughout the play to discredit as merely paper money, backed by nothing but a lust of the blood and a permission of the will, three suffering human beings—Desdemona first and next Emilia and now Othello— have stepped forward to redeem with gold.

CHAPTER EIGHT

"WE CĀME CRYĨŊG HITHER"

King Lear

I

OR many of us today, *King Lear* seems the uttermost reach of Shakespeare's achievement. Not, certainly, because of its perfections as a well-made play, but because of what we understand to be the grandeur and terror of its vision of what it means to be human. It challenges us like Gerard Manley Hopkins's mind-mountain — "cliffs of fall, Frightful, sheer, no-man-fathomed"[79] — its abysses wrapped in the enigma of our own ignorance of the meaning of existence, its peaks echoing with cries of triumph and despair that we are hardly sure are not our own.

There are, of course, reasons for this preoccupation. As compared with *Hamlet*, the nineteenth century's favorite, *King Lear* speaks of a world more problematical. Action in *Hamlet* takes place within an order, however corrupt and hypocritical. At the human level, there is the ritualized life of the Renaissance court (of which the duel is the ultimate symbol), its violences hedged and mitigated by rules that, if broken, must be broken covertly: very much the conditions obtaining in Victorian and other European societies of that time. At the cosmic level, a vague but still essentially Christian order frames the arenas of human activity; and we go from thoughts about the all-night crowing of cocks at Christmas to the Almighty's prohibition of suicide to a praying king likening his murder to Cain's and on from there to flights of angels singing a sweet prince to his rest. As for the prince himself, he was easily perceived as a version of a figure much brooded on by nineteenth-century authors: the man of decency and conscience confronting a corrupt society and world.

King Lear's world, like our century, is larger, looser, cruder, crueller. Gods, if any, seem to be chthonic gods who when appealed to in the thunder do not answer; can be imagined, like boys with flies, to "kill us for their sport" (4.1.37), and when invoked to defend Cordelia manifestly pay no attention. In the *Lear* world, moreover, as sometimes seems increasingly true of our own, the greeds and lusts of the mighty know no restraints apart from the greed and lust of competitors, and the play can be seen, now usually *is* seen (in marked contrast to the nineteenth-century view of it as a triumph of love "that suffereth long and is kind, . . . hopeth all things, endureth all things") as a cry of despair. Despair without closure, and in a play without closure if we intimate at the end through repeated bursts of distant thunder, as was done in perhaps the best-known recent production, that the whole cycle now begins anew.

2

We have no records of *Lear*'s effectiveness in performance before the closing of the theaters in 1642 nor during the interval between their reopening and 1681. But from that year until 1838, Shakespeare's *King Lear* was seen on the stage only in the revision by Nahum Tate, who gave it a happy ending and made other changes too silly to mention here. Tate's happy ending, in which Cordelia is spared to marry Edgar and King Lear retrieves his kingdom, may be looked on as the appropriate expression of an age deeply convinced that there was an order of justice underlying the appearances of things which it was the function of literature to reveal and imitate, not to hide.

A hundred and fifty-seven years later, Macready rescued the play from its neoclassic trappings, but he and his successors continued to hold it at arm's length. They historicized it, situated it among Druids, or in ancient Britain immediately after the departure of the Romans, swathed all its fierce edges in scene-changes, realistic storm effects, and trees with individual leaves that shook. This way of dealing with the play was the natural expression of an age whose best poet (who happily did not often practice his preachment) said that poetry was made of the real language of real men, and whose most systematic critic believed he had engaged what was important about literature when he talked of *race, milieu, mo-ment*.[80] It is only today that audiences may again hope to see this play performed in something approaching its original grandeur, as a work of the mythic imagination to which a comparable imaginative response must be made if we are not to be put off by its stiff allegorisms, on the one hand, its melodramatic implausibilities, on the other.

It may be that the play also draws us because its "tragic-heroic" con-tent, like that of our contemporary plays, is ambiguous and impure. This is not simply to refer to its well-known vein of grotesqueries, or those events and speeches which have the character of poignant farce and even of inspired music-hall fooling, like the Fool's mouthings, Edgar's gyra-tions, Gloucester's leap. The play altogether blurs the ordinary tragic-heroic norms. Consider the death of the protagonist, for instance. This is usually in Shakespeare climactic and distinctive, has sacrificial implica-tions, dresses itself in ritual, springs from what we know to be a Renais-sance mystique of stoical self-dominion. How differently death comes to Lear! Not in a moment of self-scrutiny that stirs us to awe or exaltation or regret at waste, but as a blessing at which we must rejoice with Kent, hardly more than a needful afterthought to the death that counts dra-matically, Cordelia's. To die with no salute to death, with the whole con-sciousness launched toward another; to die following a life-experience in which what we have been shown to admire is far more the capacity to endure than to perform: this is unique in Shakespeare, and sits more easily with our present sensibility (which is pathologically mistrustful of heroism) than the heroic resonances of the usual Shakespearean close.

The miscellaneousness and very casualness of death in *King Lear* is perhaps also something to which the generations that know Auschwitz are attuned. In the other tragedies, as a student of mine once noticed in a highly original report, there is always a hovering suggestion that death is noble, that the great or good, having done the deed or followed the des-tiny that was in them to do or follow, go out in a blaze of light. So Romeo and Juliet seem to go. So Cleopatra goes, turning to air and fire to meet Mark Antony. Hamlet goes in a glimpse of some felicity, Othello in a recollection of a deed of derring-do and justice, even Macbeth in a kind of negative glory like the transcendent criminal he has become. But *King Lear* repudiates this:

> The dramatic emphasis is on the generality of death; death is not noble or distinctive; nearly every character dies and for nearly every sort of reason. The reiterated fact of the multiple deaths is processional in quality. It is like an enormous summarial obituary. The Fool disappears of causes mysterious; Oswald, tailor-made servant, is killed by Edgar; Goneril and Regan are poisoned and dagger-slain; Gloucester dies offstage of weariness, conflicting emotion, and a broken heart; Kent is about to die of grief and service; Edmund is killed by his brother in a duel; Cordelia dies (by a kind of mistake — "Great thing of us forgot!") at a hangman's hands; and King Lear dies of grief and deluded joy and fierce exhaustion. . . . Death is neither punishment nor reward: it is simply the nature of things.[81]

To this we may add, I think, a third factor that brings *King Lear* close to our business and bosoms as the twentieth century fades. Intimations of World's End run through it like a yeast. In the scenes on the heath, the elements are at war as if it were indeed Armageddon. When Lear awakes with Cordelia at his side, he imagines that already apocalypse is past, she is a soul in bliss, he bound upon a wheel of fire. Appearing in the last act with Cordelia dead in his arms, he wonders that those around him do not crack "heaven's vault" (5.3.260) with their grief, and they wonder in turn if the *pietà* they behold is "the promised end" (5.3.264) or "image of that horror." These are but some of the overt allusions. Under them everywhere run tides of doomsday passion that seem to use up and wear away people, codes, expectations, all stable points of reference, till only a profound sense remains that an epoch, in fact a whole dispensation, has forever closed.

> The oldest hath borne most: we that are young
> Shall never see so much, nor live so long. (5.3.326)

To this kind of situation, we of the late twentieth century are likewise sensitively attuned. I shall quote from another brilliant paper, partly

because the comment is eloquent, but chiefly because I think it is significant that everywhere in these latter days minds young and old respond to
King Lear as never before. "Every great critic," this student writes,

> from Johnson on, including many who were and are hostile to
> the play, at some time or other begins to think of the sea. The most
> moving example of this common image, perhaps, is Hazlitt's: he
> speaks of the passion of King Lear as resembling an ocean, "swell-
> ing, chafing, raging, without bound, without hope, without bea-
> con, or anchor," and of how on that sea Lear "floats, a mighty
> wreck in the wide world of sorrows." . . . The sea plays no direct
> part in the action. But the smell of it and the sound of it are
> omnipresent. The sea licks up at Dover relentlessly, its "murmur-
> ing surge" is endless and inescapable and everywhere — an arche-
> type not of an individual drowning, but of the flooding of the
> world. *King Lear* is alive again: it is our myth, our dream, as we
> stand naked and unaccommodated, listening to the water rise up
> against our foothold on the cliff of chalk.[82]

This statement is incomplete. It leaves out of account the strong
undertow of victory in the play which carves on those same chalk walls
Lear's "new acquist" of self-knowledge and devotion to Cordelia, the
majesty of his integrity and endurance, the invincibleness of his hope.
These give to an audience's applauses at the close of a great performance
a quality of exaltation. The statement is incomplete; but what it includes
and what it leaves out both make clear why *King Lear* above all others has
become the Shakespearean tragedy for our time.

3

I turn now to the play itself, to make primarily three comments: one on
the special character of its action, one on the special character of the
world in which this action is housed, and one, stemming from both of
these, on what I take to be the play's tragic theme, summed up best in
Lear's words to Gloucester in Dover fields: "We came crying hither"
(4.6.175).

As we watch it in the theater, *King Lear* comes to us first of all as an experience of violence and pain. No other Shakespearean tragedy, not even *Titus*, contains more levels of raw ferocity, physical as well as moral. In the action, the exquisite cruelties of Goneril and Regan to their father are capped by Gloucester's blinding on-stage, and this in turn by the wanton indignity of Cordelia's murder. In the language, as Miss Spurgeon has pointed out, allusions to violence multiply and accumulate into a pervasive image as of "a human body in anguished movement — tugged, wrenched, beaten, pierced, stung, dislocated, flayed, scalded, tortured, and finally broken on the rack."[83]

Miss Spurgeon's comment formulates the play in terms of passiveness and suffering. But the whole truth is not seen unless it is formulated also in terms of agency and aggression. If the *Lear* world is exceptionally anguished, it is partly because it is exceptionally contentious. Tempers in *King Lear* heat so fast that some critics are content to see in it simply a tragedy of wrath. Unquestionably it does contain a remarkable number of remarkably passionate collisions. Lear facing Cordelia, and Kent facing Lear, in the opening scene; Lear confronting Goneril at her house with his terrifying curse; Kent tangling with Oswald outside Gloucester's castle; Cornwall run through by his own servant, who warns Regan that if *she* had a beard he'd "shake it on this quarrel"; Edgar and Edmund simulating a scuffle in the first act, and later, in the last act, hurling charge and countercharge in the scene of their duel; the old king himself defying the storm: these are only the more vivid instances of a pattern of pugnacity which pervades this tragedy from beginning to end, shrilling the voices that come to us from the stage and coloring their language even in the tenderest scenes. The pattern gives rise to at least one locution which in frequency of occurrence is peculiar to *King Lear* — to "outface the winds and persecutions of the sky" (2.3.11), to "outscorn the to-and-fro-conflicting wind and rain" (3.1.10), to "outjest his heart-struck injuries," to "outfrown false Fortune's frown" (5.3.6). And it appears as a motif even in that pitiful scene at Dover, where the old king, at first alone, throws down his glove before an imaginary opponent — "There's my gauntlet; I'll prove it on a giant" (4.6.90) — and, afterward, when the blind Gloucester enters, defies him too: "No, do thy worst, blind Cupid; I'll not love" (4.6.136). So powerful is this vein of belligerence in the linguistic texture of the play that pity itself is made, in Cordelia's words, something that her father's white hairs must "challenge." Even "had you not been their father," she says in an apostrophe to the sleeping king, referring to the suffering he has been caused by his other daughters, "these white flakes Did challenge pity of them" (4.7.30).

It goes without saying that in a world of such contentiousness most of the *dramatis personae* will be outrageously self-assured. The contrast with the situation in *Hamlet*, in this respect, is striking and instructive. There, as I have argued on an earlier page, the prevailing mood tends to be interrogative. Doubt is real in *Hamlet*, and omnipresent. Minds, even villainous minds, are unquiet and uncertain. Action does not come readily to anyone except Laertes and Fortinbras, who are themselves easily deflected by the stratagems of the King, and there is accordingly much emphasis on the fragility of the human will. All this is changed in *King Lear*. Its mood, I would suggest (if it may be caught in a single word at all), is imperative. The play asks questions, to be sure, as *Hamlet* does, and far more painful questions because they are so like a child's, so simple and unmediated by the compromises to which much experience usually impels us: "Is man no more than this?" (3.4.97), "Is there any cause in nature that makes these hard hearts?" (3.6.75), "Why should a dog, a horse, a rat have life, And thou no breath at all?" (5.3.307). Such questionings in *King Lear* stick deep, like Macbeth's fears in Banquo.

Yet it is not, I think, the play's questions that establish its distinctive coloring on-stage. It is rather its commands, its invocations and appeals that have the quality of commands, its flat-footed defiances and refusals: "Come not between the dragon and his wrath" (1.1.122) — "You nimble lightnings, dart your blinding flames Into her scornful eyes!" (2.4.160) — "Blow, winds, and crack your cheeks! rage! blow!" (3.2.1) — "Thou shalt not die. Die for adultery? No!" (4.6.110) — "A plague upon you, murderers, traitors, all! I might have saved her" (5.3.270). In the psychological climate that forms round a protagonist like this, there is little room for doubt, as we may see from both Lear's and Goneril's scorn of Albany.

157

No villain's mind is unquiet. Action comes as naturally as breathing and twice as quick. And, what is particularly unlike the situation in the earlier tragedies, the hero's destiny is self-made. Lear does not inherit his predicament like Hamlet; he is not duped by an antagonist like Othello. He walks into disaster head on.

This difference is of the first importance. *King Lear*, to follow R. W. Chambers in applying Keats's memorable phrase, is a vale of soul-making, where the will is agonizingly free.[84] As if to force the point on our attention, almost every character in the play, including such humble figures as Cornwall's servant and the old tenant who befriends Gloucester, is impelled soon or late to take some sort of stand—to show, in Oswald's words, "What party I do follow" (4.5.40). One cannot but be struck by how much positioning and repositioning of this kind the play contains. Lear at first takes up his position with Goneril and Regan, France and Kent take theirs with Cordelia, Albany takes his with Goneril, and Gloucester with Cornwall and Regan.

But then all reposition. Kent elects to come back as his master's humblest servant. The Fool elects to stay with the great wheel, even though it runs downhill. Lear elects to become a comrade of the wolf and owl rather than return to his elder daughters. Gloucester likewise has second thoughts and comes to Lear's rescue, gaining his sight though he loses his eyes. Even Albany has second thoughts and lives, he says, only to revenge those eyes. In the actions of the old king himself, the taking of yet a third position is possibly implied. For after the battle, when Cordelia asks, "Shall we not see these daughters and these sisters? (5.2.7), Lear replies (with the vehemence characteristic of him even in defeat), "No, no, no, no!" and goes on to build, in his famous following lines, that world entirely free of pugnacity and contentiousness in which he and Cordelia will dwell: "We two alone will sing like birds i' th' cage."

Movements of the will, then, have a featured place in *King Lear*. But what is more characteristic of the play than their number is the fact that no one of them is ever exhibited to us in its inward origins or evolution. Instead of scenes recording the genesis or gestation of an action — scenes of introspection or persuasion or temptation like those which occupy the

heart of the drama in *Hamlet, Othello,* and *Macbeth — King Lear* offers us
the moment at which will converts into its outward expressions of action
and consequence — and this fact, I suspect, helps account for the special
kind of painfulness that the play always communicates to its audiences.
In *King Lear* we are not permitted to experience violence as an external-
ization of a psychological drama which has priority in both time and
significance, and which therefore partly palliates the violence when it
comes. This is how we do experience, I think, Hamlet's vindictiveness to
his mother, Macbeth's massacres, Othello's murder: the act in the outer
world is relieved of at least part of its savagery by our understanding of
the inner act behind it. The violences in *King Lear* are thrust upon us
quite otherwise — with the shock that comes from evil which has nowhere been inwardly accounted for, and which, from what looks like a
studiedly uninward point of view on the playwright's part, must remain
unaccountable, to characters and audience alike: "Is there any cause in
nature that makes these hard hearts?"

4

The relatively slight attention given in *King Lear* to the psychological
processes that ordinarily precede and determine human action suggests
that here we may be meant to look for meaning in a somewhat different
quarter from that in which we find it in the earlier tragedies. In *Hamlet,*
Shakespeare had explored action in its aspect of dilemma. Whether or
not we accept the traditional notion that Hamlet is a man who cannot
make up his mind, his problem is clearly conditioned by the unsatisfactory nature of the alternatives he faces. Any action involves him in a kind
of guilt, the more so because he feels an already existing corruption in
himself and in his surroundings which contaminates all action at the
source: "Virtue cannot so inoculate our old stock but we shall relish of
it" (3.1.117). Hence the focus of the play is on those processes of consciousness that can explain and justify suspension of the will.

In *Othello,* by contrast, Shakespeare seems to be exploring action in its
aspect of error. Othello faces two ways of understanding love, Iago's and
Desdemona's — which is almost to say, in the play's terms, two systems of

valuing and two ways of being—but we are left in no doubt that one of the ways is wrong. Even if we take Iago and Desdemona, as some critics do, to be dramatic emblems of conflicting aspects in Othello's own nature, the play remains a tragedy of error, not a tragedy of dilemma. "The pity of it, Iago" is that Othello makes the wrong choice when the right one is open to him and keeps clamoring to be known for what it is even to the very moment of the murder. The playwright's focus in this play is therefore on the corruptions of mind by which a man may be led into error, and he surrounds Iago and Desdemona with such overtones of damnation and salvation as ultimately must attend any genuine option between evil and good.

King Lear, as I see it, confronts the perplexity and mystery of human action at a later point. Choice remains in the forefront of the argument, but its psychic antecedents have been so effectively shrunk down in this primitivized world that action seems to spring directly out of the bedrock of personality. We feel sure no imaginable psychological process could make Kent other than loyal, Goneril other than cruel, Edgar other than "a brother noble" (1.2.172). The meaning of action, here, appears to lie rather in its effects than in antecedents, and particularly in its capacity, as with Lear's in the opening scene, to generate energies that will hurl themselves in unforeseen and unforeseeable reverberations of disorder from end to end of the world.

The elements of that opening scene are worth pausing over, because they seem to have been selected to bring before us precisely such an impression of unpredictable effects lying coiled and waiting in an apparently innocuous posture of affairs. The atmosphere of the first episode in the scene, as many a commentator has remarked, is casual, urbane, even relaxed. In the amenities exchanged by Kent and Gloucester, Shakespeare allows no hint to penetrate of Gloucester's later agitation about "These late eclipses" (1.2.101), or about the folly of a king's abdicating his responsibilities and dividing up his power. We are momentarily lulled into a security that is not immediately broken even when the court assembles and Lear informs us that he will shake off all business and "Unburdened crawl toward death" (1.1.41). I suspect we are invited to sense, as Lear speaks, that this is a kingdom too deeply swaddled in forms of all kinds — too comfortable and secure in its "robes and furred gowns" (4.6.162); in its rituals of authority and deference (of which we have just heard and witnessed samples as Gloucester is dispatched offstage, the map demanded, and a "fast intent" [1.1.38] and "constant will" [1.1.43] thrust on our notice by the king's imperious personality); and in its childish charades, like the one about to be enacted when the daughters speak.

Possibly we are invited to sense, too, that this is in some sort an emblematic kingdom — almost a paradigm of hierarchy and rule, as indeed the scene before us seems to be suggesting, with its wide display of ranks in both family and state. Yet perhaps too schematized, too regular — a place where complex realities have been too much reduced to formulas, as they are on a map: as they are on that visible map, for instance, on which Lear three times lays his finger in this scene ("as if he were marking the land itself," says Granville-Barker), while he describes with an obvious pride its tidy catalogue of "shadowy forests" and "champains," "plenteous rivers and wide-skirted meads" (1.1.64). Can it be that here, as on that map, is a realm where everything is presumed to have been charted, where all boundaries are believed known, including those of nature and human nature; but where no account has been taken of the heath which lies in all countries and in all men and women just *beyond* the boundaries they think they know?

However this may be, into this emblematic, almost dreamlike, situation erupts the mysterious thrust of psychic energy that we call a choice, an act; and the waiting coil of consequences leaps into threatening life, bringing with it, as every act (considered absolutely) must, the inscrutable where we had supposed all was clear, the unexpected though we thought we had envisaged all contingencies and could never be surprised. Perhaps it is to help us see this that the consequences in the play are made so spectacular. The first consequence is Lear's totally unlooked-for redistribution of his kingdom into two parts instead of three, and his rejection of Cordelia. The second is his totally unlooked-for banishment of his most trusted friend and counselor. The third is the equally unlooked-for rescue of his now beggared child to be the Queen of France; and what the unlooked-for fourth and fifth will be, we already guess from the agreement between Goneril and Regan, as the scene ends, that something must be done, "and i' th' heat" (1.1.306). Thereafter the play seems to illustrate, with an almost diagrammatic relentlessness and thoroughness, the unforeseen potentials that lie waiting to be hatched from a single choice and act: nakedness issues out of opulence, madness out of sanity and reason out of madness, blindness out of seeing and insight out of blindness, salvation out of ruin. The pattern of the unexpected is so completely worked out, in fact, that it appears to embrace even such minor devices of the plot as the fact that Edmund, his fortune made by two letters, is undone by a third.

Meantime, as we look back over the first scene, we may wonder whether the gist of the whole matter has not been placed before us, in the play's own emblematic terms, by Gloucester, Kent, and Edmund in that brief conversation with which the tragedy begins. This conversation touches on two actions, we now observe, each loaded with menacing possibilities, but treated with a casualness at this point that resembles Lear's in opening his trial of love. The first action alluded to is the old king's action in dividing his kingdom, the dire effects of which we are almost instantly to see. The other action is Gloucester's action in begetting a bastard son, and the dire effects of this will also speedily be known. What is particularly striking, however, is that in the latter instance the principal effect is already on the stage before us, though its nature is undisclosed, in the person of the bastard son himself. Edmund, like other "consequences," looks tolerable enough till revealed in full: "I cannot wish the fault undone, the issue of it being so proper" (1.1.16), says Kent, meaning by proper "handsome"; yet there is a further dimension of meaning in the word that he and we will only later understand.

Like other consequences, too, Edmund looks to be predictable and manageable — in advance. "He hath been out nine years," says Gloucester, who has never had any trouble holding consequences at arm's length before, "and away he shall again" (1.1.31). Had Shakespeare reflected on the problem consciously — and it would be rash, I think, to be too sure he did not—he could hardly have chosen a more vivid way of giving dramatic substance to the unpredictable relationships of act and consequence than by this confrontation of a father with his unknown natural son—or to the idea of consequences come home to roost, than by this quiet youthful figure, studying "deserving" (1.1.30) as he prophetically calls it, while he waits upon his elders.

5

In *King Lear* then, I believe it is fair to say, the inscrutability of the energies that the human will has power to release is one of Shakespeare's paramount interests. By the inevitable laws of drama, this power receives a degree of emphasis in all his plays, especially the tragedies. The difference in *King Lear* is that it is assigned the whole canvas. The crucial option, which elsewhere comes toward the middle of the plot, is here presented at the very outset. Once taken, everything that happens after is made to seem, in some sense, to have been set in motion by it, not excluding Gloucester's recapitulation of it in the subplot. Significantly, too, the act is not one which could have been expected to germinate into such a harvest of disaster (the old king's longing for public testimony of affection seems in itself a harmless folly: it is not an outrage, not a crime, only a foolish whim) any more than Cordelia's death could have been expected to follow from her truthfulness or Gloucester's salvation to be encompassed by a son whom he disowns and seeks to kill.

All this, one is driven to conclude, is part of Shakespeare's point. In the world he creates for Lear, action is cut loose not simply from the ties that normally bind it to prior psychic causes, but from the ties that usually limit it to commensurate effects. The logic of the play is mythic: it abandons verisimilitude to find out truth, like the story of Oedipus; or like the *Rime of the Ancient Mariner*, with which, in fact, it has some interesting affinities. Both works are intensely emblematic. Both treat of crime and punishment and reconciliation in poetic, not realistic, terms. In both the fall is sudden and unaccountable, the penalty enormous and patently exemplary. The wilful act of the mariner in shooting down the albatross has a nightmarish inscrutability like Lear's angry rejection of the daughter he loves best; springs from a similar upsurge of egoistic wilfulness; hurls itself against what was until that moment a natural "bond" (1.1.93), and shatters the universe. Nor do the analogies end with this. When the mariner shoots the albatross, the dark forces inside him that prompted his deed project themselves and become the landscape, so to speak, in which he suffers his own nature: it is his own alienation, his own waste land of terror and sterility that he meets. Something very similar takes place in Shakespeare's play. Lear, too, suffers his own nature, encounters his own heath, his own storm, his own nakedness and defenselessness, and by this experience, like the mariner, is made another man.

To some in Shakespeare's audience the scenes on the heath may have brought an additional shock of recognition. It was not simply that they could see there, as we do, a countryside not located in any imaginable England or at any imaginable time but in an eternal moment of human possibility. Nor was it simply that the torrential passion of the old king would come to them trailing long memories of the psychomachia of the morality plays, with Kent, Gloucester, and the Fool playing parts that might formerly have been assigned such names as Watchful, Good Will, Innocent.

What must have struck some of Shakespeare's contemporaries far more forcibly than this, however, was that here a structure they had long associated with pastoral romance, the most popular of their literary and dramatic genres, had been turned topsy-turvy and charged with undreamed-of power. In the action of pastoral romances, which is nearly as predictable as the action of an American Western, the protagonist ordinarily moves out in a sweeping arc from the world of everyday, where he has met with problems or experiences that threaten to disintegrate him, to an Arcadian countryside or forest, where nature is fully in sympathy with things human, and there undergoes a learning process that consists in part of discovering his own problem reflected in those he meets. Having confronted his problem in another, having sometimes in the process undergone something like a ritual death and rebirth, he is able to return to the everyday world restored to serenity and often to temporal felicity. The broad characteristics of the pattern may be studied in Sidney, in Montemayor, in Sannazaro, and in such of Shakespeare's own works as *A Midsummer Night's Dream, As You Like It, A Winter's Tale, The Tempest*, and perhaps others.

That Shakespeare has based the ground plan of *King Lear* on a version of this pattern can be seen from a glance at *As You Like It*. In both plays, we have an extruded ruler, and an ugly thunderhead of passion which closes the doors of "nurture" to the more sympathetic members of the *dramatis personae* and impels them to seek "nature." There is a wind which is urged to "Blow, blow" because it is not so biting as ingratitude; a Fool, who knows he has been in a better place, but is loyal. There are rustic primitives, who in *As You Like It* are the comical William and Audrey, in *King Lear* Tom of Bedlam and the country people who figure in his mad talk. There are good and evil brothers, the good brother in both plays leading an old man — in *King Lear*, his father, in *As You Like It*, an old servant who has been as a father to him; and there is a daughter of the extruded ruler, herself an exile, who is reunited to her father before the play ends.

Obviously, it is the differences here that count. Yet even the differences have a surrealistic resemblance. *As You Like It* moves from extrusion to a magical forest where everyone meets, as in a glass, reflections of what he is. To the good Duke, the forest discovers

> tongues in trees, books in the running brooks,
> Sermons in stones, and good in everything. (2.1.16)

To Orlando, it discovers first a community of "kindness" — that is to say, natural feeling — when he meets the Duke and his men preparing food and is invited to partake. Such "kindness" is precisely what he has vainly sought at home, and what he himself exemplifies as he carries Adam on his back and forages sword in hand to feed him. Soon after this, the forest discovers love to Orlando. To Jaques, by contrast, the forest brings the stricken deer, abandoned and self-pitying like himself, whose "sobbing" he accompanies with his own "weeping" (2.1.38). To Rosalind it brings tongues in trees, but not in the same way as to her father: to her the trees speak of love and in rhyme; their "fruit" is Orlando, found by Celia under an oak "like a dropped acorn" (3.2.224). Touchstone, as we might expect, unearths in the forest an Audrey; Silvius woos a Phoebe; Celia, who has given up everything to accompany Rosalind, meets with an Oliver, who has also learned by this time to give up. To each visitor the forest brings according to his capacity; and following an exhibition of Rosalind's "magic," which in some respects resembles a ritual death and rebirth (her withdrawal as Ganymede to reappear as Rosalind), all except Jaques leave Arcadia for the world.

King Lear alludes to such patterns but turns them upside down. It moves from extrusion not to pastoral but to the greatest anti-pastoral ever penned. Lear's heath is the spiritual antipodes of the lush romance Arcadias. Nature proves to be indifferent or hostile, not friendly. The figures are not Arcadian, but the wretched fiend-haunted villagers of Edgar's hallucinations. The reflections of his condition that Lear meets are barrenness, tempest, and alienation, the defenseless suffering of his Fool, the madness of a derelict beggar who is "the thing itself" (3.4.101). And though a ritual death of sorts occurs at the close of this anti-pastoral, followed much later by a rebirth, all that is thus won is no sooner won than snatched away.

6

To turn from a play's action to its world is not, when the dramatist is Shakespeare, to take up a new subject but to reconsider the old in a new light. The strains of violence and aggression stressed earlier in connection with the play's action could as well be treated as an aspect of its world. The bareness and spareness so often cited as features of its world penetrate equally the character and action. The austerity and rigor that these have in *King Lear* may best be appreciated by comparing Hal and Falstaff, in whom the dramatist's exuberant invention multiplies variety, to Lear and his Fool, where invention plays intensely but always along the same arc; or by recalling *Othello*, with all its supernumerary touches of actual domesticity in Desdemona, actual concerns of state in the Moor; or *Hamlet*, with its diversions and digressions among guardsmen,

recorders, gossip of city theaters, its mass of historical and literary allusions, its diversities of witty, sophisticated, and self-conscious speech.
Lear, too, contains diversities of speech — ritual and realistic styles described by W. B. C. Watkins,[85] iterations singled out by Bradley to
characterize Cordelia[86] (they are, in fact, characteristic of several of the
play's speakers), "oracular fragments of rhapsody" in the mad scenes (the
phrase is Granville-Barker's),[87] imperatives, preachments, questionings,
and, last but not least, the Fool's wry idiom, vehicle of the hard-won wisdom of the poor, made up largely of proverb, riddle, maxim, fable, and
ballad. *Lear* has such diversities, but as Winifred Nowottny has argued
convincingly, all are marked, even the most passionate and poignant, by
a surface "absence of contrivance,"[88] which allows flashes of profound
feeling to flare up unexpectedly in the most unpretentious forms of
speech, yet seems to tell us at the same time (the very measure of its art-
fulness in fact) that "feeling and suffering . . . are beyond words." "The
play is deeply concerned," she writes, "with the inadequacy of language
to do justice to feeling or to afford any handhold against abysses of
iniquity and suffering."[89]

Here, too, it strikes me, the play is of a piece. As it uses for the most
part the barest bones of language to point at experiences that lie beyond
the scope of language, so it uses stripped-down constituents of personality (character that is entirely *esse*, that does not alter but develops to be
always more completely the thing it was) to point to complexities of
being and of human reality that lie beyond the scope of the ordinary
conventions of dramatic character.

But these are matters that come through to us more clearly in the
study than onstage. There can be no question that the most powerful
single dimension of the play's world for its spectators is its continual
reference to and evocation, through eye and ear alike, of the nature and
significance of human society. A "sense of sympathy and human relatedness," as Miss Welsford has said, is what the good in this play have or win
through to.[90] In the world of *King Lear*, this is the ultimate gift, spring of
man's joy and therefore of his pain. When Lear dies, as I mentioned in
the beginning, with his whole being launched toward another, with even

his last gasp an expression of hope that she lives, the image before us is deeply tragic; yet it is also, in the play's terms, a kind of victory. This is a matter we must come back to. What needs to be considered first is the circumstantial "sociality" of the Lear world which defines and gives body to this closing vision of human achievement and its cost.

In writing *King Lear*, Shakespeare's imagination appears to have been so fully oriented toward presenting human reality as a web of ties commutual that not only characterization and action, but language, theme, and even the very *mise en scène* are influenced. The play's imagined settings — divisible into several distinct landscapes as "shadowy forests" and "champains" (1.1.64) fade off first into "low farms" and "poor pelting villages," (2.3.17) then into the bare and treeless heath, then into glimpses of high-grown grain at Dover on the brink of the giddy cliff that only exists in Edgar's speech and his father's imagination — are always emphatically social. Even on that literally and emblematically lonesome heath we are never allowed to forget the nearby presence of what T. S. Eliot calls in his *Dry Salvages* "the life of significant soil." Somewhere just beyond the storm's rim and suitably framing the rain-swept beggared king, Shakespeare evokes through Tom of Bedlam's speeches a timeless community of farms and villages where the nights are measured between "curfew" and "the first cock" (3.4.108), the beggars are "whipped from tithing to tithing" (3.4.125), the green mantle of the standing pool is broken by the castaway carcasses of the "old rat and the ditch-dog" (3.4.124), and the white wheat is mildewed by "the foul Flibbertigibbet," who also gives poor rustics "the web and the pin, squints the eye and makes the hairlip" (3.4.108). Likewise at Dover, around the two old men, one mad, one blind, Shakespeare raises another kind of society, equally well adapted to the movement of the plot, courtly, sophisticated, decadent. A society of adulterers and "simp'ring dame[s]." A society where "a dog's obeyed in office," the beadle lusts for the whore he whips, "the usurer hangs the cozener," and "robes and furred gowns hide all" (4.6.117ff).

By these surrealist backgrounds and conflations, Shakespeare dilates his family story into a parable of society of all times and places. The characters themselves show signs of having been shaped with such a parable in view. As a group, they are significantly representative, bringing before us both extremes of a social and political spectrum (monarch and beggar), a psychic spectrum (wise man and fool), a moral spectrum (beastly behavior and angelic), an emotional spectrum (joy and despair), and, throughout, a "contrast of dimension," as Miss Nowottny has called it,[91] that draws within one compass both the uttermost human anguish which speaks in "She's dead as earth" (5.3.262) and the strange limiting "art of our necessities" which speaks in "undo this button" (5.3.310).

As individuals, on the other hand, these same characters, especially the younger ones, show a significant and perhaps studied diversification. According to one producer of the play, we meet with "heartless intellect" in Edmund, "impure feelings" in Goneril, "unenlightened will" in Cornwall, "powerless morality" in Albany, "unimaginative mediocrity" in Regan.[92] I should not care to adopt these particular descriptions, but they serve to call attention to what everyone has recognized to be a somewhat schematic variety in the play's *dramatis personae*, as if the playwright were concerned to exhibit the widest possible range of human potentiality. This general "anatomy" of mankind, if it is such, is further enhanced by the well-known antiphonal characterizations of Lear and Gloucester and even by the double quality of the old king himself as Titan and (in Cordelia's phrase) "poor perdu." (4.7.35) Thus, from the play's opening moments, when we are shown all the powers of the realm collected and glimpse both aspects of the king, we are never allowed to lose sight of the fact that the people in front of us make up a composite image of the state of man, in every sense of the word "state."

7

Shakespeare's concern with "relation" as the ultimate reality for human beings also expresses itself strongly in the plot of *King Lear* and in the language of social use and habit to which the plot gives rise and which it repeatedly examines. To an extent unparalleled in the other tragedies, the plot of the play depends on and manipulates relations of service and of family—the two relations, as W. H. Auden has reminded us in an

arresting essay, from which all human loyalties, and therefore all societies, derive.[93] Family ties, which come about by nature, cannot be
dissolved by acts of will: in this lies the enormity of Lear's action in the
opening scene and of his elder daughters' actions later. Service ties,
however, being contractual, *can* be dissolved by acts of will, only the act
must be ratified on both sides. Kent, refusing to dissolve his relation with
his master, illustrates the crucial difference between the two types of af-
filiation. The essentials of the service bond can be restored even though
Kent is unrecognized and in disguise. The essentials of the natural bond
between Cordelia and Lear, or Edgar and Gloucester, can never be
restored apart from mutual recognition and a change of heart.

Ties of service and ties of nature lie closely parallel in the play and
sometimes merge. It has been argued that one way of interpreting the
broad outlines of the story would be to say that the lessons Lear must
learn include the lesson of true service, which is necessarily part of the
lesson of true love. Once Lear has banished true love and service in the
persons of Cordelia and Kent, it is only to be expected that he will have
trouble with false service and false love in a variety of forms, including
Oswald, his daughters, and his knights, and that he should need, once
again, the intercession of true service in the form of the disguised Kent.
Gloucester, too, we are told, has to learn to distinguish true service.
Beginning by serving badly, he is badly served in turn by Edmund, and
only after he becomes a true servant, going to Lear's rescue at the risk of
his life, is he himself once more served truly, first by his old tenant, and
subsequently by Edgar.

The term "service," with its cognates and synonyms, tolls in the language of *King Lear* like that bell which reminded John Donne we are all
parts of a single continent, but it is only one of a host of socially oriented
terms to do so. Almost as prominent, and equally pertinent to the playwright's concern with human relatedness, are the generic terms of social
responsibility: "meet," "fit," "proper," "due," "duty," "bond," and the
generic appellations of social status and social approbation and disappro-
bation: "knave," "fool," "villain," "rogue," "rascal," "slave," and many
more. Often these are simply vehicles of the willfulness that crackles in

this frantic disintegrating realm where kings are beggars, but several of them carry in solution anxious questions about the ties that hold together the human polity, which from time to time the action of the play precipitates out. When Cornwall, challenged by his own servant after Gloucester's blinding, exclaims incredulously "My villain!" and Regan adds scornfully "A peasant stand up thus!" the ambiguities that may attach to servitude are brought into question with a precision that enables us to appreciate the immediately following references to Gloucester as "treacherous villain" and "eyeless villain" (3.7.78ff), and to the now slain rebel servant as "this slave." In Byam Shaw's production, as Muriel St. Clare Byrne describes it, a highly imaginative *exeunt* was adopted for Regan and Cornwall at this moment, which must have brought home to any audience the implications of a world in which language could be so perversely and solipsistically misused.

> Mortally wounded, terror and pain in voice and gesture, Cornwall turned to his wife: "Regan, I bleed apace. . . . Give me your arm." [3.7.97] Ignoring him, almost disdainfully, she swept past to the downstage exit. He staggered back, groping for support; no one stirred to help him. Open-mouthed, staring-eyed, death griping his heart, he faced the dawning horror of retribution as the jungle law of each for himself caught up on him and he knew himself abandoned even by his wife.[94]

Other "titles" that the play first manipulates and then explores in visually expressive episodes are "gentleman" and "fellow." Kent is introduced to us and to Edmund as "this noble gentleman" in the first lines of the play, a title which he later amplifies into "gentleman of blood and breeding" (3.1.40). Oswald is also introduced to us first as a gentleman — "my gentleman" (1.3.1) — by Goneril, and receives the title again at a significant moment when Edgar, speaking as a peasant, has to defend his father's life against him. In 2.2 these two very different definitions of gentility, Oswald and Kent, clash outside Gloucester's castle. The "gentleman of blood and breeding" puts Goneril's "gentleman" to rout by power of nature, but by power of authority — that great graven image of authority which, as Lear says later in a reference likely to recall this episode, makes "the creature run from the cur" (4.6.154) — he is ejected (and punished) in favor of one whose true titles, Kent tells us, make him no gentleman, but "the composition of a knave, beggar, coward, pander, and the son and heir of a mongrel bitch" (2.2.18).

Or again, the play asks (and this is perhaps its most searching exploration visually as well as verbally), what is it that makes a man a "fellow"? Is it being born to menial status, as for the many serving men to whom the word is applied? Is it total loss of status, as for Edgar, Kent, and Lear, to each of whom the word is also applied? Or is it simply being a human being — everyone's fellow by virtue of a shared humanity? During the heath scenes, when Lear, Kent, Edgar, and the Fool become fellows in misery as well as in lack of status, this question is given a poignant visual statement. Gloucester, coming to relieve Lear, rejects one member of the motley fellowship, his own son Poor Tom: "In, fellow, there into the hovel" (3.4.165); but Lear, who has just learned to pray for all such naked fellows, refuses to be separated from his new companion and finally is allowed to "take the fellow" (3.4.168) into shelter with him. For as Edgar will ask us to remember in the next scene but one,

> the mind much sufferance doth o'erskip,
> When grief hath mates, and bearing fellowship.
> (3.6.104)

8

Questions like these point ultimately to larger questions, over which the action of the play, like Hamlet's melancholy, "sits on brood." One of these has to do with the moral foundations of society. To what extent have our distinctions of degree and status, our regulations by law and usage, moral significance? To what extent are they simply the expedient disguises of a war of all on all, wherein humanity preys on itself (as Albany says) "Like monsters of the deep"? (4.2.50).

This anxiety, though it permeates the play, is pressed with particular force in the utterances of the mad king to Gloucester in the fields near Dover. Here, as so often in Shakespeare and most notably in Hamlet's "To be or not to be" soliloquy, we encounter an occasion when the barriers between fiction and reality are suddenly collapsed, and the Elizabethan audience was made to realize, as we are, that it was listening to an indictment far more relevant to its own social experience than to any this king of ancient Britain could be imagined to have had. Furthermore, here onstage, as during the scene on the heath, a familiar convention was again being turned upside down and made electric with meaning. A king of the realm — like their own king, guarantee of its coinage ("they cannot touch me for coining"), commander of its troops ("There's your press money"), chief beneficiary of its *paideia* ("They flattered me like a dog"), fountain of its justice ("I pardon that man's life"), sacred object of its reverence ("O! let me kiss that hand!") — was not only presented mad, crowned with weeds, but in his madness registered for all to hear the bankruptcy of the very body politic and body moral of which he was representative and head:

> Plate sin with gold,
> And the strong lance of justice hurtless breaks;
> Arm it in rags, a pigmy's straw does pierce it.
> None does offend, none — I say none! I'll able 'em.
> Take that of me, my friend, who have the power
> To seal th' accuser's lips. Get thee glass eyes
> And, like a scurvy politician, seem
> To see the things thou dost not. (4.6.162)

No one, I suspect, who had responded to the role of the king in Shakespeare's history plays, or the king's role in contemporary drama generally, could miss the shock in these lines, coming as they did from "the thing itself" (3.4.101). If we suppose, further, that the structural conventions of the Elizabethan theater, with its "very solid three-dimensional symbols of order" representing "home, city, and king,"[95] sometimes induced in observers a deeper identification, a sense that they were witnessing in the career of the stage monarch a "sacred combat" or ritual struggle that enacted the corporate quest for well-being and self-knowledge in the person of the king, we may guess that the shock of this reversal was profound indeed. But we need not suppose so much. Even the most casual playgoer, who had looked about him reflectively in Jacobean England, must have experienced a shudder of self-recognition as Lear's "sermon" proceeded. The gulf between medieval social ideals and contemporary actualities was imposing by Shakespeare's time a significant strain on sensitive minds, the kind of strain that (in a way we are painfully familiar with in our own age) can madden men, as in a sense it has maddened Lear. "The ideal was still Christian," writes Crane Brinton, who has put the matter as pithily as anyone, "still an ideal of unity, peace, security, organization, status; the reality was endemic war, divided authority even at the top, [and] a great scramble for wealth and position."[96]

Lear's vision of society in Dover's fields is a vision of this gulf. To a limited extent it relates to his own sufferings, but principally to the society for which it was written, and, I would wish to add, to all societies as such. Under the masks of discipline, Lear's speeches imply, in any imaginable society on earth, there will always lurk the lust of the simpering dame, the insolence of the dog in office, the hypocrisy of the usurer who hangs the cozener, the mad injustice of sane humanity's choices, like Lear's in disowning Cordelia. Institutions are necessary if society is to exist at all; but as the play here eloquently points out, and as Lear from this point on himself knows, they are not enough. What human relatedness truly means, stripped of its robes and furred gowns and all marks of status and images of authority, we are shown in the ensuing scenes of mutual humility and compassion between Lear and Cordelia, Edgar and Gloucester.

A second question that the play keeps bringing before our imaginations in its social dimension is the problem of human identity. It sees this, in part, as a function of status, and it is doubtless not without meaning that so many of the play's persons undergo drastic alterations in the "statistical" sphere. Cordelia is deprived of her place in state and family; Kent, of his earldom; Edgar, of his sonship and patrimony; Gloucester, of his title and lands; Lear, of the whole fabric of familiar relations by which he has always known himself to be Lear and through the loss of which he falls into madness. Yet the matter is also presented to us at a deeper level than that of status. When, at Goneril's, Lear cries out,

"This is not Lear. . . . Who is it that can tell me who I am?" (1.4.216) or, on the heath, staring at Edgar's nakedness, "Is man no more than this?" (3.4.97) we realize that his questionings cast a shadow well beyond the limits of the immediate situation as he understands it, a shadow that involves the problem of human identity in its ultimate sense, which has lost none of its agonizing ambiguity with the passage of nearly four centuries. *Is* man, in fact, no more than "this"? — a poor bare forked animal in the wind and rain — or is man an ethical conception, a normative term, which suffers violence whenever any human being has been reduced to the condition of "bare forked animal" (3.4.102), whenever "man's life is cheap as beast's" (2.4.262) because the "need" has been too much "reasoned," whenever "man's work" (5.3.39) (as with Edmund's officer who hangs Cordelia) excludes drawing a cart or eating dried oats but not the murder of his own kind? As the waters rise against our foothold on the cliff of chalk, this has become our question too.

9

The ultimate uncertainty in *King Lear* to which all others point is, as always in tragedy, the question of humanity's fate. With its strong emphasis on inexorable and unimaginable consequences winding into a web to which every free and willful act contributes another toil, *King Lear* may claim a place near the absolute center, "The true blank" (1.1.159) (so Kent might call it) of tragic experience. "The tragedy of Adam," writes Northrop Frye, following Milton in tracing "the archetypal human tragedy" in the narrative of Genesis, "resolves, like all other tragedies, in the manifestation of natural law. He enters a world in which existence is itself tragic, not existence modified by an act, deliberate or unconscious."[97]

Existence is tragic in *King Lear* because existence is inseparable from relation; we are born from and to it; it envelops us in our loves and lives as parents, children, sisters, brothers, husbands, wives, servants, masters, rulers, subjects — the web is seamless and unending. When we talk of virtue, patience, courage, joy, we talk of what supports it. When we talk of tyranny, lust, and treason, we talk of what destroys it. There is no human action, Shakespeare shows us, that does not affect it and that it

does not affect. Old, we begin our play with the need to impose relation — to divide our kingdom, set our rest on someone's kind nursery,
and crawl toward our death. Young, we begin it with the need to respond
to relation — to define it, resist it even in order to protect it, honor it, or
destroy it. Humanity's tragic fate, as *King Lear* presents it, comes into
being with our entry into relatedness, which is our entry into humanity.

In the play's own terms this fate is perhaps best summarized in the
crucial concept of "patience." By the time he meets Gloucester in Dover
fields, Lear has begun to learn patience; and patience, as he defines it
now, is not at all what he had earlier supposed. He had supposed it was
the capacity to bear up under the outrages that occur to oneself in a corrupt world; and so he had cried, when Regan and Goneril joined forces
against him, "You heavens, give me that patience, patience I need!"
(2.4.266). Now, with his experience of the storm behind him, his mind
still burning with the lurid vision of a world where "None does offend,
none" (4.6.165) because all are guilty, he sees further. His subject is not
personal suffering in what he here says to Gloucester; his subject is the
suffering that is rooted in the very fact of being human, and its best
symbol is the birth cry of every infant, as if it knew already that to enter
humanity is to be born in pain, to suffer pain, and to cause pain.

> Thou must be patient. We came crying hither:
> Thou know'st, the first time that we smell the air
> We wawl and cry. (4.6.174)

Or as George Gascoigne had put it, giving an old sentiment a new turn
in his translation of Innocent III's *De Contemptu Mundi:* "We are all
borne crying that we may thereby expresse our misery; for a male childe
lately borne pronounceth A [for Adam] and a woman childe pronounceth E [for Eve]: So that they say eyther E or A: as many as descend from
Eva. . . . Eche of these soundes is the voyce of a sorrowful creature,
expressing the greatnesse of his grefe."[98]

Lear's words to Gloucester, I take it, describe this ultimate dimension
of patience, in which the play invites us to share at its close. It is the
patience to accept the condition of being human in a scheme of things

where the thunder will not peace at our bidding; where nothing can stay the unfolding consequences of a rash act, including the rash acts of bearing and being born; where

> The worst is not
> So long as we can say "This is the worst."
> (4.1.27)

Yet where the capacity to grow and ripen — in relation and in love — is in some mysterious way bound up with the capacity to lose, and to suffer, and to endure:

> Men must endure
> Their going hence, even as their coming hither:
> Ripeness is all. (5.2.9)

From one half of this tragic knowledge, Lear subsequently wavers — as Gloucester wavers from what Edgar thought he had learned at Dover Cliff. Lear would need no crumbs of comfort after the battle if his sufferings could at last be counted on to bring rewards — if, for example, he could pass his declining years in peace and happiness with Cordelia. He wants to believe that this is possible. He has made the choice that he should have made in the beginning. He has allied himself with those who in the world's sense are fools; and he is prepared to accept the alienation from the world that this requires, as the famous passage at the opening of the last scene shows. In this passage he puts aside Goneril and Regan forever; he does not even want to see them. He accepts eagerly the prison which marks his withdrawal from the world's values, for he has his own new values to sustain:

> We two alone will sing like birds i' th' cage.
> When thou dost ask me blessing, I'll kneel down
> And ask of thee forgiveness. So we'll live,
> And pray, and sing, and tell old tales, and laugh
> At gilded butterflies, and hear poor rogues
> Talk of court news; and we'll talk with them too —
> Who loses and who wins, who's in, who's out —
> And take upon 's the mystery of things
> As if we were God's spies. (5.2.9)

They will be in the world, but not of it. On this kind of sacrifice, he adds, "The Gods themselves throw incense" (5.2.21).

But to speak so is to speak from a knowledge that no human experience teaches. If it could end like this, if there were guaranteed rewards like this for making our difficult choices, the play would be a melodrama, and our world very different from what it is. So far as human wisdom goes, the choice of relatedness must be recognized as its own reward, leading sometimes to alleviation of suffering, as in the case of Gloucester's joy in Edgar, but equally often to more suffering, as in the case of Lear. For Lear, like many another, has to make the difficult choice only to lose the fruits of it. Not in his own death—as Kent says, "He hates him That would upon the rack of this tough world Stretch him out longer" (5.3.314)—but in Cordelia's. Cordelia, our highest choice, is what we always want the gods to guarantee. But to this the gods will not consent. Hence when Albany exclaims, at Edmund's confession that he has ordered Cordelia's death, "The gods defend her!" (5.3.257), the gods' answer to that is, as Bradley pointed out long ago, "Enter Lear, with Cordelia in his arms."[99]

In his last speech, the full implications of the human condition evidently come home to Lear. He has made his choice, and there will be no reward. Again and again, in his repetitions, he seems to be trying to drive this final tragic fact into his human consciousness, where it never wants to stick:

No, no, no life!
Why should a dog, a horse, a rat have life
And thou no breath at all? Thou'lt come no more,
Never, never, never, never, never! (5.3.306)

He tries to hold this painful vision unflinchingly before his consciousness, but the strain, considering everything else he has been through, is too great—consciousness itself starts to give way: "Pray you, undo this button. Thank you, sir" (5.3.310). And with it the vision gives way too: he cannot sustain it; he dies, reviving in his heart the hope that Cordelia lives: "Look on her! Look her lips, Look there, look there!"

10

We are offered two ways of being sentimental about this conclusion, both of which we must make an effort to avoid. One is to follow those who argue that, because these last lines probably mean that Lear dies in the joy of thinking Cordelia lives, some sort of mitigation or transfiguration has been reached which turns defeat into total victory. "Only to earthbound intelligence," says Professor O. J. Campbell, "is Lear pathetically deceived in thinking Cordelia alive. Those familiar with the Morality plays will realize that Lear has found in her unselfish love the one companion who is willing to go with him through Death up to the throne of the Everlasting Judge."[100] I think most of us will agree that this is too simple. Though there is much of the Morality play in *Lear*, it is not used toward a morality theme, but, as I have tried to suggest in this essay, toward building a deeply metaphysical metaphor, or myth, about the human condition, the state of man, in which the last of many mysteries is the enigmatic system of relatedness in which he is enclosed.

The other sentimentality leads some to indulge a fashionable cynicism and to derive from the fact that Lear's joy is mistaken, or, alternatively, from the fact that in the Lear world "even those who have fully repented, done penance, and risen to the tender regard of sainthood can be hunted down, driven insane, and killed by the most agonizing extremes of passion," the conclusion that "we inhabit an imbecile universe."[101] Perhaps we do — but Shakespeare's *King Lear* provides no evidence of it that till now we lacked. That love, compassion, hope, and truth are "subjects all," not only to "envious and calumniating time," but to purest casualty and mischance has been the lament of poets since Homer. Shakespeare can hardly have imagined that in *King Lear*'s last scene he was telling his audiences something they had never known, or was casting his solemn vote on one side or other of the vexing philosophical and theological questions involved in the suffering of the innocent and good.

The scene has, besides, his characteristic ambiguity and balance. No world beyond this one in which "all manner of things will be well" is asserted; but neither is it denied: Kent happens to take it for granted and will follow his master beyond that horizon as he has beyond every other: "My master calls me, I must not say no" (5.3.323). Edgar has come to soberer assessments of reality than he was given to making in the fore-part of the play, but his instinctive kindness (we may assume) is unabated and has survived all trials. Lear's joy in thinking that his daughter lives (if this is what his words imply) is illusory, but it is one we need not be-grudge him on his deathbed, as we do not begrudge it to a dying man in hospital whose family has just been wiped out. Nor need we draw elabo-rate inferences from its illusoriness about the imbecility of our world; in a similar instance among our acquaintances, we would regard the illu-sion as a godsend, or even, if we were believers, as God-sent.

In short, to say that "the remorseless process of *King Lear*" forces us to "face the fact of its ending without any support from systems of moral . . . belief at all"[102] is to indulge the mid-twentieth-century *frisson du néant* at its most sentimental. We face the ending of this play, as we face our world, with whatever support we customarily derive from sys-tems of belief or unbelief. If the sound of David crying "Absalom, my son," the image of Mary bending over another broken child, not to mention all that earth has known of disease, famine, earthquake, war, holocaust, and prison since men first came crying hither — if our moral and religious systems can survive this, and the record suggests that for many good men they do and can, then clearly they will have no trouble in surviving the figure of Lear as he bends in his agony, or in his joy, above Cordelia. Tragedy never tells us what to think; it shows us what we are and may be. And what we are and may be was never, I submit, more memorably fixed upon a stage than in this kneeling old man whose heartbreak is precisely the measure of what, in our world of relatedness, it is possible to lose and possible to win. The victory and the defeat are simultaneous and inseparable.

If there is any "remorseless process" in *King Lear*, it is one that begs us to seek the meaning of our human fate not in what becomes of us, but in what we become. Death, as we saw, is miscellaneous and commonplace; it is life whose quality may be made noble and distinctive. Suffering we all recoil from; but we know it is a greater thing to suffer than to lack the feelings and virtues that make it possible to suffer. Cordelia, we may choose to say, accomplished nothing; yet we know it is better to have been Cordelia than to have been her sisters. When we come crying hither, we bring with us the badge of all our misery; but it is also the badge of the vulnerabilities that give us access to whatever grandeur we achieve.

CHAPTER NINE

THE MANY FACES OF

Macbeth

I

AFTER *Lear, Macbeth* seems at first glance a simple play. Seen in one light, it simply tells the brutal story of a Scottish usurper whom Shakespeare had read about in one of his favorite source-books, Raphael Holinshed's *Chronicles of England, Scotland, and Ireland.* Holinshed's Macbeth is an arresting figure, not so much because of his murderous career, which seems to have been only a little in excess of the habits of his time, as because he is said during his first ten years of rule to have "set his whole intention to mainteine justice," and during his last seven years to have begun to "shew what he was, instead of equitie practising crueltie."[103]

Shakespeare, though no historian, knew that no man wears a mask of virtue for ten years, only to reveal that he was "really" a butcher all along. This oddity in Holinshed's conception may have challenged him to speculations that ended in a conception of his own: that of an heroic and essentially noble human being who, by visible stages, deteriorates into a butcher. The great crimes of literature, it has been well said, are mostly committed by persons who would ordinarily be thought incapable of performing them like Othello, like Brutus in *Julius Caesar,* like Raskolnikov in Dostoevsky's *Crime and Punishment.* The hero that Shakespeare draws in *Macbeth* is no exception. At the beginning of the play, even the thought of murder stands his hair on end, makes his heart knock at his ribs (1.3.135). By the end, he is too numb to care. His wife's death scarcely stirs him, and the wild cry of her women in their grief only reminds him of what he can no longer feel:

The time has been my senses would have cooled
To hear a night-shriek, and my fell of hair
Would at a dismal treatise rouse and stir
As life were in't. I have supped full with horrors.
Direness, familiar to my slaughterous thoughts,
Cannot once start me. (5.5.10)

2

Coming at the play from another angle, we realize that its medieval story of the rise and fall of a usurper has been colored by, and also in some sense mirrors, a number of contemporary interests and events. In 1605, for instance, just a year before the probable date of the play's composition and first performance, came the revelation of the Gunpowder Plot, a plan to blow up King, Lords, and Commons in Parliament as they convened for the new session of that year on the fifth of November. The plot was made known through an anonymous letter only ten days before the intended massacre, and the climate of shock and suspicion that prevailed throughout England, especially London, immediately thereafter has almost certainly left its mark in the play's haunted atmosphere of blood, darkness, stealth, treachery, and in the vividness with which it communicates the feeling that a whole community based on loyalty and trust has been thrown into terror by mysterious agencies (both unnatural and natural) working through it like a black yeast. Several of the conspirators were from Warwick, Shakespeare's own county, and may have been known to him. If so, there was no doubt personal as well as dramatic relevance in such observations of the play as Duncan's "There's no art To find the mind's construction in the face" (1.4.12), or Macbeth's "False face must hide what the false heart doth know" (1.7.82). At the very least, such statements, however they were meant by their author, would have held an exceptional charge of meaning for the play's first audiences in 1606.

Witchcraft, too, is among the contemporary interests that the play draws into its murderous web. Witchcraft was a live issue at all times in the sixteenth and seventeenth centuries, but it loomed especially large in the public mind after the Scottish James I came to power, following the great Elizabeth, in 1603. James considered himself an authority on witches, had published a book on demonology in 1599 affirming their existence and their baleful influence in human affairs, and, in 1604, a year after his accession to the throne, inaugurated new statutes against them. Thus, the whole topic was accentuated at just about the time of the writing of the play.

Except in one phrase (1.3.6) and in the stage directions, the play always refers to the witches as *weyard* — or *weyward* — *sisters*. Both spellings are variations of *weird*, which in Shakespeare's time did not mean "freakish," but "fateful" — having to do with the determination of destinies. Shakespeare had met with such creatures in Holinshed, who regularly refers to the supernatural agents with whom Macbeth has dealings as "the three sisters," or "the three weird sisters," i.e., the three Fates. The witches in the play, however, are by no means so unambiguously defined. They have considerable power of insight and suggestion, we gather, but they do not determine a man's will, and Macbeth never blames them for influencing what he has done, only for tricking him into a false security. They are presented to us, moreover, in a climate of suggestion that is fully as demeaning as it is aggrandizing. If they belong with one part of their nature to an extra-human world of thunder, lightning, rain, and demonic powers (1.1), and, as Banquo says, "look not like th' inhabitants o' th' earth" (1.3.41), they have nevertheless some of the attributes of defeminized old women; their familiar demons assume shapes no more terrible than those of cat and toad; and the actions with which they identify themselves — killing swine, wheedling chestnuts, and persecuting the "rump-fed ronyon's" (1.3.6) sea-going husband — show a pettishness and spite that seem perhaps more human than diabolical.

On the other hand, the weyard sisters are obviously more impressive than the ordinary garden variety of seventeenth-century witch, the village crone or hallucinated girl, and their collusion with such dire agents as Lady Macbeth calls upon (1.5.45) and Macbeth invokes (4.1.50) seems unmistakable. The obscurity with which Shakespeare envelops their nature and powers is very probably deliberate, since he seems to intend them to body forth, in a physical presence on stage, precisely the mystery, the ambiguity, the question mark (psychological as well as metaphysical) that lies at the root of human wrong-doing, which is always both local and explicable, universal and inexplicable, like these very figures. In their relations with Macbeth, they are obviously objective "real" beings with whom he talks. Yet they are also in some sense representative of potentialities within him and within the scheme of things of which he is a part.

What is emphatically to be noticed is that the weyard sisters do not suggest Duncan's murder; they simply make a prediction, and Macbeth himself takes the matter from there. The prediction they make, moreover, is entirely congenial to the situation, requires no special insight. Having made himself in this last battle more than ever the great warrior-hero of the kingdom and its chief defender, what more natural than that the ambitious man should be moved in the flush of victory to look ahead, hope, imagine? Hence, while recognizing the objectivity of the sisters as diabolical agents, we may also look on them as representing the potentialities for evil that lurk in every success, agents of a nemesis that seems to attend always on the more extreme dilations of the human ego.

Besides the lore of witchcraft, in which he was intensely interested, and the great Plot which threatened to destroy him together with his Parliament, James's own tenure of the English throne seems to be celebrated, at least obliquely, in Shakespeare's play. His family, the Stuarts, claimed descent from Banquo, and it is perhaps on this account that Shakespeare departs from Holinshed, in whose narrative Banquo is Macbeth's accomplice in the assassination of Duncan, to insist on his "royalty of nature" and the "dauntless temper of his mind" (3.1.50). Many critics see a notable compliment to James in the dumb show of kings descending from Banquo ("What, will the line stretch out to th' crack of doom?" (4.1.117) which so appalls Macbeth at the cave of the weyard sisters. Some commentators, influenced by its Scottish background and its use of a story involving one of James's reputed ancestors, go so far as to suppose that the play was actually composed for a royal occasion and conceivably by royal command. What is certain, in any case, is that the playwright has effectively transformed a remote and primitive story—which at first looks simple—into a theatrical event tense with contemporary relevance. The almost routine assassination of a weak, good-natured king in Holinshed becomes, in Shakespeare's hands, a sensitive and terrifying exposition of the abyss a man may open in himself and in the entire sum of things by a naked act of self-will.

3

This brings us to the third face of *Macbeth*, its character as parable, as myth. For all its medieval plot and its framework of Jacobean feeling, the play has a universal theme: the consuming nature of pride, the rebellion it incites to, the destruction it brings. In some ways Shakespeare's story resembles the story of the Fall of Satan. Macbeth has imperial longings, as Satan has; he is started on the road to revolt partly by the circumstance that another is placed above him; he attempts to bend the universe to his will, warring against all the bonds that relate men to each other—reverence, loyalty, obedience, truth, justice, mercy, and love. But again, as in Satan's case, to no avail. The principles his actions violate prove in the event stronger than he, knit up the wounds he has made in them, and combine to plunge him into an isolation, or alienation, that reveals itself (not only in social and political but in psychological terms) to be a kind of Hell. As Milton's Satan was to put it later in *Paradise Lost:* "Which way I fly is Hell; myself am Hell."

In other ways, the story Shakespeare tells may remind us of the folk-tale of which Marlowe's *Dr. Faustus* is one version: a man sells his soul to the Devil in return for superhuman powers only to find in the end that his gains are illusory, his losses unbearable. It is true, of course, that Shakespeare's hero is attracted by the Scottish throne, not by magic or by power in general; and it is likewise true that he signs no formal contract like his predecessor. Still, the resemblances remain. Macbeth does open his mind to diabolical promptings:

This supernatural soliciting
Cannot be ill, cannot be good. If ill,

187

Why hath it given me earnest of success,
Commencing in a truth? I am Thane of Cawdor.
If good, why do I yield to that suggestion
Whose horrid image doth unfix my hair
And make my seated heart knock at my ribs
Against the use of nature? (1.3.130)

He imagines himself, moreover, to have received immunities of a superhuman sort:

I will not be afraid of death and bane
Till Birnam Forest come to Dunsinane. (5.3.59)

But swords I smile at, weapons laugh to scorn,
Brandished by man that's of a woman born. (5.7.12)

And he finds in the end, like Faustus, that his gains amount to nothing:

I have lived long enough. My way of life
Is fall'n into the sere, the yellow leaf,
And that which should accompany old age,
As honor, love, obedience, troops of friends,
I must not look to have; but, in their stead,
Curses not loud but deep, mouth-honor, breath,
Which the poor heart would fain deny, and dare not.
  (5.3.22)

The very immunities he thought had been guaranteed him prove deceptive, for Birnam Wood comes to high Dunsinane after all, and so does an antagonist not born of woman in the usual sense. In the end, Macbeth knows that what he had begun to fear after Duncan's murder, in the course of meditating Banquo's, is true: he has given his soul to the Devil to make the descendants of Banquo, not his own descendants, kings. All his plans have become instrumental to a larger plan that is not his:

They hailed him father to a line of kings.
Upon my head they placed a fruitless crown

And put a barren sceptre in my gripe,
Thence to be wrenched with an unlineal hand,
No son of mine succeeding. If 't be so,
For Banquo's issue have I filed my mind;
For them the gracious Duncan have I murdered,
Put rancors in the vessel of my peace
Only for them, and mine eternal jewel
Given to the common enemy of man
To make them kings — the seeds of Banquo kings.
(3.1.60)

4

As Freud noticed long ago, the two Macbeths complement each other in their reactions to the crime. Her fall is instantaneous, even eager, like Eve's in *Paradise Lost;* his is gradual and reluctant, like Adam's. She needs only her husband's letter about the weyard sisters' prophecy to precipitate her resolve to kill Duncan. Within an instant she is inviting murderous spirits to unsex her, fill her with cruelty, thicken her blood, convert her mother's milk to gall, and darken the world "That my keen knife see not the wound it makes" (1.5.50). Macbeth, in contrast, vacillates. The images of the deed that possess him simultaneously repel him (1.3.130, 1.7.1). When she proposes Duncan's murder, he temporizes: "We will speak further" (1.5.69).

Later, withdrawing from the supper they have laid for Duncan to consider the matter alone, he very nearly decides not to proceed. It takes all her intensity, all her scorn of what she wrongly chooses to call unmanliness, to steel him to the deed. Throughout this first crime, we notice, it is she who assumes the initiative and devises what is to be done (1.5.64, 1.7.60). Yet we would certainly be wrong to see her as monster or fiend. On the contrary, she is perhaps more than usually feminine. She is conscious of her woman's breasts, her mother's milk (1.5.45); knows "How tender 'tis to love the babe that milks me" (1.7.55); and, when she thinks to carry out the murder herself, fails because the sleeping King too much reminds her of her father (2.2.12). We may infer from this that she is no strapping Amazon; Macbeth calls her his dearest "chuck" (3.2.45), and she speaks, when sleep-walking, of her "little hand" (5.1.48). Thus such evidence as there is suggests that we are to think of her as a womanly woman, capable of great natural tenderness, but one who, for the sake of her husband's advancement and probably her own, has now wound up her will almost to the breaking point.

An equally important contrast between the two Macbeths appears sharply in the scene following the murder, one of the most powerful scenes that Shakespeare ever wrote. Their difference of response at this point is striking — not only because he is shaken to the core and cannot conceal it, whereas she shows an iron discipline throughout, but also because his imagination continues as in the past to be attuned to a world of experience that is closed to her. That world is visionary and even hallucinatory, we can readily see, but at the same time, it is the mark of a keener moral sense, a fuller consciousness of the implications of what they have done, than she possesses.

The difference between his and her responses is related to a form of double vision that extends thoughout the play. Shakespeare establishes for us from the beginning one perspective on his story that is symbolic and mythical, a perspective that includes both the objective weyard sisters, on the one hand, and the subjective images of horror and retribution that rise like smoke from Macbeth's protesting imagination, on the other. The play also establishes, as a second perspective, the ordinary historical world of Scotland, where Duncan is king, Macbeth becomes king, Malcolm will be king, and the witches are skinny old women with beards. In general, Macbeth enacts his crimes in the historical world, experiences them in the symbolic world, and out of this experience, new crimes arise to be enacted in the former. To put it in different terms, a force that seems to come from outside the time-world of history impinges on history, converting history into an experience for Macbeth that is timeless and mythical. We are asked to sense that his crime is not simply a misdeed in the secular political society of a given time and place, but simultaneously a rupture in some dimly apprehended ultimate scheme of things where our material world of evil *versus* good and virtue *versus* vice gives way to a spiritual world of sin *versus* grace and hell *versus* heaven.

5

The suggestiveness of Shakespeare's play in this larger sense is inexhaustible. Every element it contains lives with a double life, one physical, one metaphysical. Consider night, for instance. Night settles down halfway through the first act and stays there through much of the rest of the play: 1.6–7, 2.1–4, 3.2–5, 4.1, and 5.1 are night scenes, and several more, undetermined in the text, could be effectively presented as such, e.g., 1.5 and 4.2–3. All this is ordinary nighttime, of course, but it is obviously much more. "Thick," "murky," full of "fog and filthy air," it "entombs" the face of earth (2.4.9), blots out the stars and the moon, "strangles" even the sun (2.4.7). Duncan rides into it to his death, as does Banquo. Lady Macbeth evokes it (1.5.48) and then finds herself its prisoner, endlessly sleepwalking through the thick night of a darkened mind. Macbeth succumbs to its embrace so completely that, in the end, even a "night-shriek" cannot stir him.

Or again, consider blood. "What bloody man is that?" are the play's first words, following the first weyard sisters' scene. Like the night, blood is both ordinary and special. It sticks like real blood: "His secret murders sticking on his hands," says Angus of Macbeth (5.2.17). It smells as real blood smells: "Here's the smell of the blood still," says Lady Macbeth (5.1.47) hopelessly washing. Yet it finally covers everything Macbeth has touched, in ways both qualitative and quantitative that real blood could not. The sleeping grooms are "all badged" with it, their daggers "Unmannerly breeched with gore." Duncan's silver skin is "laced" with it (2.3.108), Banquo's murderer has it on his face (3.4.14), Banquo's hair is "boltered" with it (4.1.123), and Macbeth's feet are soaked in it (3.4.136). Perhaps the two most bloodcurdling lines in the play, when expressively spoken, are Macbeth's lines after the ghost of Banquo is gone: "It will have blood, they say: blood will have blood" (3.4.122) and Lady Macbeth's moaning cry as she washes and washes: "Yet who would have thought the old man to have had so much blood in him?" (5.1.35).

Macbeth's style of speech in the play has something of this same double character. The startling thing about much of it is its inwardness, as if it were spoken not with the voice at all, but somewhere deep in the arteries and veins, communing with remote strange powers.

> Light thickens, and the crow
> Makes wing to th' rooky wood;
> Good things of day begin to droop and drowse,
> Whiles night's black agents to their preys do rouse.
> (3.2.50)

Between the two battles that open and close the play, Macbeth's language seems frequently to lean away from the historical world of Scotland toward the registering of such experience as rises, timeless and spaceless, both within his mind and beyond it. Thence come thronging those images that "unfix my hair" (1.3.135), the presences that will "blow the horrid deed in every eye" (1.7.24), the voices that cry "Sleep no more!" (2.2.34), the ghost that returns from the dead to mock him for what he has failed to achieve, and the apparitions that are called with great effort from some nether (but also inner) world only to offer him the very counsels that he most wants to hear.

These continuous blurrings of the "real" with the "unreal," intrusions of what is past and supposedly finished into the present (Banquo's ghost, 3.4) and even into the theoretically still formless future (Banquo's descendants, 4.1), provide an appropriate sort of environment for Macbeth and his wife. Lady Macbeth is easily "transported," we learn from her first words to her husband, "beyond This ignorant present" to feel "The future in the instant" (1.5.54). In a similar way, Macbeth's imagination leaps constantly from what is now to what is to come, from the weyard sisters' prophecy to Duncan's murder, from being "thus" to being "safely thus" (3.1.48), from the menace of Banquo to the menace of Macduff, and from a today that is known to an unknown "To-morrow, and to-morrow, and to-morrow" (5.5.19). Shakespeare vividly records in these ways the restlessness of the Macbeths' ambition and at the same time the problem that ambition, like every other natural urge to self-realization, poses for human beings and their relationships to each other.

6

To understand this problem in the dramatic and poetic terms Shakespeare gives it, it is helpful to look at two of the play's most often noticed features. One is feasting. Macbeth withdraws from the supper he has laid for Duncan to weigh the arguments for killing him (1.7). The entertainment, which he has himself ordered, marks his adherence to the community of mutual service that we find implied in the scene at Duncan's court (1.4). Here is a society, we realize, that depends on thane cherishing king — "The service and the loyalty I owe," Macbeth tells Duncan, "In doing it pays itself" — and on king cherishing thane: "I have begun to plant thee," Duncan assures Macbeth, "and will labor To make thee full of growing" (1.4.28). When Macbeth withdraws, therefore, we see him retreating from the shared community of the supper that he has provided for Duncan and the other thanes into the isolation that his intended crime against that community implies. Once he has withdrawn and his withdrawal is sealed by murder, he can never rejoin the community he has ruptured. This he discovers at the feast in 3.4, when the ghost of Banquo preempts his place. The only community left him after this is the community of dark powers we see him appealing to in 4.1, where the weyard sisters dance about a hell-broth (also a feast?) of dislocated fragments. After 3.4, we never see Macbeth in the company of more than one or two other persons, usually servants, and in the last act his forces ebb inexorably away till there is only himself. Similarly, and with similar implications, after 3.4 we never see Macbeth and his wife together. Instead of being united by the crime, they are increasingly separated by it, she gradually lost in the inner hell that she finds so "murky" in the sleepwalking scene, he always busier in the outer hell that he has made Scotland into.

The other much commented on feature is children. Four children have roles in the play: Donalbain, Malcolm, Fleance, and the son of Macduff. Two children are among the apparitions raised by the weyard sisters in 4.1: "a Bloody Child" and "a Child Crowned, with a tree in his hand." Allusions to children occur often. We hear of the child or children Lady Macbeth must have sometime had (1.7.54), of the son Macbeth wishes he had now to succeed him (3.1.64), and of pity, who comes "like a naked new-born babe Striding the blast" to trumpet forth Macbeth's murderous act till "tears shall drown the wind" (1.7.21). Plainly, in some measure, all these "children" relate to what the play is telling us about time. Macbeth, in his Scottish world (though not in his demonic one), belongs like the rest of us to a world of time: he has been Glamis, he is Cawdor, and he shall be (so the weyard sisters predict) "King hereafter" (1.3.50). The crux, of course, is *hereafter.* Macbeth and his wife seek to make hereafter now, to wrench the future into the present by main force, to master time. But this option, the play seems to be saying, is always disastrous for human beings. The only way human beings can constructively master time is Banquo's way, letting it grow and unfold from the present as the Stuart line of kings is to grow and unfold from Fleance. The more Macbeth seeks to control the future, the more it counters and defeats him (in Fleance, Donalbain, Malcolm, the bloody child, the crowned child) and the more he is himself cut off from its creative unfolding processes — having *had* children we are told, but having now only a "fruitless" crown, a "barren" scepter. "No son of mine succeeding" (3.1.64).

Toward the play's end, Malcolm and his soldiers move in on Dunsinane with their "leavy screens" (5.6.1), and very soon after this Macduff, the man who "was from his mother's womb Untimely ripped," meets Macbeth (5.8), slays him, then reappears with his head fixed on a pike. What did Shakespeare intend us to make of this? All that can be said for certain is that the situation on stage in these scenes has some sort of allusive relation to the three apparitions that were summoned at Macbeth's wish by the weyard sisters. The first was an armed head — matched here at the play's end, apparently, by Macbeth's armed head on a pike. The second was a bloody child, who told him that none of woman born could harm him. This child is evidently to be associated with Macduff. The third apparition was a crowned child holding a tree — an allusion, we may suppose, to Malcolm, child of Duncan, who is soon to be crowned King, who is part of the future that Macbeth has tried in vain to control, and who now with his men, holding the green branches of Birnam Wood, seems calculated to remind us of the way in which Nature, green, fertile, "full of growing," (1.4.29) moves inexorably to "overgrow" a man who has more and more identified himself with death and all such destructive uses of power as the armed head suggests.

If these speculations are at all well founded, what takes place in the final scenes is that a kind of Living Death, a figure who has alienated himself from all the growing processes, goes out to war encased in an armor that he believes to be invulnerable on the ground that nothing in the scheme of nature, nothing born of woman, can conquer Death. But he is wrong. Death can always be conquered by the bloody child, who, being ripped from the womb as his mother lay dying, is indicative of the life that in Nature's scheme of things (like the green leaves in Birnam Wood) is always being reborn from death.

7

To leave the play on this abstract and allegorical plane, however, is to do it wrong. What comes home most sharply to us as we watch these last scenes performed is the twistings and turnings of a ruined but fascinating human being, a human being capable of profound even if disbalanced insights, probing the boundaries of our common nature ever more deeply in frantically changing accesses of arrogance and despair, defiance and cowardice, lethargy and exhilaration, folly and wisdom. Underscoring this, we have the succession of abrupt changes from place to place, group to group, and speaker to speaker that marks scenes 2 to 8 in Act 5, an unsettling discontinuity which does much to dramatize our sense of a kingdom coming apart at the seams. In the background, too, we hear the gradually swelling underbeat of the allied drums, called for by the stage directions in 5.2, 4, 6, and 8, and audible elsewhere if the director desires. This gives a sensory dimension to the increasing prosperity of Malcolm's cause, and can be made particularly dramatic and significant in 5.5. Here, following the scene's opening, we hear Macbeth's drums for the only time in the play. Then comes the famous soliloquy, where he assures us that life is an empty fraud, a "tale told by an idiot." If, at the close of this, when the door to Dunsinane opens to admit the messenger bearing the news of Birnam Wood, we hear again in the distance the steady beat of the allied drums signifying the existence of a very different point of view about the value of life, the impact is powerful.

Perhaps the most telling sensory effect in these final scenes is the call of trumpets. We hear them first on the appearance of Macduff, whose command may remind us of Macbeth's earlier prognostication about "heaven's cherubin" riding the winds and blowing the fame — or in-famy — of the murder of Duncan through the whole world:

Make all our trumpets speak, give them all breath,
Those clamorous harbingers of blood and death. (5.6.9)

We then hear their alarums with the next entry of Macduff, who is now searching for Macbeth, and again with the exit of Malcolm; alarums once more when Macduff and Macbeth begin to fight and when they go fighting off stage; and finally, three massed flourishes of trumpets, one as Malcolm enters after the sounding of retreat, a second as Macduff and the other thanes hail Malcolm king, and a third as all go out, Macbeth's head waving somberly on Macduff's spear (5.8.35). The former age has been wiped away and the new age inaugurated, fittingly, to the sound of the trumpets of a Judgment.

All this, we understand, is as it must be. Alike as ruler and man, Macbeth has been tried and found wanting. Yet we realize, as we hear Malcolm speak of "this dead butcher and his fiend-like queen" (5.8.69) — and we realize it all the more because of these last scenes, in which a great man goes down fighting, bayed around by enemies external and internal, natural and even supernatural, committed to the Father of Lies but taking the consequences like a man — how much there is that judgment does not know, and how much there is that, through Shakespeare's genius, we do.

CHAPTER TEN

THE STILLNESS AND THE DANCE

Antony and Cleopatra

I

THE last of Shakespeare's greatest tragedies, in my view, is *Antony and Cleopatra:* the delight of audiences, the despair of critics. Its delight for audiences springs, in part at least, from its being inexhaustible to contemplation, as Coleridge implies when he speaks of its "giant strength," the "happy valiancy" of its style, and calls it of all Shakespeare's plays "the most wonderful."[104] No doubt its delight for today's audiences owes something also to its being the most accessible of the major Shakespearean tragedies to twentieth-century sensibilities, especially those not much experienced in drama apart from that of the realistic stage. There are no witches in *Antony and Cleopatra* to require a mild suspension of disbelief, no ghosts, no antic madmen, no personages who are paragons of good or evil, nor even any passions (such, for example, as Coriolanus's contempt for the Roman commoners) which require of today's spectator an act of imaginative adjustment.

True, the play's story of the ruin of a great man by an enchantress (if that *is* its story) must have carried more plausibility in 1607 than it does today, when our enchantresses, brash and busty, seem unlikely to endanger anyone who has got past his freshman year, and our great men are in depressingly short supply. Nonetheless, the enchantment formula has the virtue of being familiar to us, however shrunken the modern instances, and it has, besides, for those who insist on realism, the sanction of history, or at least such history as Plutarch, Appian, and Lucius Florus knew how to write.

I suppose it has, too, the sanction of what a present fashion likes to call our fantasy-life. There is no woman, one may be permitted to believe, who has not somewhere in her being a touch, or twitch, of Cleopatra; no man who has not entertained, at some time, the dream of exercising a magnanimity like Antony's, setting his beloved in a hail of barbaric pearl and gold, disposing of men and measures with an imperious nod, and falling, if fall he must, with a panache that makes women weep and strong men suck in their waistlines. Even the Victorian lady who is reported to have whispered to her husband at the close of a performance of *Antony and Cleopatra*, "How unlike the home-life of our own dear Queen!" may be presumed to have lingered a little longer than usual over her toilette the next day.

2

So much for audiences. For critics, the case is different. If the play is inexhaustible to contemplation, it is at the same time remarkably inaccessible to interpretation, or at any rate to a consensus of interpretation, as the critical record shows. There seems to be a delicacy combined with intricacy in the play's interior balance that no criticism can lay hold of for long without oversimplifying or oversetting, including the criticism speculatively offered here. Magnanimous emperor, calculating politician, charismatic leader, reckless lover and risk-taker, posturer, angry husband — all these figures are contained in Antony, yet he is not reducible to any of them or even to all together. Cleopatra is actress, trickster, trull, and loving wife; she is "wrinkled deep in time" (1.5.29) yet timeless, "Eastern star" (5.2.307) and "morsel, cold upon Dead Caesar's trencher," (3.13.116) "Royal Egypt" (4.15.74) but "commanded By such poor passion as the maid that milks And does the meanest chares" (4.15.76). Yet relevant as these categories are in her case too, she manages to escape them, as the widely disparate estimates of her conduct made by spectators as well as readers show. Even at the play's end, there remains a sense in which, as the 116th sonnet says of another "star," her "worth's unknown, although [her] height be taken."

The play, moreover, like the lovers, makes no confidences. Soliloquies and asides, though engaged in by Enobarbus, are evidently foreign to Shakespeare's conception of heroic character in this play, or at least to his conception of the optimum relation between these protagonists and us. We are never brought close to them by a secret shared, a motive, conscious or unconscious, suddenly divulged. We watch them always from a distance, uncertain how far to accept their actions — and which actions — at face value, how far to believe the commentary of the ob-servers in which Shakespeare again and again frames them, and even how to reconcile one action with the next. Antony is never allowed for an instant to reflect for our benefit on his betrayal of Cleopatra in marrying Octavia or on his betrayal of Octavia and Caesar in returning to Cleo-patra or, as we might perhaps especially expect, on the meaning of his past experiences as he dies. We learn only that he lived "the greatest prince o' th' world, The noblest" (4.15.54) (a summary which consider-ably begs the question), and dies now, not basely or cowardly in sur-render to Caesar, but by his own hand, "a Roman, by a Roman Valiantly vanquished" (4.15.54).

As for Cleopatra, Enobarbus tells us what *he* makes of her cajoleries with Thidias, and he is in some sense our guide:

> Sir, sir, thou art so leaky
> That we must leave thee to thy sinking, for
> Thy dearest quit thee. (3.13.63)

Yet this episode is followed by one of the most endearing reconcilia-tion scenes ever written, one in which I see no shred of evidence to show that Cleopatra is lying and Antony her dupe:

ANTONY: Alack, our terrene moon
Is now eclipsed, and it portends alone
The fall of Antony!
CLEOPATRA: I must stay his time.
ANTONY:
To flatter Caesar, would you mingle eyes
With one that ties his points?
CLEOPATRA: Not know me yet?
ANTONY:
Cold-hearted toward me?

CLEOPATRA: Ah, dear, if I be so,
From my cold heart let heaven engender hail,
And poison it in the source, and the first stone
Drop in my neck: as it determines, so
Dissolve my life! The next Caesarion smite,
Till by degrees the memory of my womb,
Together with my brave Egyptians all,
By the discandying of this pelleted storm,
Lie graveless, till the flies and gnats of Nile
Have buried them for prey!
ANTONY: I am satisfied.
(3.13.153)

Antony is satisfied, but critics understandably have not been. For if this expresses her real feelings, what was she up to with Thidias, and what did the playwright wish us to make of Enobarbus's remark about the leaky ship, from which, presumably, the rats are fleeing? On the other hand, if these lines must be dismissed as rhetoric, so must almost every other expression of emotion in the play, for they are all of a hyperbolic piece, including Cleopatra's grief at Antony's death and her dream of him re-counted to Dolabella.

Similar questions, we realize, haunt our impressions of her interview with Caesar, when her treasurer either gives her game away or affects to, and also of the two failures of her ships at Actium. Why, at that first bat-tle, does she fly? Is it simple fear ("Forgive my fearful sails" [3.11.55])? Or does her woman's intuition suspect that the ultimate contest against Caesar is already lost? Or that a victory for Antony would be a defeat for her, since in that event he might be struck again by that "Roman thought" (1.2.79) which earlier deprived her of him? Or is it perhaps her hope, by taking herself out of the battle, to strengthen her negotiating position, no matter to whom the victory falls?

The second occasion is yet more puzzling. This time the fleet not only yields to the foe, but "yonder They cast their caps up and carouse together Like friends long lost," and Antony's inference from this that he has been "betrayed" by Cleopatra, "Beguiled . . . to the very heart of loss" (4.12.10), seems unexceptionable. How else to account for a surrender without (apparently) a single blow struck? Yet Cleopatra's emissary, Diomedes, later tells Antony and us that no such treason occurred, at least none in which she had a hand:

> for when she saw
> (Which never shall be found) you did suspect
> She had disposed with Caesar, and that your rage
> Would not be purged, she sent you word she was dead.
> (4.14.121)

I labor the obvious in these instances because I believe that Shakespeare means us to take note of what he is about. I cannot persuade myself, as some recent critics have done, that his failure to supply "the directives to the audience that are obviously needed" springs from inattention or fatigue, the play being so clearly in all other respects the product of a poetic consciousness supremely alert, and even, I would wish to add, rather plainly disposed to jolt us from our usual automatisms and stock responses. For what else can be the intent of that unusual structure, already mentioned, whereby every major action of the lovers is enveloped in a choral commentary that we are simultaneously aware does not quite adequately represent it? What else can be the intent of establishing so many wide polarities — Rome and Egypt, nature and art, war and love, indulgence and austerity, loyalty and self-interest, sincerity and affectation, and many others — and of so steadfastly refusing to resolve them or adjudicate between them?

Even a great deal of the play's language seems calculated to question or explode our habitual safe norms and logical expectations. It bristles with startling oxymorons, contradictions, and abrupt reversals that every playgoer will recall: the bellows that cools, not kindles (1.1.9); the fans that heat the cheek they cool "and what they did undid" (2.2.203); the woman "wrinkled deep in time" (1.5.29) whom age, however, cannot wither, who makes "defect perfection," and, when breathless, "pow'r breathe[s] forth" (2.2.232); the man who can say "with a wound I must be cured" (4.14.78) and whose bounty "grew the more by reaping"

(5.2.86); the prayer that prays and yet unprays itself—"Husband win, win brother, Prays, and destroys the prayer" (3.4.18); our "most persisted deeds" that yet "compel" us to lament them (5.1.29); the "lover's pinch, Which hurts, and is desired" (5.2.294); the asp that is both death and lover, or death and infant, or possibly all three (5.2.302ff).

Again, I stress the obvious. What these effects convey is the same intricate balance of opposing impulses and conflicting attitudes that characterize the play throughout. Somewhere dimly behind them we may sense not only the playwright's effort to achieve a style that will accommodate the story he has to tell in its extremes of grandeur and folly, dignity and humiliation, but, just possibly, the mood of serious play (I suspect this is among the meanings Coleridge meant to assign to his "happy valiancy") that seems to shine out in all Renaissance works that draw heavily on the vein of paradox.

Not impossibly, Shakespeare was himself conscious of his propinquity in this instance to that honorable tradition. With a heroine who was historically guaranteed both whore and queen, yet who, in popular story, had additionally been looked on as an exemplar of fidelity, one of love's own martyrs; with a hero, too, who was credited with being one of the greatest soldiers in the world and at the same time one of the greatest lovers and carousers; and with a source, or a set of sources, certain to attract a poet's mind toward the ancient question whether the world can ever be well lost, and if so, for what return, he must have been considerably less clairvoyant about the implications of his materials than he usually shows himself to be if he did not see that in *Antony and Cleopatra* he was engaged in the central act of the paradoxist, which is to defend the indefensible, or at least to defend something which is widely held to be indefensible, like Erasmus's "Folly" or Donne's "Inconstancy in Women."

Plato's Gorgias, we are told, set himself the paradoxical task of praising Helen, who had brought ruin by her adulterous beauty to all Greece, and succeeded so well at it that his successors supposed he had been serious and took her thereafter for a proper object of praise. It was not the last time that this would happen. Milton's effort to lift Satan, who

had brought ruin to all mankind, out of the category of common buga-
boo and fiend (a spectacular exercise in defending the indefensible), was
to enjoy, after an interval, a similar success in certain quarters, as was
Swift's praise of stoic apathy in the fourth book of *Gulliver.* We know far
less of course of Shakespeare's intentions because we know far less of
him. But whatever they were, it is safe to say that he has left us a pair of
reckless and irresponsible lovers so well praised that audience and critic
alike still find it impossible to sort out their sympathies. In other words,
the paradox of his theme, whether he himself saw it or not, continues to
"do his kind," as the clown says of the worm (5.2.262): it continues to be
faithful to the nature of paradox, which is "to be paradoxical, to do two
things at once, two things which contradict . . . one another."[105]

3

Considered as pure story, the play that Shakespeare makes of Antony and
Cleopatra would have delighted Chaucer's Monk. For it obviously owes
much, at least in its general outline, to the medieval tragic formula of the
fall-of-princes and mirror-for-magistrates tradition, which the Monk
enunciates to the Canterbury pilgrims, and which was still, in 1607,
owing to a good deal of Elizabethan dramatic practice including Shakespeare's own, far better known than Plutarch to playhouse audiences.
Tragedy, according to this formula, is what happens when eminent historical personages lose their foothold on the pinnacle of wealth or power
and plummet down to ruin with a gratifying homiletic crash. Implied in
Plutarch's narrative inevitably, though only desultorily stressed there and
sometimes lost in masses of detail better suited to biography than to
homily, the theme of lost (or gained) imperium became for Shakespeare
the central issue.

For this reason, his Antony is brought before us at the zenith of his
eminence, when his soldiership ("twice the other twain" in the view of
Pompey, comparing him with Lepidus and Caesar — 2.1.34) is critically
in demand. He already holds the whole of the gorgeous East in fee and
now is about to be freed from threats, on one side by his reconciliation
with Caesar and marriage to Caesar's sister; on the other, by the victories

of his lieutenant Ventidius in Parthia. He is also, we quickly learn, about to throw all this away for the fascinating creature shown us in four of the first five scenes and in Enobarbus's description of Cleopatra on the Cydnus. For conquest has several forms, it seems. There is more than one kind of stronghold to attract a soldier:

> those his goodly eyes
> That o'er the files and musters of the war
> Have glowed like plated Mars, now bend, now turn
> The office and devotion of their view
> Upon a tawny front; (1.1.2)

and there is more than one kind of attitude that may be taken toward the imperium of Rome:

> Let Rome in Tiber melt and the wide arch
> Of the ranged empire fall! Here is my space,
> Kingdoms are clay. (1.1.33)

In short, from the moment we are introduced to Antony, we are made aware of the undertow that will sweep him away, and this is kept so vividly before us in every scene thereafter — by Cleopatra, Enobarbus, Caesar, Pompey, the soothsayer, and Antony himself — that it is only a small exaggeration to say that Shakespeare's story of Antony's fall and of its consequences moves from the first scene of Act 1 to the last scene of Act 5 uninterruptedly, despite the presence of certain early scenes in which, ostensibly, his political fortunes are on the rise.

The play has other features, too, that if not derived from the medieval formula are at any rate in tune with it. Treatment of the protagonists from the outside and from a certain aesthetic distance, so as to enhance the element of spectacle and with it our impression that we behold in them a sort of paradigm or exemplum in the *de casibus* tradition, is one such feature that I have already underscored. So is the corollary reliance on choric commentary rather than interior meditation to point up the stages leading to the disaster, and particularly the emphasis laid by this means (and in every other imaginable way) on the grandeur of the world the protagonists inhabit and on their own special magnificence and magnanimity, in order to increase the pathos of their fall, however much that fall may be shown to be self-caused.

The play is further attuned to the formula in insisting simultaneously on what is *not* self-caused, on fortune, accident, destiny, doom — all that in the original medieval context might have been called the will of God and here is hinted at least to be the will of one god: "'Tis the god Hercules, whom Antony loved, Now leaves him" (4.3.15). Shakespeare may have been moved to this equivocal management by a bemusing sentence in his source. For Plutarch says of Cleopatra's plea to be allowed to join the wars against Caesar (in Plutarch's narrative, delivered to Antony through a bribed Canidius): "These fair persuasions won him; for it was predestined that the government of all the world should fall into Octavius Caesar's hands." Hence it was Antony's decision, except that it was also destiny's.

Just so, in the play, though our attention is repeatedly called to Antony's misjudgments, a sense of impersonal fate runs deep. Caesar, as Bradley says, is "the Man of Destiny, the agent of forces against which the intentions of an individual could avail nothing," one from whom "the feeling of fate comes through to us."[106] The language repeatedly proclaims this. Whereas "noble" is the play's characterizing term for Antony (despite his sometimes ignoble deeds like the whipping of Thidias), Caesar's characterizing term is "fortune." This word, with its cognates and synonyms, appears some forty times in *Antony and Cleopatra*, more than twice as often as in any other of the major tragedies, and repeatedly in connection with Caesar, whose invisible "genius" it appears to be. Antony's own genius, the soothsayer assures him immediately after his marriage to Octavia, "is Noble, courageous, high, unmatchable," but placed near Caesar's it is overpowered; "and of that natural luck, He beats thee 'gainst the odds" (2.3.19). From that point on, Caesar regularly beats Antony against the odds, and is spoken of increasingly as "fortunate Caesar" (4.14.76), "full-fortuned Caesar" (4.15.24), the man whom Antony has to address after Actium as "Lord of his fortunes" (3.12.11), and the man whose "luck," we are told by Cleopatra, he learns eventually to mock: "I see him rouse himself," she says of Antony as she is dying, "To praise my noble act. I hear him mock The luck of Caesar" (5.2.283).

Something similar seems to hold true for Cleopatra. Though Antony chooses her and we are shown the familiar feminine skills with which she draws him, the play keeps alive a complementary assurance that a power works through her which is also, in some sense, a fate. She is for everyone an "enchantress," a "fairy" (4.8.12), a "witch" (4.12.37), a "charm" (4.12.25), a "spell" (4.12.30), and she moves, even for the Romans, in an ambience of suggestion that seems to give these terms a reach beyond their conventional horizons of gallantry and erotic praise. The sun makes love to her; the air, "except for vacancy" (2.2.217), would have gone to see her triumphant landing from the Cydnus; her sighs and tears are greater storms and tempests than almanacs can report; she is cunning past man's thought; her variety is infinite; and the fetters in which she binds, like those of Merlin's Vivien, are "strong," as is also — to recall a phrase of Caesar's when he sees her in death — her "toil of grace":

> She looks like sleep,
> As she would catch another Antony
> In her strong toil of grace.
> (5.2.344)

That phrase captures her mystery superbly because its range of meaning is indeterminable. Is the emphasis in "toil" on the cruel snare of the hunter or on the delighting web of the accomplished woman's charms? Do the boundaries of "grace" include simply the feline movements of the experienced beast of prey, or do they extend to the worldly accomplishments cited by Claudius in giving young Laertes permission to return to Paris: "Time be thine, And thy best graces spend it at thy will" (1.2.62) or do they glance also toward the enigmatic territories touched on by Prospero when, in praising Ariel for his simulation of the harpy, he sums up in five words the meaning of the disasters in *The Tempest* and (some critics would have it) of those in *Antony and Cleopatra* as well?

Bravely the figure of this harpy hast thou
Performed, my Ariel; *a grace it had, devouring.*
(3.3.83)

My point, of course, is not that there is a right answer to these questions, but rather that the play teases us into asking them. Shakespeare's medieval inheritance remains strong enough to enable him to show us a catastrophe that Antony has quite literally made love to as if it were simultaneously a "doom" (3.13.78).

4

The "fall" story chiseled out of Plutarch receives in the finished play many kinds of imaginative extension, as every spectator will remember. One of these is the intricately elaborated context of mobility and mutability within which the fall is shown to occur, so that here as elsewhere in Shakespeare a play's characteristic "world" and its major action tend to become expressions of each other.

Our sense of a world in flux in *Antony and Cleopatra* is created primarily through the imagery, as many have pointed out, but in the theater it reaches us yet more directly through continual shifts of place (to mention only those of the first three acts: from Egypt to Rome to Egypt to Messina to Rome to Egypt to Misenum to Syria to Rome to Egypt to Athens to Rome to Actium to Egypt), and in the number and brevity of the episodes and scenes. In its episodic character, in fact, the play again seems mindful of the medieval past, each scene acted, as it were, from an appropriate historical "maison" or pageant-wagon, as in the cyclical plays. Today, the text of *Antony and Cleopatra* is usually divided into forty-two scenes, and while these need not be taken seriously as divisions of the action, since the folio text has neither scenes nor acts, their number indicates to us how often we are asked to register that one time, place, mood, or person gives way before another.

To this we must add the equally striking circumstance that *Antony and Cleopatra* in performance contains just under two hundred distinct entrances and exits (rather more than one per minute of playing time) and that a great many of these acquire a special impact on our senses, either from being ceremonial and accompanied by much fanfare or from their effect in bringing about emotionally significant leave-takings and re-unions. People flow to and away from each other in *Antony and Cleopatra* with relentless frequency and ease — Antony from Cleopatra and to her, to Caesar and from him; Octavia from Caesar and to him, to Antony and from him; Enobarbus from Antony, then (in heart) to him; and Cleo-patra — who can say? This pattern is climaxed by the great reunions and leave-takings of the close. Antony, after being reunited with Cleopatra in her monument, takes his last farewell of her ("I am dying, Egypt, dying" [4.15.18]); Cleopatra takes hers of Caesar and the world ("Give me my robe, put on my crown" [5.2.279]); and both farewells are preludes, so the lovers insist, to a further reunion in the Elysian fields, or on the Cydnus, where the great passion will begin anew. Nothing seems to be granted finality in *Antony and Cleopatra*, perhaps not even death.

Mobility and mutability are not confined to spatial and geographical forms, but penetrate the play at every point. They are reiterated in the allusions to the ebbing and flowing of the tides; the rising and setting (or eclipse and extinction) of stars, moons, and suns; the immense reversals of feeling in the lovers and in Enobarbus; the career of Pompey, whose powers, "crescent" in 2.1, are by 3.5 scattered and the man himself dead; and the steady erosion of persons whom for a moment we have known or heard of as presences: Fulvia, Lepidus, Pompey, Pacorus, Enobarbus, Alexas, and Eros all are dead before Antony dies; Menas and Menecrates, Philo and Demetrius, Ventidius and Scarus have disappeared without a trace, along with Mardian; Canidius and Decretas (besides Alexas and Enobarbus) have turned their coats, and Cleopatra may or may not have been several times on the verge of turning hers.

In addition, the style itself generates impressions of this kind. John-son's account of the play rightly emphasizes the "hurry," the "quick succession" of events that calls the attention forward; and part of the effect he has in mind comes clearly from the style, which pours rather than broods (as in *Macbeth*), which is sensuous rather than intellectual (as in *Hamlet*), and which, as Pope said of Homer's, animates everything it touches: from Philo's view of Antony in 1.1, where eyes glow, bend, turn, and the heart remembers buckles it has burst in the scuffles of great fights, to Cleopatra's view of him in 5.2, where he bestrides, rears, crests; quails and shakes the orb with rattling thunder; gives in a perpetual autumn; sports like a dolphin above the ocean of his pleasure; and scatters crowns and coronets from his pockets as if they were small change.

Most striking of all, perhaps, is Shakespeare's use of the grammatical mood that, of all moods, best expresses mobility and mutability: the optative. Most of the great speeches in the play are "options" — in the radical sense. At all levels, high and low, playful and serious, hearts continually press forward with their longings, so much so that by placing even a few of them in sequence one may easily recapitulate the action.

Let Rome in Tiber melt. (1.1.33)

Let me be married to three kings in a forenoon and widow them all. . . . Find me to marry me with Octavius Caesar, and companion me with my mistress. (1.2.25)

> Upon your sword
> Sit laurel victory, and smooth success
> Be strewed before your feet! (1.3.99)

Let his shames quickly
Drive him to Rome. (1.4.72)

> But all the charms of love,
> Salt Cleopatra, soften thy waned lip!
> Let witchcraft join with beauty, lust with both!
> (2.1.20)
> Let her live
> To join our kingdoms and our hearts; and never
> Fly off our loves again. (2.2.151)

Would I had never come from thence, nor you thither. (2.3.12)

Melt Egypt into Nile! and kindly creatures
Turn all to serpents! (2.5.78)

In thy fats our cares be drowned,
With thy grapes our hairs be crowned.
(2.7.114)

> Sink Rome, and their tongues rot
That speak against us! (3.7.15)

> O that I were
Upon the hill of Basan, to outroar
The hornèd herd! (3.13.126)

This is a selection simply, and from the first three acts. Thereafter, for obvious reasons, the optative mood quickens, to culminate at last in three of the best known utterances in the play:

We'll bury him; and then, what's brave, what's noble,
Let's do't after the high Roman fashion,
And make death proud to take us. (4.15.89)

I dreamt there was an Emperor Antony.
O, such another sleep, that I might see
But such another man! (5.2.76)

> Husband, I come:
Now to that name my courage prove my title!
(5.2.286)

To all these impressions of a world in motion, much is added in performance by the playwright's insistent stress on messages and messengers — though here, doubtless, other effects and purposes must also receive their due. To ignore a man's messenger who has a legitimate claim on you, as Antony does in 1.1, or to have such a messenger whipped, as he does in 3.13, or, like Cleopatra in 2.5, to assault a messenger for the bad news he carries: these are Shakespeare's equivalents in this play of Hamlet's melancholy, Lear's quick wrath — marks of the tragic personage's incapacity or unwillingness to adjust to the world he lives in. Messengers also, of course, enhance our sense of power and of the rearrangements that take place in power as the play wears on. Cleopatra's inexhaustible supply of emissaries and her determination to "unpeople Egypt" (1.5.78) rather than let Antony in Rome go a day without a letter bear testimony to her political stature at the outset of the play as well as to her passion. Later on, the fact that Antony, who has had "superfluous kings for messengers" (3.12.5), is reduced to using his children's school-master to carry a message to Caesar serves as an index to the audience as well as to Caesar that his wing has indeed been "plucked" (3.12.3). Such effects are of course highly visual in performance, and capable in some contexts of communicating exquisite ironies. In the last scene, for in-stance, Caesar's messengers come and go again and again in a fine show of strategy and efficiency, but then comes the messenger no one antici-pated, a bumpkin and malapropist bearing figs, who is escorted in by Caesar's own guard; and he proves to be the messenger that counts.

Beyond this, the play's emphasis on messengers reminds us that, in so volatile and mutable a world, opinion and report are matters of huge concern. All these people have an immense curiosity about each other, especially the Romans about Cleopatra, which they can only satisfy with fresh news. "From Alexandria," says Caesar to Lepidus the first time we see him, "This is the news" (1.4.3), and he goes on to detail Antony's ill courses there. After the triumvirs have made peace in Rome, Enobarbus is no sooner left alone with Maecenas and Agrippa than they throw out bait about life in Egypt that they hope he will rise to: "Eight wild boars roasted whole at a breakfast, and but twelve persons there. Is this true?" says Maecenas (2.2.180). Pompey plays a like game with Antony, hinting at the time when Cleopatra kept an assignation with Julius Caesar by having herself rolled up inside a mattress and carried to him (2.6.68); while Lepidus, in the brawl on Pompey's galley, speculates drunkenly — but inquiringly — about pyramises and crocodiles (2.7.24).

This is merely the surface of "report" in the play. It soon turns out that almost everyone we meet is passionately conscious of report in other senses: not simply the public report of Rome, which Caesar is concerned as far as possible to manipulate and even Antony and Cleopatra from time to time feel the need to placate or consciously defy, but the report of history. This too is an aspect of the play that insists on its aesthetic distance from us, on its character as spectacle and exemplum. Caesar is walking into history, and is keenly conscious of it; in fact, he hopes to guarantee a good "report" for himself by composing it: "Go with me to my tent," he says to Agrippa and Maecenas, after Antony's death has been announced to him:

> where you shall see
> How hardly I was drawn into this war,
> How calm and gentle I proceeded still
> In all my writings. Go with me, and see
> What I can show in this. (5.1.73)

Enobarbus, too, throughout his hesitations about leaving Antony, looks forward to what "story" will say of him if he stays —

> The loyalty well held to fools does make
> Our faith mere folly: yet he that can endure
> To follow with allegiance a fall'n lord,
> Does conquer him that did his master conquer
> And earns a place i' th' story. (3.13.42)

— though it must be admitted he reckoned without Plutarch, who gives his going over to Caesar and his repentance short shrift, and says nothing whatever about his hesitations. Again, in his death scene, all alone, he appeals to the "blessèd moon" (4.9.7) to bear him witness, "When men revolted shall upon record Bear hateful memory," that he repents his betrayal of his master, and then, as if resigning himself to an eternity of bad notices in the *theatrum mundi*, concludes:

> O, Antony,
> Nobler than my revolt is infamous,
> Forgive me in thine own particular,
> But let the world rank me in register
> A master leaver and a fugitive. (4.9.18)

The lovers' own consciousness of being ever on parade before the reviewing stand of world opinion is particularly acute. Antony's anguished

"I have offended reputation" (3.11.49) after Actium means more than simply that he has stained his individual honor, or even his immediate public image; he has also deviated from the world's conception of what a Roman soldier is and does, guarded and passed on from generation to generation in world opinion. When he takes Cleopatra in his arms at the play's beginning, he is conscious of the world as audience; in fact, he invokes it:

> The nobleness of life
> Is to do thus; when such a mutual pair
> And such a twain can do 't, in which I bind,
> On pain of punishment, the world to weet
> We stand up peerless. (1.1.36)

When he anticipates their reunion in the Elysian fields, he thinks of the audience they will have there:

> Where souls do couch on flowers, we'll hand in hand,
> And with our sprightly port make the ghosts gaze.
> (4.14.51)

And when Eros takes his own life rather than kill him, the thought that captivates his imagination is that Eros and Cleopatra will have won a nobler place in history than his: "My queen and Eros Have by their brave instruction got upon me A nobleness in record" (4.14.97).

This, too, as everyone will remember, is the concern that occupies Cleopatra as she steels herself after Antony's death to do "what's brave, what's noble . . . after the high Roman fashion," and so win fame, not obloquy, in the chronicles of times to come (4.15.89). Her wish that her women "show" her "like a queen" in her "best attires" (5.2.227) — though no doubt partly vanity and partly calculated staginess for Caesar's last view of her — is partly too, one feels, her sense of what is suitable, in the record that will be forthcoming, "for a princess Descended of so many royal kings" (5.2.325). Caesar's parting words about her have the quality of an epitaph, and seal the immortality in "report" that now awaits all three:

She shall be buried by her Antony.
No grave upon the earth shall clip in it
A pair so famous. High events as these
Strike those that make them; and their story is
No less in pity than his glory which
Brought them to be lamented. (5.2.356)

5

The imaginative extension that Shakespeare gives to the story of Antony's fall by surrounding it with a world in which, as Mutability says in *The Faerie Queene*, "Nothing doth firme and permanent appeare, But all things tost and turnèd by transverse," has its counterpart in the extension he gives the love affair. Everyone who reads or sees the play is struck at once by the hyperbolic character of the value the lovers set on each other, or at any rate the hyperbolic character of their own conception of that value: "There's beggary," as Antony puts it, "in the love that can be reckoned" (1.1.15).

The play as a whole, supporting but also qualifying this attitude, sets moving around it an enormous traffic of evocation, primarily of two sorts. One sort moves the love affair in the general direction of allegory and myth. In some sense, the play hints, there looms behind Antony's choice of "Pleasure" the great model of Hercules at the Crossroads — a popular motif of Renaissance painting and engraving about which much has been written by iconographers — choosing between Virtue and Pleasure, who are represented in two females as opposite in their qualities as Octavia and Cleopatra, or Rome and Egypt. It has been pointed out, too, that behind the play's references to a great warrior feminized — Cleopatra putting her robes on Antony, for instance, and wearing his sword Philippan, or Canidius's remark after the decision to fight at Actium by sea: "so our leader's led, And we are women's men" (3.7.69) — may be discerned another favorite Renaissance exemplum: Hercules's servitude in woman's dress to Omphale. This Plutarch explicitly compares to Antony's in his *Comparison of Demetrius with Antonius:*

But to conclude, [Demetrius] neuer had ouerthrow or misfortune through negligence, nor by delaying time to follow his owne pleasure; as we see in painted tables, where *Omphale* secretly stealeth away *Hercules* clubbe, and took his Lyon skinne from him: euen so *Cleopatra* oftentimes vnarmed *Antonius*, and enticed him to her, making him lose matter of great importance, and very needful iournies, to come and be dandled with her.[107]

To these the play adds two further analogies, Aeneas and Dido, and Mars and Venus, whose implications are far less clear. Though at first Antony might be said to imitate Aeneas in abandoning his Dido for a Roman destiny and a Latin marriage, his later career substantively revises the Virgilian story in that he abandons Rome and empire for his African queen and, in the only overt allusion the play makes to Virgil's lovers, anticipates that he and Cleopatra in the afterworld will be admired more than they for their eminence in love: "Dido and her Aeneas shall want troops, And all the haunt be ours" (4.14.53). Does Shakespeare nod here, forgetting Virgil's own depiction in Book 6 of the estrangement of Dido from Aeneas on his visit to the underworld? Or is this simply Antony's exuberant imagination undertaking to bring reality closer to the heart's desire, as he does so often elsewhere? Or does Shakespeare, for whatever reasons, choose to see Aeneas in the Chaucerian and generally medieval perspectives that had already made of Dido, as of Cleopatra, an exemplar of faithful love?

Similar questions must be asked about the playwright's association of his lovers with Mars and Venus. Are we chiefly to remember Homer, in whose *Odyssey* the two Olympians, trapped in an adulterous affair and exposed in the absurdity of love's postures in a net they cannot break, move our superior laughter — as do, in one of their dimensions, Antony and Cleopatra? Are we to remember, too, the Renaissance taste for paintings and engravings that show a Mars vanquished by Venus, victim or trophy of love's power, her *amorini* sporting with his armor, and he himself languid or asleep, or in some instances, chained and fettered to her throne — the image Othello so roundly repudiates when he assures the Venetian senators that Desdemona's company will not feminize him?

And is it pertinent to recall further that at least in Renaissance paintings the intention of these images often turns out to be more complex than at first glance we might suppose? For the two deities, in some instances, are to be understood as emblems of contrary qualities, male force and female grace, now in a work of art ideally reconciled; and even, in other instances, as the contrary powers of Strife and Love, which tie the universe together and from whose union, according to Plutarch, the goddess Harmony was born.[108]

Antony, like Mars in the paintings, grows conscious of love's "fetters";[109] loses or is threatened with loss of manhood, as the fanning eunuchs in 1.1 warn us; and at long last acknowledges himself (as he was also obliged to do the day she came down the Cydnus) Cleopatra's captive in a "Triumph of Love." But the crucial question that remains — in the play as in the painted figures of Mars and Venus — is what the triumph means. I believe that Shakespeare throws some light on the perplexities of this question in the scene that reunites the lovers after the middle day of Actium, when for the time being Antony and his men have had the victory (4.8). As he enters, still clad in full armor, he thanks his soldiers with characteristic élan and generosity. Then he sees Cleopatra, stops (as I read the scene) in his tracks bedazzled (leaving us in the audience to imagine his emotions as he finds himself once more in his old role of redoubtable captain returning to a radiant queen), and then, with an intensity of adoration that ignores all onlookers, bursts forth in one of the most winning speeches of the play:

> O thou day o' th' world,
> Chain mine armed neck; leap thou, attire and all,
> Through proof of harness to my heart, and there
> Ride on the pants triumphing. (4.8.13)

The image of Cleopatra riding the great beats of Antony's heart (a heart that, as we know from earlier comment, "in the scuffles of great fights hath burst The buckles on his breast" [1.1.7]) as if it were a high-mettled steed on which she is carried in a Triumph that he — her prisoner, "chained" — adorns, is breathtaking and becomes more so when we reflect on what we see. For though in the language she is conqueror and he her captive, in the scene he is conqueror too and has indeed freely bestowed this conquest on her, as his victorious presence, in full armor, attests. The episode forces upon our consciousness a recognition of the very different kind of "triumph" that they have within their power as lovers from the kind for which Caesar seeks them, and the two competing value systems, theirs and Caesar's, hang for a brief instant in the eye as well as in the ear, as she runs to be embraced. Then, leaning back and devouring him with her gaze, she kindles sublimely to the occasion, catching his image in an answering image of her own:

> Lord of lords!
> O infinite virtue, com'st thou smiling from
> The world's great snare uncaught? (4.8.16)

Does she, by her "world's great snare," mean the wars? Does she, on the contrary, mean Caesar, who is soon to become "universal landlord" (3.13.72) and "Sole sir o' th' world" (5.2.120)? Or does she simply mean, as a recent editor phrases it, "all the snares the world can set," understanding by "world" everything, inner as well as outer, that the play accumulates to threaten love? No matter. As with Roman triumphs versus Antony's "triumphing," we are obviously to let this "snare" reverberate against another order of captivity altogether, an order implicit at this moment in Antony's "chain my armed neck" (4.8.14), explicit earlier in his "These strong Egyptian fetters I must break" (1.2.112), and evoked again, tellingly, at the play's end, when, as we saw, Caesar speaks of "her strong toil of grace" (5.2.346). There, once again, the two attitudes will hang against each other in the mind and invite us to consider that there are more kinds of captivity and of triumph than any Caesar dreams of.

6

The other sorts of evocation that Shakespeare sets in motion in *Antony and Cleopatra* derive from the themes and conventions of Renaissance love poetry, notably the sonnet. Individualizing and psychological, these strongly counter the play's tendencies toward moral exemplum and allegory, establishing it still more intransigently in the domain of paradox, where contradiction thrives. Though the ultimate effect of this body of evocation is to bring before the mind of the spectator a unified and highly plausible experience of passion, we may nevertheless separate out for our present purpose two divergent strains, answering to the *amo* and *odi* of the Latin love poets, the *amare* and *amaro* of the Italian.

The *odi-amare* strain in *Antony and Cleopatra* is best grasped by comparison and contrast with Shakespeare's treatment of it in his sonnets to and about the Dark Lady. In both cases, we have an affair between experienced lovers, "orbited nice" (to borrow a phrase of John Crowe Ransom's), in an intense relationship that contains comedy and tragedy, and, to the man at least, brings disgust and pain as often as love and pleasure. In both we find a mistress very like a parody of the delicate blonde *belle dame sans merci* of the sonneteering convention, who is always indescribably remote and chaste; a woman who in the sonnets is notably blackhaired as well as hearted, and in the play, whatever we may decide about her heart, has a tawny skin ("with Phoebus' amorous pinches black," 1.5.28), and a voluptuous disposition. Both mistresses have a remarkable — in the sonnets it is also sinister — power to make ill things look attractive, "For vilest things," says Enobarbus, at the end of his famous account of Cleopatra, so

> Become themselves in her, that the holy priests
> Bless her when she is riggish. (2.2.239)

The poet of the sonnets confronts the same puzzle:

> Whence hast thou this becoming of things ill,
> That in the very refuse of thy deeds
> There is such strength and warrantise of skill
> That in my mind thy worst all best exceeds?
> Who taught thee how to make me love thee more,
> The more I hear and see just cause of hate?
> (Sonnet 150)

These are lines that a lesser Antony, trimmed and barbered to the sonnet's narrow room, might have uttered after watching Cleopatra put out her hand for Thidias to kiss.

Such "treason" is precisely a further resemblance between the sonnet's story and the play's. Both mistresses, in one sense or other, are capable of playing their lovers false; have, or have had, other men; and though Cleopatra is not, so far as we are ever reliably told, unfaithful to Antony within the time of the play, she uses locutions in referring to her former affair with Pompey's father that may suggest a conscious or unconscious link tying her to the treacherous dark lady in the poet's mind. For as she waits for Antony to return from Rome — feeding herself "With most delicious poison," (1.5.27) as she puts it — she muses how when Julius Caesar was alive, she was already "A morsel for a monarch," and how "great Pompey"

> Would stand and make his eyes grow in my brow;
> There would he anchor his aspect, and die
> With looking on his life. (1.5.31)

The individual words in these lines are alive with erotic possibilities; just how alive one can best see by placing them beside the appropriate verses of Sonnet 137, where likewise a woman is the sea, and men are the ships that anchor there:

> If eyes, corrupt by over-partial looks,
> Be anchored in the bay where all men ride,
> Why of eyes' falsehood hast thou forgèd hooks
> Whereto the judgment of my heart is tied?
> Why should my heart think that a several plot
> Which my heart knows the wide world's common place?
> Or mine eyes seeing this, say this is not,
> To put fair truth upon so foul a face?

Allowing again for the difference between dramatic speech and lyric, this could be Antony speaking after Thidias has been taken to be whipped, for it is certainly his theme:

> You have been a boggler ever:
> But when we in our viciousness grow hard
> (O misery on't!) the wise gods seel our eyes,

In our own filth drop our clear judgments; make us
Adore our errors, laugh at 's while we strut
To our confusion. (3.13.110)

To conclude, both affairs "puddle" — this is Desdemona's word for
the effect of Othello's jealousy — the clear spirit of the lover. Both describe what, at one level of the experience, or at least when viewed in one
way (in *Antony and Cleopatra*, usually the Roman way), is unqualified lust:
"Th' expense of spirit in a waste of shame" (Sonnet 129). And both
eventuate in a perpetual unrest which rises to peaks of anguish and self-
loathing akin to madness. Antony feels that he has been poisoned with
the shirt of Nessus, and in his last towering rage Cleopatra takes him to
have run mad:
more mad
Than Telamon for his shield; the boar of Thessaly
Was never so embossed. (4.13.1)

The speaker of the sonnets sees his condition in like terms. It is an
incurable disease which brings on madness and must end in death because his reason, like Antony's reasoning Enobarbus in the play, has
given him up for lost. When seen against Antony's continuous fluctua-
tions from disgust to reconciliation, and against the movements of Enobarbus, who acts as reason's spokesman in the play, the whole of Sonnet
147 becomes luminous:

My love is as a fever, longing still
For that which longer nurseth the disease,
Feeding on that which doth preserve the ill,
Th' uncertain sickly appetite to please.
My reason, the physician to my love,
Angry that his prescriptions are not kept,
Hath left me, and I desperate now approve
Desire is death, which physic did except.
Past cure I am, now reason is past care,
And frantic-mad with evermore unrest;
My thoughts and my discourse as madmen's are,
At random from the truth vainly expressed:

For I have sworn thee fair, and thought thee bright
Who art as black as hell, as dark as night.

Such likenesses are seductive; but they are also extremely unspecific, and it would be folly to argue from them that the love affair in the play in any precise way reflects that in the sonnet sequence. The tone of the sonnet love affair is, in any case, far more acrid, cynical, corrosive. The play's lovers are repeatedly caught up into regions of feeling, and touch on images and idioms of romantic amplification and adulation that the lover who speaks in the Dark Lady sonnets avoids, or uses only to belittle; and the literary territory on which Shakespeare levies for this affirmative side of his *odi et amo* polarity is visibly a system of Petrarchan attitudes and conventions whose general emphasis on immutability and steadfastness creates a significant antithesis to our sense of a world in flux.

To be remarked in this connection, first of all, is the exuberant vein of compliment that Antony so often has recourse to, tributes of the perfect lover to his dazzling lady. Cleopatra's eye, he tells us, "becked forth" his wars "and called them home" (4.12.26). Her bosom was his "crownet," his "chief end." "Eternity" was in her lips and eyes, "Bliss" in her brows' bent (1.3.35). Her hand, even in one of his great rages, remains for him "this kingly seal, And plighter of high hearts" (3.13.125). Her beauty and vitality, like those of every sonneteer's mistress, make her equal to the sun ("O thou day o' th' world" [4.8.13]) and to the moon ("our terrene moon Is now eclips'd" [3.13.153]). Her tears outvalue empires ("Fall not a tear, I say: one of them rates All that is won and lost" [3.11.69]), and when she dies, brightness falls from the air ("since the torch is out, Lie down, and stray no farther" [4.14.46]).

All these praises Cleopatra reciprocates with an abandon that is new to the tradition only because the speaker is a woman: Antony is her "man of men" (1.5.72), her "Lord of lords" (4.8.16), "infinite virtue" (4.8.17), "the crown o' th' earth" (4.15.63), "jewel" (1.81), and "nature's piece 'gainst fancy" (5.2.99), that is to say, nature's masterpiece surpassing anything the imagination can create. For her, too, attraction continues even when she is most repelled: "Though he be painted one way like a Gorgon, The other way's a Mars" (2.5.116); and for her, too, light goes out of the world with his death: "Ah, women, women, look! Our lamp is spent, it's out!" (4.15.87):

> O sun,
> Burn the great sphere thou mov'st in, darkling stand
> The varying shore o' th' world! (4.15.9)

— for there is nothing remarkable left to see on earth, even by "the visiting moon" (4.15.68).

There is no exuberance quite like this in the sonnets, nor is there room for such radical amplifications as the stage allows. One thinks particularly of the commonplace comparison of love's sighs and tears to winds and floods,[110] comically transformed by Enobarbus's comment on Cleopatra's emotional resources —

> We cannot call her winds and waters sighs and tears: they are greater storms and tempests than almanacs can report. This cannot be cunning in her; if it be, she makes a shower of rain as well as Jove. (1.2.144)

Or one thinks of the handsome version of the absent-yet present formula contained in Antony's final words to her as he leaves for Rome —

> Our separation so abides and flies
> That thou residing here goes yet with me,
> And I hence fleeting here remain with thee.
> (1.3.102)

Particularly striking is the old image of the beloved's name entombed in the lover's breast, adapted by Mardian to give verisimilitude to his baroque tale of Cleopatra's death (and by Shakespeare, I suspect, to give a possibly sexual and certainly risible edge to the whole proceeding):

> The last she spake
> Was "Antony! most noble Antony!"
> Then in the midst a tearing groan did break
> The name of Antony; it was divided
> Between her heart and lips: she rend'red life,
> Thy name so buried in her. (4.14.29)

Other formulas from the sonneteer's thesaurus have been so thoroughly renovated in the playwright's imagination that their identity is difficult to be sure of. The idea, for example, that love's bondage is the highest freedom ("To enter in these bonds, is to be free," says Donne),[111] which presumably survives among the meanings intended by Shakespeare, though not by Caesar, in the reference to Cleopatra's "strong toil of grace," and which is almost certainly implicit in the great reunion of the lovers already noticed: "Chain mine armed neck," "Com'st thou smiling from The world's great snare uncaught?" Or the idea of the lover's dream of his beloved, which brings her so vividly before his senses that he wakes longing for its return, and even questioning the reality of what he wakes to as compared with his dream-vision. This experience is given in the play to the beloved after her lover's death ("O, such another sleep, that I might see But such another man" [5.2.77]), and the weighing of the two realities of dream and wake, the latter intensified by Dolabella's skepticism, is handled with a teasing virtuosity.

CLEOPATRA:
Think you there was or might be such a man
As this I dreamt of?
DOLABELLA: Gentle madam, no.
CLEOPATRA:
You lie, up to the hearing of the gods.
But if there be nor ever were one such,
It's past the size of dreaming: nature wants stuff
To vie strange forms with fancy, yet t' imagine
An Antony were nature's piece 'gainst fancy,
Condemning shadows quite. (5.2.93)

7

Easily the two most important derivatives in *Antony and Cleopatra* from the formulas of love poetry are the conception of love-as-space, and the closely related conception of love-as-war. These, I believe, are the presiding structural ideas of the play, and the presence of the latter is felt at every point. All the conventions of the sonneteers and courtly love poets on this theme — Sidney's "dear captainness," Petrarch's "O dolce mia guerriera," the common notion of the beloved as "dearest enemy" (1 Henry IV, 3.2.123), the metaphors of love's encounters, duels, sieges, arrows, armor, the puns on killing, dying, and being slain, still vigorous as late as Pope's time — all these unverbalize themselves in *Antony and Cleopatra* to become explicitly or implicitly exemplified in the dramatic action. The lady's arming her knight for combat appears in the play in the form of an actual aubade scene (4.4), where Venus-Cleopatra fumbles tenderly with Mars-Antony's armor. The "warrior-lady" appears in the form of a warrior-lady who goes to the wars in fact: "And as the president of my kingdom will Appear there for a man" (3.7.17). The "death-wound" given the sonnet-lover by his mistress's eyes, as in Sidney's twentieth ("Fly, fly, my friends, I have my death wound; fly!") substantiates in the play into a real death wound, for which the mistress is responsible even if she does not give it, and into a situation whose likeness to the one imagined in Sidney is signaled by Decretas's cry: "Thy death and fortunes bid thy followers fly."

Similarly, the lyric lover's ingenious play on "love" and "honor" —

I could not love thee, dear, so much,
Loved I not honor more

— finds at Shakespeare's hands a massive development in terms of Antony's predicament throughout the play; and likewise the lyric lover's semantic game with supposedly alternative kinds of warfare —

Till I have peace with thee, warr other Men,
And when I have peace, can I leave thee then?

Here lett me warr; in these arms lett me lye;
Here lett me parlee, batter, bleede and dye

— enlarges into whole scenes of anguish when, in the play, the two wars prove to be inseparable and love's war the more ruinous of the two.

For in Antony, passion is not the isolable experience that it is in Donne and Lovelace.[112] It is a part of all he is, and therefore part and parcel of his soldiership, in which it finds expression and which finds expression in it. Warring cannot be isolated from loving:

I made these wars for Egypt, and the Queen,
Whose heart I thought I had, for she had mine.

Nor can loving be isolated from warring, from the political and military ascendancy that a million loyal supporters guarantee:

Whose heart I thought I had, for she had mine,
Which, whilst it was mine, had annexed unto 't
A million moe, now lost.

Decay of love is tied irrevocably to decay of imperial glory:

she, Eros, has
Packed cards with Caesar, and false-played my glory
Unto an enemy's triumph; (4.114.15 ff)

and conversely, his Roman enemy's "triumph" (used here with a pun on "trump"), if it has been assisted by Cleopatra, precludes forever the kind of triumph in which his "dearest enemy" once rode "on the pants triumphing." (4.8.16)

The other presiding idea, love-as-space (space that is to be discovered, explored, claimed, possessed), is of course intimately allied to love-as-war, but serves, I think, a subtler function, opening immediately into the play's geographical magnitudes. For the lover, throughout the tradition we are considering, love constitutes an "empire"; and the beloved (from love's infinitely expansionist and sometimes erotically exploratory point of view) is considered spatially in various ways: as countryside, garden, orchard, park, tillage ("I'll be thy park, and thou shalt be my deer";[113] "She made great Caesar lay his sword to bed; He ploughed her, and she cropped" [2.2.228]); or as a rich new land for voyages of discovery and commerce — spice island, continent, or hemisphere:

O my America! my new-found-land,
My kingdome safeliest when with one man man'd,
My Myne of precious stones, My Emperie,
How blest am I in this discovering thee![114]

or best of all as a world:

> For love, all love of other sights controules,
> And makes one little roome, an every where.
> Let sea-discoverers to new worlds have gone,
> Let Maps to other, worlds on worlds have showne,
> Let us possesse one world, each hath one, and is one.[115]

What Shakespeare does in the play is to give this literary formula — together with the psychological and emotional "truth" it incorporates, the heart's systolic and diastolic fervor now amplifying the person of the beloved to include in her person all being and all meaning, now contracting all being and meaning so that they may be contained in her person — a reinterpretation in dramatic terms. The play's political and geographical grandeurs, its struggles of great personages for "empire," enable him to create, in a subtle psychological sense to which Kenneth Burke has shrewdly called attention,[116] an objective correlative, or "ostentation," of the expansionist phase of passion, with its rapturous self-assertions, shows of power, and displaced gestures of aggression. In this light may be seen Antony's greeting to Cleopatra through Alexas:

> Say the firm Roman to great Egypt sends
> This treasure of an oyster; at whose foot,
> To mend the petty present, I will piece
> Her opulent throne with kingdoms. All the east
> (Say thou) shall call her mistress. (1.5.43)

Both lovers write large, in the marketplace of Alexandria and on the maps of Asia, the erotic energies of their union, as Caesar's description of the occasion seems to understand:

CAESAR:
> Contemning Rome, he has done all this and more
> In Alexandria. Here's the manner of 't:
> I' th' market-place on a tribunal silvered,
> Cleopatra and himself in chairs of gold
> Were publicly enthroned; at the feet sat

Caesarion, whom they call my father's son,
And all the unlawful issue that their lust
Since then hath made between them. Unto her
He gave the stablishment of Egypt; made her
Of lower Syria, Cyprus, Lydia,
Absolute queen.

MAECENAS: This in the public eye?

CAESAR:

I' th' common show-place, where they exercise.
His sons he there proclaimed the kings of kings:
Great Media, Parthia, and Armenia
He gave to Alexander; to Ptolemy he assigned
Syria, Cilicia, and Phoenicia. She
In the habiliments of the goddess Isis
That day appeared, and oft before gave audience,
As 'tis reported, so. (3.6.1)

With the same tumescent overtones, at the close, Cleopatra cherishes her dream of an Antony who is emotionally and spatially realized simultaneously, a sort of psycho-cosmos whose arm crests the world and whose voice is propertied as all the tunèd spheres.

The contrary or contractive impulses of passion find *their* correlative, one supposes, in Cleopatra's monument and the long decrescendo that brings Antony to it. There, whatever it may signify, the lovers are reunited for the last time in the play; Antony dies in Cleopatra's arms (the only "space" now left him); and she also dies, robed and crowned, on a throne that is in fact a bed. "Every where" — to read the reverse face of Donne's coin — has now become "one little roome." The paths of glory have led (like all paths) to a grave. And love has been dissolved in death, except that dying has proved to be a manifestation of love, in more senses than one. Though to go beyond this is to risk saying far too much, additional ghostly figures from Petrarchan and other repertories — of the beloved as a fortress under siege by death and time; of Desire as an infant at the breast of nurse Beauty; of the worm (serpent and what more?) as death's but also love's and immortality's agent, as the clown's malapropisms seem to hint; and of another kind of "monument," more durable than brass and loftier than the pyramids — may well continue to float troublingly, for some, about the final scenes.

8

Antony's death is followed by a moment when Cleopatra faints and lies as still as he:

CHARMIAN: O quietness, lady!
IRAS: She's dead too, our sovereign.
(4.15.69)

Then her women succeed in rousing her, she speaks her resolve to do as he has done, and they go out together, *"bearing off Antony's body."* Cleopatra's death is followed by a similar moment, more prolonged. After she is dead, Charmian straightens her crown, speaks proudly to Caesar's guard (who has rushed in to check on his prisoners) of what has been done — what has been "well done, and fitting for a princess Descended of so many royal kings" — then falls herself. There is an entry by Dolabella, and a full ceremonial entry by *"Caesar and all his Train, marching."* They theorize about the deaths, Caesar renders his epitaph, which receives the lovers into "story," and announces a solemn funeral, after which, "to Rome." They go out again marching, one presumes, carrying Cleopatra's bed, her motionless figure sitting or half-reclining on it, robed and crowned.

The sensory effect of both these moments is very powerful. Basically, in stage terms, it comes from the difference between absolute stillness and purposeful movement. In the movers, life goes on, as we know it must; their history will be fulfilled. In the immobile, history has already been fulfilled; it has departed from them, and something else has replaced it. But what? Is it a dignity, such as perhaps we always attribute to those who have drunk the whole of experience, the ultimate stillness as well as the movement that leads there? Is it an exultation that they are, as Shakespeare says elsewhere, "past the tyrant's stroke" (*Cymbeline*, 4.2.265), past the whips and scorns of time? Is it a serenity got from the same source as poets when they are laid asleep in body to become a living soul, seeing into the life of things? Or is it simply that absolute stillness has some sort of indefinable absolute claim on the human imagination, being the thing most opposite to what we know at first hand in the diurnal world, where, as in this play, everything slips and slides and rots itself with motion?

Whatever the explanation, I never read or see these two scenes acted without concluding that the unresolved polarities they contain—life against death, movement against stillness, change against something that has shackled accidents and bolted up change, history against something that is no longer temporal—has something to say to us about Shakespeare's procedure in the play as a whole with its long series of similarly unresolved oppositions: Egypt and Rome, politics and love, public life and private, loyalty and self-interest, grandeur and humility, mobility and constancy, and many more pairs that one may accumulate by reading the critics. For the play seems founded, in my own experience of it—not founded accidentally, but creatively, painstakingly—on the same sort of defiant pluralism that we find in other deeply paradoxical works, such as *The Praise of Folly* or *Don Quixote*. As in Erasmus, we have in the play one perspective which knows that Folly is always folly, a consuming and illicit passion always ruinous, and another perspective which sees that some follies may be less foolish than the world's cherished wisdom, an imperium in the embrace of Cleopatra more life-giving than an imperium in Rome. Neither perspective cancels the other out, both are "true."

In Cervantes, the representative of an imagined literary world of perfect chivalry is set down in seventeenth-century Spain, suffers bravely and comically the incongruities that result, refuses to be discomfited, and at last persuades us that his vision of things has a valency of its own. Something of this sort happens also in our play. Antony, ever attracted by the sweeping magnanimity of his nature to an imagined literary world of perfect devotion between man and woman (as the first line he speaks to us shows: "There's beggary in the love that can be reckoned" [1.1.15]) is set down in the slippery Roman world he has himself helped create, suffers deeply—but always too, like Quixote, a little comically—from the incongruities between the code he is attracted to and that world's demands, yet refuses equally to be discomfited (either by Cleopatra's treasons or his own), and in the end wagers with his life that there is a valency in the code's perspective, though again it can never cancel out the world's perspective, since both are true.

Shakespeare's play is not a *Praise of Folly*, despite certain affinities that were mentioned at the beginning of this essay. Still less is it a *Don Quixote de la Mancha*. It has its own metabolism. Yet I think the thrust of history in it, the pressures of mobility and mutability which lead inexorably to Antony's ruin and Caesar's triumph, are countered, to a degree, by the traditions of ideal devotion, and of escape from mutability through love, that are implied in the Petrarchan and romance idiom in which both lovers have been immersed by their creator.

Plainly, the world of history is unfriendly to these principles, as it is unfriendly also to Quixote's chivalric fiction, and in the end they are likely to be compromised or betrayed, as happens repeatedly in the play. Yet they speak for something that is durable in the human heart, something no more but also no less true to our experience than the nightmare of history from which, like Stephen Dedalus, we all struggle in our several fashions to escape; and I believe that Shakespeare saw this, as he moved in the romances that follow *Antony and Cleopatra* toward defining an alternative. It is an alternative that has never failed in its power to move the imagination, whether we think, like Dante, of the love that moves the sun and other stars; or, like Spenser, of the time to come when "all shall changèd bee, And from thenceforth none no more change shall see"; or, like Keats, of the bright star whose steadfastness he longs to reconcile with his living breathing passion for Fanny Brawne; or, most recently, like T. S. Eliot, of the still center without which there would be no turning wheel:

> Except for the point, the still point,
> There would be no dance, and there is only the dance.[117]

Is this the madness of poets? Or may there be, as even Polonius suspects, a method in it?

CHAPTER ELEVEN

WHAT HAPPENS IN SHAKESPEAREAN

TRAGEDY

I

No account of Shakespeare's virtuosity as a dramatist, and more importantly as a tragic dramatist, would be complete without an effort to examine some of the principles of construction (often repeated from play to play but in such varying guises that they rarely command our conscious attention) which give his tragedies their distinctive "feel," their form and pressure. And the right place to begin, it seems to me, is with A. C. Bradley's pioneering analysis in the second of his famous lectures, published some ninety years ago. Bradley's concern was with what would today be called the clearer outlines of Shakespearean practice — the management of exposition, conflict, crises, catastrophe; the contrasts of pace and scene; the over-all patterns of rise-and-fall, variously modulated; the slackened tension after the crisis and Shakespeare's devices for countering this; and the faults.[118]

Bradley is quite detailed about the faults. Sometimes, he says, there are too rapid shiftings of scene and *dramatis personae*, as in the middle section of *Antony and Cleopatra*. Sometimes there is extraneous matter, not required for plot or character development, like the player's speech in *Hamlet* about the murder of Priam, or Hamlet's advice later to the same player on speaking in the theater. Sometimes there are soliloquies too obviously expositional, as when Edgar disguises to become Poor Tom in *King Lear*. Or there is contradiction and inconsistency, as with double time in *Othello*. Or flatulent writing: "obscure, inflated, tasteless," or "pestered with metaphors." Or "gnomic" insertions, like the Duke's couplet interchange with Brabantio in *Othello*, used "more freely than, I suppose, a good playwright now would care to do." And finally, to make an end, there is too often, he says, a sacrificing of dramatic appropriateness to get something said that the author wants said. Thus the comments of the Player King and Claudius on the instability of human purpose arise because Shakespeare "wishes in part simply to write poetry, and partly to impress on the audience thoughts which will help them to understand, not the player-king nor yet King Claudius, but Hamlet himself." These failings, Bradley concludes, belong to an art of drama imperfectly developed, which Shakespeare inherited from his predecessors and acquiesced in, on occasion, from "indifference or want of care."

Though Bradley's analysis is still the best account we have of the outward shape of Shakespearean tragedy, a glance at his list of faults and especially his examples reminds us that a vast deal of water has got itself under the critical bridges since 1904. It is not simply that most of the faults he enumerates would no longer be regarded as such, but would instead be numbered among the characteristic practices of Shakespearean dramaturgy, even at its most triumphant. Still more striking is the extent to which our conception of the "construction" of the tragedies has itself changed. The matters Bradley described have not ceased to be important — far from it. Still, it is impossible not to feel that he missed something — that there is another kind of construction in Shakespeare's tragedies than the one he designates, more inward, more difficult to define, but not less significant. This other structure is not, like his, generated entirely by the interplay of plot and character. Nor is it, on the other hand, though it has been fashionable to suppose so, ultimately a verbal matter. It is poetic, but it goes well beyond what in certain quarters today is called (with something like a lump in the throat) "the poetry." Some of its elements arise from the playwright's visualizing imagination, the consciousness of groupings, gestures, entrances, exits. Others may even be prior to language, in the sense that they appear to belong to a paradigm of tragic "form" that was consciously or unconsciously part of Shakespeare's inheritance and intuition as he worked.

At any rate, it is into this comparatively untraveled and uncharted territory of inward structure that I should like to launch some tentative explorations. I shall occasionally look backward as far as *Julius Caesar* (1599), *Richard II* (1595?–1597), and even *Romeo and Juliet* (1595–6); but in the main I shall be concerned here with the tragedies of Shakespeare's prime, from *Hamlet* (1600–1601) to *Coriolanus* (1607–8). In these seven or eight years, Shakespeare's golden period, he consolidated a species of tragic structure that for suggestiveness and flexibility has never been matched.[119]

First, the hero. The Shakespearean tragic hero, as everybody knows, is an overstater. His individual accent will vary with his personality, but there is always a residue of hyperbole. This, it would seem, is for Shakespeare the authentic tragic music, mark of a world where a man's reach must always exceed his grasp and everything costs not less than everything.

> Wert thou as far
> As that vast shore washed with the farthest sea,
> I would adventure for such merchandise. (*Romeo*, 2.2.82)

> 'Swounds, show me what thou'lt do:
> Woo't weep? woo't fight? woo't fast? woo't tear thyself?
> Woo't drink up esill? eat a crocodile?
> I'll do't. (*Hamlet*, 5.1.261)

> Nay, had she been true,
> If heaven would make me such another world
> Of one entire and perfect chrysolite,
> I'ld not have sold her for it. (*Othello*, 5.2.144)

> Death, traitor! nothing could have subdued nature
> To such a lowness but his unkind daughters. (*Lear*, 3.4.68)

> Will all great Neptune's ocean wash this blood
> Clean from my hand? (*Macbeth*, 2.2.59)

> I, that with my sword
> Quartered the world, and o'er green Neptune's back
> With ships made cities, . . . (*Antony*, 4.14.57)

233

> I go alone,
> Like to a lonely dragon, that his fen
> Makes feared and talked of more than seen.
> (*Coriolanus*, 4.1.29)

This idiom is not, of course, used by the hero only. It is the language he is dressed in by all who love him and often by those who do not:

> This was the noblest Roman of them all . . .
> His life was gentle, and the elements
> So mixed in him that Nature might stand up
> And say to all the world, "This was a man!"
> (*Caesar*, 5.5.68)

> The courtier's, soldier's, scholar's eye, tongue, sword;
> Th' expectancy and rose of the fair state,
> The glass of fashion and the mold of form,
> Th' observed of all observers, . . . (*Hamlet*, 3.1.151)

> Can he be angry? I have seen the cannon,
> When it hath blown his ranks into the air,
> And, like the devil, from his very arm
> Puffed his own brother: — and can he be angry?
> (*Othello*, 3.4.134)

> On the Alps
> It is reported thou didst eat strange flesh,
> Which some did die to look on. (*Antony*, 1.4.66)

> Let me twine
> Mine arms about thy body, whereagainst
> My grainèd ash an hundred times hath broke,
> And scarred the moon with splinters.
> (*Coriolanus*, 4.5.107)

But by whomever used, it is a language that depends for its vindication — for the redemption of its paper promises into gold — upon the hero, and any who stand, heroically, where he does. It is the mark of his, and their, commitment to something beyond "the vast waters Of the petrel and the porpoise," as T. S. Eliot has it in *East Coker,* a commitment to something—not merely death—which shackles accidents and bolts up change and palates no dung whatever.

Thus the hyperbole of tragedy stands at the opposite end of a tonal scale from the hyperbole of comedy which springs from and nourishes detachment:

> When I was about thy years, Hal, I was not an eagle's talent in the waist; I could have crept into any alderman's thumb-ring. (*1 Henry IV,* 2.4.313)

> O she misused me past the endurance of a block! An oak but with one green leaf on it would have answered her; my very visor began to assume life and scold with her. (*Much Ado,* 2.1.214)

> He has a son, who shall be flayed alive; then 'nointed over with honey, set on the head of a wasp's nest; then stand till he be three quarters and a dram dead; then recovered again with aqua-vitae or some other hot infusion. Then, raw as he is, and in the hottest day prognostication proclaims, shall he be set against a brick-wall, the sun looking with a southward eye upon him, where he is to behold him with flies blown to death. (*Winter's Tale,* 4.4.771)

> Comic overstatement aims at being preposterous. Until it becomes so, it remains flat. Tragic overstatement, on the other hand, aspires to be believed, and unless in some sense it is so, remains bombast.

2

Besides the hyperbolist, in Shakespeare's scheme of things, there is always the opposing voice, which belongs to the hero's foil. As the night the day, the idiom of absoluteness demands a vocabulary of a different intensity, a different rhetorical and moral wave length, to set it off. This other idiom is not necessarily understatement, though it often takes the form of a deflating accent and very often involves colloquialism—or perhaps merely a middling sort of speech—expressive of a suppler outlook than the hero's and of other and less upsetting ways of encountering experience than his hyperbolic, not to say intransigent, rigorism. "'Twere to consider too curiously to consider so" (5.1.193), says Horatio of Hamlet's equation between the dust of Alexander and a bunghole, and this enunciates perfectly the foil's role. There is no tragedy in him because he does not consider "curiously"; there are always more things in earth and heaven than are dreamt of in his philosophy.

Each of the Shakespearean tragedies contains at least one personage to speak this part, which is regularly assigned to someone in the hero's immediate entourage — servitor, wife, friend. In *Romeo and Juliet* it is of course Mercutio, with his witty resolution of all love into sex. In *Julius Caesar* it is Cassius, whose restless urgent rhythms, full of flashing images, swirl about Brutus's rounder and abstracter speech, like dogs that bay the moon:

BRUTUS:

I do believe that these applauses are
For some new honors that are heaped on Caesar.

CASSIUS:

Why, man, he doth bestride the narrow world
Like a Colossus, and we petty men
Walk under his huge legs and peep about
To find ourselves dishonorable graves. (1.2.133)

In the famous forum speeches this second voice is taken over temporarily by Antony, and there emerges a similar but yet more powerful contrast between them. Brutus's prose — in which the actuality of the assassination is intellectualized and held at bay by the strict patterns of an obtrusively formal rhetoric, almost as though corporal death were transubstantiated to "a ballet of bloodless categories" — gives way to Antony's sinewy verse about the "honorable men" (3.2.83), which draws the deed, and its consequence, the dead Caesar, ever closer till his own vengeful emotions are kindled in the mob.

In *Hamlet* the relation of foil to hero undergoes an unusual adaptation. Here, since the raciest idiom of the play belongs to the hero himself, the foil, Horatio, is given a quite conventional speech, and, to make the contrast sharper (Hamlet being of all the heroes the most voluble), as little speech as may be. Like his stoicism, like his "blood and judgment" — "so well commeddled, That they are not a pipe for Fortune's finger To sound what stop she please." (3.2.66) — Horatio's "Here, sweet lord" (3.2.50), "O, my dear lord," "Well, my lord" are, presumably (as the gentleman in *Lear* says of Cordelia's tears), "a better way" (4.3.19) than Hamlet's self-lacerating virtuosities and verbosities. But of course we do not believe this and are not meant to: who would be Horatio if he could be Hamlet?

Plainly, this is one of the two questions that all the tragic foils exist to make us ask (the other we shall come to presently). Who, for instance, would be Enobarbus, clear-sighted as he is, in preference to Antony? His brilliant sardonic speech, so useful while he can hold his own career and all about him in the comic focus of detachment, withers in the face of his engagement to ultimate issues, and he dies speaking with an imagery, accent, and feeling which are surely meant to identify him at the last with the absoluteness of the heroic world, the more so since his last syllables anticipate Cleopatra's:

> Throw my heart
> Against the flint and hardness of my fault;
> Which, being dried with grief, will break to powder,
> And finish all foul thoughts. O Antony,
> Nobler than my revolt is infamous,
> Forgive me in thine own particular,
> But let the world rank me in register
> A master leaver and a fugitive:
> O Antony! O Antony! (4.9.15)

Such unequivocal judgments are a change indeed on the part of one who could earlier rally cynically with Menas about "two thieves kissing" (2.6.96) when their hands meet.

King Lear is given two foils. The primary one is obviously the Fool, whose rhymes and riddles and jets of humor in the first two acts set off both the old king's brooding silences and his massively articulated longer speeches when aroused. But in the storm scenes, and occasionally elsewhere, one is almost as keenly conscious of the relief into which Lear's outrageous imprecations are thrown by the mute devoted patience of his servant Kent. For both foils — and this of course is their most prominent function as representatives of the opposing voice — the storm itself is only a storm, to be stoically endured, in the one case, and, in the other, if his master would but hear reason, eschewed:

> O nuncle, court holy-water in a dry house is better than this rain-water out o' door. Good nuncle, in; ask thy daughters blessing. . . . (3.2.10)

Doubtless the Fool does not wish to be taken quite *au pied de la lettre* in this — his talk is always in the vein of the false daughters', his action quite other. But neither for him nor for Kent does facing the thunder have any kind of transcendent meaning. In Lear's case, it has; the thunder he hears is like the thunder heard over Himavant in *The Waste Land;* it has what the anthropologists call "mana"; and his (and our) consuming questions are what it means — and if it means — and whose side it is on.

In my view, the most interesting uses of the opposing voice occur in *Macbeth* and *Othello*. In *Macbeth* Shakespeare gives it to Lady Macbeth, and there was never, I think, a more thrilling tragic counterpoint set down for the stage than that in the scene following the murder of Duncan, when, as we saw earlier, her purely physical reading of what has happened to them both is met by his metaphysical intuitions. His "noise" (2.2.14) to her is just the owl screaming and the crickets' cry. The voice of one crying "Sleep no more" (2.2.34) is only his "brain-sickly" (2.2.45) fear. The blood on his hands is what "A little water clears us of" (2.2.66). "Consider it not so deeply" (2.2.29), she says at one point, with an echo of Horatio in the graveyard. "These deeds must not be thought After these ways." But in the tragic world which always opens on transcendence, they must; and this she herself finds before she dies, a prisoner to the deed, endlessly washing the damned spot that will not out. "What's done cannot be undone" is a language that like Enobarbus she has to learn.

Othello's foil of course is Iago, about whose imagery and speech there hangs, as recent commentators have pointed out, a constructed air, an ingenious, hyperconscious, generalizing air, essentially suited to one who, as W. H. Clemen has said, "seeks to poison . . . others with his images."[120] Yet Iago's poison does not work more powerfully through his images than through a corrosive habit of abstraction applied in those unique relations of love and faith where abstraction is most irrelevant and most destructive. Iago has learned to "sickly o'er" the irreducible individual with the pale cast of class and kind:

Blessed fig's-end! The wine she drinks is made of grapes. . . . (2.1.247)

These Moors are changeable in their wills. . . . If sanctimony and a frail vow betwixt an erring barbarian and a supersubtle Venetian be not too hard for my wits . . . (1.3.344)

Come on, come on! You are pictures out of doors,
Bells in your parlors, wildcats in your kitchens,
Saints in your injuries, devils being offended,
Players in your housewifery, and housewives in your beds.
  (2.1.109)

I know our country disposition well:
In Venice they do let God see the pranks
They dare not show their husbands. (3.3.201)

Othello's downfall is signaled quite as clearly when he drifts into this rationalized dimension —

          O curse of marriage,
That we can call these delicate creatures ours,
And not their appetites! — (3.3.268)

leaving behind his true vernacular, the idiom of "My life upon her faith!" (1.3.294) as when his mind fills with Iago's copulative imagery. Shakespeare seems to have been well aware that love is the mutual knowing of uniqueness. And also that there are areas of experience where, as a great saint once said, one must first believe in order that one may know.

3

To one who should ask why these paired voices seem to be essential ingredients of Shakespearean tragedy, no single answer can be given. They occur partly, no doubt, because of their structural utility, the value of complementary personalities in a work of fiction being roughly analogous to the value of thesis and antithesis in a discursive work. Partly too, no doubt, because in stage performance the antiphonal effects of the two main vocabularies, strengthened by diversity in manner, costume, placing on the stage, supply variety of mood and gratify the eye and ear. But these are superficial considerations. Perhaps we come to something more satisfactory when we consider that these two voices apparently answer to reverberations which reach far back in the human past. *Mutatis mutandis*, Coriolanus and Menenius, Antony and Enobarbus, Macbeth and Lady Macbeth, Lear and his Fool, Othello and Iago, Hamlet and Horatio, Brutus and Cassius, Romeo and Mercutio exhibit a kind of duality that is also exhibited in Oedipus and Jocasta (as well as Creon), Antigone and Ismene, Prometheus and Oceanus, Phaedra and her nurse — and also, in many instances in Greek tragedy, by the protagonist and the chorus.

If it is true, as can be argued, that the Greek chorus functions in large measure as spokesman for the values of the community, and the first actor in large measure for the passionate life of the individual, we can perhaps see a philosophical basis for the long succession of opposing voices. What matters to the community is obviously accommodation — all those adjustments and resiliences that enable it to survive; whereas what matters to the individual, at least in the heroic mood, is just as obviously integrity — all that enables a human being to remain an *individual*, one thing not many. The confrontation of these two outlooks is therefore a confrontation of two of our most cherished instincts, the instinct to be resolute, autonomous, free, and the instinct to be "realistic," adaptable, secure.

If it is also true, as I think most of us believe, that tragic drama is in one way or other a record of man's affair with transcendence (whether this be defined as gods, God, or, as by Malraux, the human "fate," which men must "question" even if they cannot control), we can see further why the hero must have an idiom — such as hyperbole — that establishes him as moving to measures played above or outside our normal space and time. For the *reductio ad absurdum* of the tragic confrontation is the comic one, exemplified in Don Quixote and his Sancho, where the comedy arises precisely from the fact that the hero only *imagines* he moves to measures above and outside our normal world; and where, to the extent that we come to identify with his faith, the comedy slides toward pathos and even the tragic absolute.

These considerations remain speculative. What is not in doubt is that dramaturgically the antiphony of two voices and two vocabularies serves Shakespeare well, and in one of its extensions gives rise to a phenomenon as peculiar and personal to him as his signature. Toward the close of a tragic play, or if not toward the close, at the climax, will normally appear a short scene or episode (sometimes more than one) of spiritual cross purposes: a scene in which the line of tragic speech and feeling generated by commitment is crossed by an alien speech and feeling very much detached.

Bradley, noting such of these episodes as are "humorous or semi-humorous," places them among Shakespeare's devices for sustaining interest after the crisis, since their introduction "affords variety and relief, and also heightens by contrast the tragic feelings." Another perceptive critic has noted that though such scenes afford "relief," it is not by laughter. "We return for a moment to simple people, a gravedigger, a porter, a countryman, and to the goings on of every day, the feeling for bread and cheese, and when we go back to the high tragic mood we do so with a heightened sense that we are moving in a world fully realized."[121]

To such comments we may add another. For the whole effect of these episodes does not come simply from variety or from the juxtaposition of bread and cheese with the high tragic mood; though these elements are certainly present in it. It arises, in the main, I think, from the fact that Shakespeare here lays open to us, in an especially poignant form, what I

241

take to be the central dialogue of tragic experience. It is a dialogue of which the Greek dialogue of individual with community, the seventeenth-century dialogue of soul with body, the twentieth-century dialogue of self with soul are perhaps all versions in their different ways: a dialogue in which each party makes its case in its own tongue, incapable of wholly comprehending what the other means. And Shakespeare objectifies it for us on his stage by the encounter of those in whom, "changed, changed utterly," a terrible beauty has been born, with those who are still players in life's casual comedy. Hamlet and the gravediggers, Desdemona and Emilia, Cleopatra and the clown afford particularly fine examples of Shakespeare's technique in this respect.

In the first instance, the mixture of profoundly imaginative feelings contained in Hamlet's epitaph for Yorick —

> I knew him, Horatio: a fellow of infinite jest, of most excellent fancy. He hath borne me on his back a thousand times. And now, how abhorred in my imagination it is! My gorge rises at it. Here hung those lips that I have kissed I know not how oft. Where be your gibes now? your gambols, your songs, your flashes of merriment that were wont to set the table on a roar? Not one now, to mock your own grinning? Quite chap-fallen? Now get you to my lady's chamber, and tell her, let her paint an inch thick, to this favor she must come. Make her laugh at that — (5.1.173)

is weighed over against the buffoon literalism of the clown-

HAMLET. What man dost thou dig it for?
FIRST CLOWN. For no man, sir.
HAMLET. What woman, then?
FIRST CLOWN. For none, neither.
HAMLET. Who is to be buried in 't?
FIRST CLOWN. One that was a woman, sir; but, rest her soul, she's dead — (5.1.121)

and against his uncompromising factualism too, his hard, dry vocabulary of detachment, without overtones, by which he cuts his métier down to a size that can be lived with:

Faith, if 'a be not rotten before 'a die, . . . 'a will last you some
eight year or nine year: a tanner will last you nine year. (5.1.154)

In this scene, Hamlet's macabre thoughts are not allowed to outweigh
the clown. A case is made for factualism and literalism. Horatio is seen to
have a point in saying it is to consider too curiously to consider as
Hamlet does. A man must come to terms with the graveyard; but how
long may he linger in it with impunity or allow it to linger in him? Such
reckonings the opposing voice, whether spoken by the primary foil or by
another, is calculated to awake in us: this is the second kind of question
that it exists to make us ask.

In a sense, then, the implicit subject of all these episodes is the predicament of being human. They bring before us the grandeur of our nature,
which contains, potentially, both voices, both ends of the moral and
psychic spectrum. They bring before us the necessity of choice, because
it is rarely given us to go through any door without closing the rest. And
they bring before us the sadness, the infinite sadness of our lot, because,
short of the "certain certainties" that tragedy does not deal with, we have
no sublunar way of knowing whether defiant "heroism" is really more to
be desired than suppler "wisdom." The alabaster innocence of Desdemona's world shines out beside the crumpled bedsitters of Emilia's —

DESDEMONA.
Wouldst thou do such a deed for all the world?
EMILIA.
Why, would not you?
DESDEMONA.   No, by this heavenly light!
EMILIA.
Nor I neither by this heavenly light.
I might do't as well i' th' dark.
DESDEMONA.
Wouldst thou do such a deed for all the world?
EMILIA. The world's a huge thing; it is a great price for a small vice.
DESDEMONA.
In troth, I think thou wouldst not.

EMILIA. In troth, I think I should . . . Who would not make her husband a cuckold to make him a monarch? I should venture purgatory for 't.

DESDEMONA.
Beshrew me, if I would do such a wrong
For the whole world.

EMILIA. Why, the wrong is but a wrong i' th' world; and having the world for your labor, 'tis a wrong in your own world, and you might quickly make it right.

DESDEMONA: I do not think there is any such woman — (4.3.62)

but the two languages never, essentially, commune — and for this reason the dialogue they hold can never be finally adjudicated.

The same effect may be noted in Cleopatra's scene with the countryman who brings her the asps. Her exultation casts a glow over the whole scene of her death. But her language when the countryman has gone would not have the tragic resonance it has if we could not hear echoing between the lines the gritty accents of the opposing voice:

Give me my robe, put on my crown; I have
Immortal longings in me. (5.2.279)

Truly, I have him; but I would not be the party that should desire you to touch him, for his biting is immortal: those that do die of it do seldom or never recover. (5.2.245)

The stroke of death is as a lover's pinch,
Which hurts, and is desired.

I heard of one of them no longer than yesterday: a very honest woman, but something given to lie; as a woman should not do but in the way of honesty — how she died of the biting of it, what pain she felt.
                                            Peace, peace!
Dost thou not see my baby at my breast,
That sucks the nurse asleep?

Give it nothing, I pray you, for it is not worth the feeding.

The "worm" — or "my baby"; the Antony Demetrius and Philo see — or the Antony whose face is as the heavens; the "small vice" (4.3.68) of Emilia — or the deed one would not do for the whole world; the skull knocked about the mazzard by a sexton's spade — or the skull which "had a tongue in it, and could sing once" (5.1.71): these are incommensurables which human nature nevertheless must somehow measure, reconcile and enclose.

4

We move now from "character" to "action," and to the question: what happens in a Shakespearean tragedy? Bradley's traditional categories — exposition, conflict, crisis, catastrophe, etc. — give us one side of this, but as we noticed earlier, largely the external side, and are in any case rather too clumsy for the job we try to do with them. They apply as well to potboilers of the commercial theater as to serious works of art, to prose as well as poetic drama. What is worse, they are unable to register the unique capacity of Shakespearean dramaturgy to hint, evoke, imply, and, in short, by indirections find directions out. The nature of some of Shakespeare's "indirections" is a topic we must explore before we can hope to confront the question posed above with other terms than Bradley's.

To clarify what I mean by indirection, let me cite an instance from *King Lear*. Everybody has noticed, no doubt, that Lear's Fool (apart from being the King's primary foil) gives voice during the first two acts to notations of topsy-turviness that are not, one feels, simply his own responses to the inversions of order that have occurred in family and state, but a reflection of the King's; or to put the matter another way, the situation is so arranged by Shakespeare that we are invited to apply the Fool's comments to Lear's inner experience, and I suspect that most of us do so. The Fool thus serves, to some extent, as a screen on which Shakespeare flashes, as it were, readings from the psychic life of the protagonist, possibly even his subconscious life, which could not otherwise be conveyed in drama at all. Likewise, the Fool's *idée fixe* in this matter, his apparent obsession with one idea (often a clinical symptom of incipient insanity) is perhaps dramatic shorthand and even sleight-of-hand for goings-on in the King's brain that only occasionally bubble to the surface in the form of conscious apprehensions: "O let me not be mad, not mad, sweet heaven" (1.5.40). "O fool, I shall go mad!" (2.4.281). Conceivably, there may even be significance in the circumstance that the Fool does not enter the play as a speaking character till after King Lear has behaved like a fool and leaves it before he is cured.

Whatever the truth of this last point, the example of the Fool in Lear introduces us to devices of play construction and ways of recording the progress of inward "action," which, though the traditional categories say nothing about them, are a basic resource of Shakespeare's playwriting, and nowhere more so than in the tragedies. We may now consider a few of them in turn.

First, there are the figures, like the Fool, some part of whose consciousness, as conveyed to us at particular moments, seems to be doing double duty, filling our minds with impressions analogous to those which we may presume to be occupying the conscious or unconscious mind of the hero, whether he is before us on the stage or not. A possible example may be Lady Macbeth's sleepwalking scene. Macbeth is absent at this juncture, has gone "into the field" (5.1.4) — has not in fact been visible during two long scenes and will not be visible again till the next scene after this. In the interval, the slaying at Macduff's castle and the conversations between Malcolm and Macduff keep him before us in his capacity as tyrant, murderer, "Hell-kite," seen from the outside. But Lady Macbeth's sleepwalking (5.1) is, I think, Shakespeare's device for keeping him before us in his capacity as tragic hero and sufferer. The "great perturbation in nature" (5.1.9) of which the doctor whispers ("to receive at once the benefit of sleep, and do the effects of watching"), the "slumb'ry agitation," the "thick-coming fancies That keep her from her rest" (5.3.38): these, by a kind of poetical displacement, we may apply to him as well as to her; and we are invited to do so by the fact that from the moment of the first murder all the play's references to sleep and its destruction have had reference to Macbeth himself.

We are, of course, conscious as we watch the scene that this is Lady Macbeth suffering the metaphysical aspects of murder that she did not believe in; we may also be conscious that the remorse pictured here tends to distinguish her from her husband, who for some time has been giving his "initiate fear" the "hard use" (3.4.143) he said it lacked, with de-humanizing consequences. Yet in some way the pity of this situation suffuses him as well as her, the more so because in every word she utters his presence beside her is supposed; and if we allow this to be true, not only will Menteith's comment in the following scene —

Who then shall blame
His pestered senses to recoil and start,
When all that is within him does condemn
Itself for being there — (5.2.22)

evoke an image of suffering as well as retribution, but we shall better understand Macbeth's striking expression, at his next appearance, in words that we are almost bound to feel have some reference to himself, of corrosive griefs haunting below the conscious levels of the mind:

Canst thou not minister to a mind diseased,
Pluck from the memory a rooted sorrow,
Raze out the written troubles of the brain
And with some sweet oblivious antidote
Cleanse the stuffed bosom of that perilous stuff
Which weighs upon the heart? (5.3.40)

Such speeches as this and as Lady Macbeth's while sleepwalking — which we might call umbrella speeches, since more than one conscious-ness may shelter under them — are not uncommon in Shakespeare's dramaturgy, as many critics have pointed out. *Lear* affords the classic examples: in the Fool, as we have seen, and also in Edgar. Edgar's speech during the storm scenes projects in part his role of Poor Tom, the eternal outcast; in part, Edmund (and also Oswald), the vicious servant, self-seeking, with heart set on lust and proud array; possibly in part, Glouces-ter, whose arrival with a torch the Fool appropriately announces (with-out knowing it) in terms related to Edgar's themes: "Now a little fire in a wild field were like an old lecher's heart" (3.4.105); and surely, in some part too, the King, for the chips and tag-ends of Edgar's speech reflect, as if from Lear's own mind, not simply mental disintegration, but a strong sense of a fragmented moral order: "Obey thy parents; keep thy words' justice; swear not; commit not with man's sworn spouse" (3.4.76).

But, in my view, the most interesting of all the umbrella speeches in the tragedies is Enobarbus's famous description of Cleopatra in her barge. The triumvirs have gone offstage, Antony to have his first view of Octavia. When we see him again, his union with Octavia will have been agreed on all parts (though not yet celebrated), and he will be saying to her, with what can hardly be supposed insincerity:

> My Octavia,
> Read not my blemishes in the world's report:
> I have not kept my square; but that to come
> Shall all be done by th' rule. Good night, dear lady. (2.3.4)

Then the soothsayer appears, reminds Antony that his guardian angel will always be overpowered when Caesar's is by, urges him to return to Egypt; and Antony, left alone after the soothsayer has gone, meditates a moment on the truth of the pronouncement and then says abruptly:

> I will to Egypt:
> And though I make this marriage for my peace,
> I' th' East my pleasure lies. (3.3.38)

There is plainly a piece of prestidigitation here. It is performed in part by means of the soothsayer's entry, which is evidently a kind of visual surrogate for Antony's own personal intuition. ("I see it in my motion, have it not in my tongue," [2.3.14] the soothsayer says, when asked for the reasons he wishes Antony to return; and that is presumably the way Antony sees it too: in his "motion," i.e., involuntarily, intuitively.) But a larger part is played by Enobarbus's account of Cleopatra. Between the exit of the triumvirs and the reappearance of Antony making unsolicited promises to Octavia, this is the one thing that intervenes. And it is the only thing that needs to. Shakespeare has made it so powerful, so colored our imaginations with it, that we understand the promises of Antony, not in the light in which he understands them as he makes them, but in the riotous brilliance of Enobarbus's evocation of Cleopatra. The psychic gap in Antony between "My Octavia" (2.3.4) and "Good night, dear lady," on the one hand, and "I will to Egypt" (2.3.38), on the other, is filled by a vision, given to us, of irresistible and indeed quasi-unearthly power of which the soothsayer's intuition is simply a more abstract formulation. Here again, by indirection, Shakespeare finds direction out.

Not all mirror situations in the tragedies involve reflection of another consciousness. Some, as is well known, emphasize the outlines of an action by recapitulating it, as when Edgar's descent to Poor Tom and subsequent gradual re-ascent to support the gored state echoes the downward and upward movement in the lives of both King Lear and Gloucester; or as when Enobarbus's defection to, and again from, the bidding of his practical reason repeats that which Antony has already experienced, and Cleopatra will experience (at least in one way of understanding Act V) between Antony's death and her own. *Hamlet*, complex in all respects, offers an unusually complex form of this. The three sons, who are, in various senses, all avengers of dead fathers, are all deflected temporarily from their designs by the maneuvers of an elder (Claudius for Laertes and Hamlet; the King of Norway, inspired by Claudius, for Fortinbras), who in two cases is the young man's uncle.

There are of course important differences between these three young men which we are not to forget; but with respect to structure, the images in the mirror are chiefly likenesses. Hamlet, outmaneuvered by Claudius, off to England to be executed, crosses the path of Fortinbras, who has also been outmaneuvered by Claudius (working through his uncle) and is off to Poland to make mouths at the invisible event, while at the same moment Laertes, clamoring for immediate satisfaction in the King's palace, is outmaneuvered in his turn. Likewise, at the play's end, all three young men are "victorious," in ways they could hardly have foreseen. The return of Fortinbras, having achieved his objective in Poland, to find his "rights" in Denmark achieved without a blow, is timed to coincide with Hamlet's achieving his objective in exposing and killing the King and Laertes's achieving his objective of avenging his father's death on Hamlet. When this episode is played before us in the theater there is little question, to my way of thinking, but that something of the glow and martial upsurge dramatized in Fortinbras's entrance associates itself to Hamlet, even as Fortinbras's words associate Hamlet to a soldier's death. Meantime, Laertes, who has been trapped by the King and has paid with his life for it, gives us an alternative reflection of the Prince, which is equally a part of the truth.

5

Fortinbras's arrival at the close of *Hamlet* is an instance of an especially interesting type of mirroring to be found everywhere in Shakespeare's work—the emblematic entrance, and exit. Sometimes such exits occur by death, as the death of Gaunt, who takes a sacramental view of kingship and nation in *Richard II*, comes just as Richard has destroyed, by his personal conduct and by "farm[ing]" (1.4.45) his realm, the sacramental relationships which make such a view possible to maintain. Gaunt has to die, we might say, before a usurpation like his son's can even be imagined; and it is, I take it, not without significance that the first word of Bolingbroke's return comes a few seconds after we have heard (from the same speaker, Northumberland) that Gaunt's tongue "is now a stringless instrument" (2.1.149). Something similar, it seems clear, occurs with the death of Mamillius in *The Winter's Tale*. Sickening with his father's sickening mind, Mamillius dies in the instant that his father repudiates the message of the oracle; and though in the end, all else is restored to Leontes, Mamillius is not.

In the tragedies emblematic entrances and exits assume a variety of forms, ranging from those whose significance is obvious to those where it is uncertain, controversial and perhaps simply a mirage. One entrance whose significance is unmistakable occurs in the first act of *Macbeth*, when Duncan, speaking of the traitor Cawdor, whom Macbeth has slain, laments that there is no art to find the mind's construction in the face, just as the new Cawdor, traitor-to-be, appears before him. Equally unmistakable is the significance of the King's exit, in the first scene of *Lear*, with the man who like himself has put externals first, "Come, noble

250

Burgundy" (1.1.266), he says, and in a pairing that can be made profoundly moving on the stage, the two men go out together.

But what are we to say of Antony's freedman Eros, who enters for the first time (at least by name) just before his master's suicide and kills himself rather than kill Antony? This is all from Plutarch's life of Antony; but why did Shakespeare include it? Did Eros's name mean something to him? Are we to see here a shadowing of the other deaths for love, or not? Or again, the carrying off of Lepidus, drunk, from the feast aboard Pompey's galley. Does this anticipate his subsequent fate? and if it does, what does the intoxication signify to which in this scene all the great men are subject in their degree? Is it ordinary drunkenness; or is it, like the drunkenness that afflicts Caliban, Trinculo, and Stephano in *The Tempest*, a species of self-intoxication, Shakespeare's subdued comment on the thrust to worldly power? Or again, what of the arrival of the players in *Hamlet?* Granted their role in the plot, does Shakespeare make no other profit from them? Are such matters as the speech on Priam's murder and the advice on acting interesting excrescences, as Bradley thought, or does each mirror something that we are to appropriate to our understanding of the play: in the first instance, the strange confederacy of passion and paralysis in the hero's mind,[122] in the second, the question that tolls on all sides through the castle at Elsinore: when is an act not an "act"?[123]

These are questions to which it is not always easy to give a sound answer. The ground becomes somewhat firmer underfoot, I think, if we turn for a concluding instance to Bianca's pat appearances in *Othello*. R. B. Heilman suggests that in rushing to the scene of the night assault on Cassio, when she might have stayed safely within doors, and so exposing herself to vilification as a "notable strumpet" (5.1.78), Bianca acts in a manner "thematically relevant, because Othello has just been attacking Desdemona as a strumpet" — both "strumpets," in other words, are faithful.[124] Whether this is true or not, Bianca makes two very striking entrances earlier, when in each case she may be thought to supply in living form on the stage the prostitute figure that Desdemona has become in Othello's mind. Her second entrance is notably expressive.

Othello here is partially overhearing while Iago rallies Cassio about Bianca, Othello being under the delusion that the talk is of Desdemona. At the point when, in Othello's mental imagery, Desdemona becomes the soliciting whore — "Now he tells how she plucked him to my chamber" (4.1.139) — Bianca enters in the flesh, and not only enters but flourishes the magic handkerchief, now degenerated, like the love it was to ensure, to some "minx's," some "hobbyhorse's" token, the subject of jealous bickering. In the theater, the emblematic effect of this can hardly be ignored.[125]

Further types of mirroring will spring to every reader's mind. The recapitulation of a motif, for instance, as in the poisoning episodes in *Hamlet*. *Hamlet* criticism has too much ignored, I think, the fact that a story of poisoning forms the climax of the first act, a mime and "play" of poisoning the climax of the third, and actual poisoning, on a wide scale, the climax of the fifth. Surely this repetition was calculated to keep steady for Shakespeare's Elizabethan audiences the political and moral bearings of the play? We may say what we like about Hamlet's frailties, which are real, but we can hardly ignore the fact that in each of the poisoning episodes the poisoner is the King. The King, who ought to be like the sun, giving warmth, radiance and fertility to his kingdom, is actually its destroyer. The "leperous distilment" (1.5.64) he pours into Hamlet's father's ear, which courses through his body with such despatch, has coursed just as swiftly through the body politic, and what we see in Denmark as a result is a poisoned kingdom, containing one corruption upon another of Renaissance ideals. The "wise councilor," who is instead a tedious windbag. The young "man of honor," who has no trust in another's honor, as his advice to his sister shows, and none of his own, as his own treachery to Hamlet shows. The "friends," who are not friends but spies. The loved one, who proves disloyal (a decoy, however reluctant, for villainy), and goes mad — through poison also, "the poison of deep grief." The mother and Queen, who instead of being the guardian of the kingdom's matronly virtues has set a harlot's blister on love's forehead and made marriage vows "as false as dicers' oaths."

And most especially the Prince, the "ideal courtier," the Renaissance man — once active, energetic, now reduced to anguished introspection; a glass of fashion, now a sloven in antic disarray; a noble mind, now partly unhinged, in fact as well as seeming; the observed of all observers, now observed in a more sinister sense; the mold of form, now capable of obscenities, cruelty, even treachery, mining below the mines of his school friends to hoist them with their own petard. All this in one way or another is the poison of the King, and in the last scene, lest we miss the point, we are made to see the spiritual poison become literal and seize on all those whom it has not already destroyed:

> a Prince's Court
> Is like a common Fountaine, whence should flow
> Pure silver-droppes in generall: But if 't chance
> Some cursed example poyson 't neere the head,
> Death, and diseases through the whole land spread.[126]

The lines are Webster's, but they state with precision one of the themes of Shakespeare's play.

Finally, in the tragedies as elsewhere in Shakespeare, we have the kinds of replication that have been specifically called "mirror scenes,"[127] or (more in Ercles' vein) scenes of "analogical probability."[128] The most impressive examples here are frequently the opening scenes and episodes. The witches of *Macbeth*, whose "foul is fair" (1.1.10) and battle that is "won *and* lost" (1.1.4) anticipate so much to come. The "great debate" in *Antony and Cleopatra*, initiated in the comments of Philo and the posturings of the lovers and reverberating thereafter within, as well as around, the lovers till they die. The watchmen on the platform in *Hamlet*, feeling out a mystery — an image that will re-form in our minds again and again as we watch almost every member of the *dramatis personae* engage in similar activity later on. The technique of manipulation established at the outset of *Othello*, the persuading of someone to believe something he is reluctant to believe and which is not true in the sense presented — exemplified in Iago's management of both Roderigo and Brabantio, and prefiguring later developments throughout the play.

Lear offers perhaps the best of all these instances. Here the "Nature" of which the play is to make so much, ambiguous, double-barreled, is represented in its normative aspect in the hierarchies on the stage before us — a whole political society from its *primum mobile*, the great King, down to lowliest attendant as well as a whole family society from father down through married daughters and sons-in-law to a third daughter with her wooers — and, in its appetitive aspect (which Edmund will formulate in a few moments) in the overt self-will of the old King and the hidden self-will, the "plighted cunning" (1.1.280) of the false daughters. As the scene progresses, the cycle of future events becomes all but visible as these hierarchies of the normative Nature, which at first looked so formidable and solid, crumble away in the repudiation of Cordelia, the banishment of Kent, the exit of Lear and Burgundy, till nothing is left standing on the stage but Nature red in tooth and claw as the false daughters lay their heads together.

6

I dwell on these effects of "indirection" in the tragedies because I believe that most of us as playgoers are keenly conscious of their presence. Perhaps I describe them badly, in some instances possibly misconceive them; but they are not my invention; this kind of thing has been pointed to more and more widely during the past nine decades by reputable observers. In short, these effects, in some important sense, are "there." And if they are, the question we must ask is, Why? What are they for? How are they used?

I return then to the query raised earlier: what *does* happen in a Shakespearean tragedy? Is it possible to formulate an answer that will, while not repudiating the traditional categories so far as they are useful, take into account the matters we have been examining?

Obviously the most important thing that happens in a Shakespearean tragedy is that the hero follows a cycle of change which is, in part, psychic change. And this seems generally to be constituted in three phases. During the first phase, corresponding roughly to Bradley's exposition, the hero is delineated. Among other things he is placed in positions that enable him to sound the particular timbre of his tragic music:

Not so, my lord; I am too much in the sun. (*Hamlet*, 1.2.67)

Seems, madam? Nay, it is; I know not "seems." (1.2.76)

My father's brother, but no more like my father
Than I to Hercules. (1.2.152)

                  My fate cries out,
And makes each petty artery in this body
As hardy as the Nemean lion's nerve. (1.4.81)

Chiming against this we are also permitted to hear the particular
timbre of the opposing voice, spoken by the foil as well as others:

                  If it be,
Why seems it so particular with thee? (1.2.74)

For what we know must be and is as common
As any the most vulgar thing to sense,
Why should we in our peevish opposition
Take it to heart? (1.2.98)

What if it tempt you toward the flood, my lord,
Or to the dreadful summit of the cliff
That beetles o'er his base into the sea,
And there assume some other horrible form,
Which might deprive your sovereignty of reason
And draw you into madness? (1.4.69)

From now on, as we saw, these are the differing attitudes toward experience that will supply the essential dialogue of the play.

The second phase is much more comprehensive. It contains the conflict, crisis, and falling action — in short, the heart of the matter. Here,
several interesting developments occur. The one certain over-all development in this phase is that the hero tends to become his own antithesis. We have met this already in Hamlet, in whom "the courtier's,
soldier's, scholar's, eye, tongue, sword" (3.1.151) suffer some savage vio-
lations before the play is done. Likewise, Othello the unshakable, whose

original composure under the most trying insults and misrepresenta-
tions almost takes the breath away, breaks in this phase into furies, grov-
els on the floor in a trance, strikes his wife publicly. King Lear, "the great
image of authority" (4.6.155) both by temperament and position, becomes a helpless crazed old man crying in a storm, destitute of everything but one servant and his Fool. Macbeth, who would have "holily"
(1.5.19) what he would have "highly," who is too full of the milk of
human kindness to catch the nearest way, whose whole being revolts
with every step he takes in his own revolt — his hair standing on end, his
imagination filling with angels "trumpet-tongued" (1.7.19), his hands
(after the deed) threatening to pluck out his own eyes — turns into the
numbed usurper, "supped full with horrors" (5.5.13), who is hardly capable of responding even to his wife's death. The development is equally
plain in Antony and Coriolanus. "The greatest prince o' th' world, The
noblest" (4.15.54), finds his greatness slipped from him, and his nobility
debased to the ignominy of having helpless emissaries whipped. The
proud and upright Coriolanus, patriot soldier, truckles in the market
place for votes, revolts to the enemy he has vanquished, carries war
against his own flesh and blood.

   This manner of delineating tragic "action," though it may be traced
here and there in other drama, seems to be on the whole a property of
the Elizabethans and Jacobeans. Possibly it springs from their concern
with "whole" personalities on the tragic stage rather than, as so often
with the ancients and Racine, just those aspects of personality that guarantee the *dénouement*. In any case, it seems to have become a consistent
feature of Shakespeare's dramaturgy and beautifully defines the sense of
psychological alienation and uprootedness that tragic experience in the
Elizabethan and Jacobean theater generally seems to embrace. Its dis-
tinctively tragic implications stand out the more when we reflect that
psychic change in comedy (if indeed comedy can be said to concern itself
with psychic change at all) consists in making, or in showing, the protagonist to be more and more what he or she always was.

   In this second phase too, either as an outward manifestation of inward
change, or as a shorthand indication that such change is about to begin

or end, belong the tragic journeys. Romeo is off to Mantua, Brutus to the Eastern end of the Roman world, Hamlet to England, Othello to Cyprus, Lear and Gloucester to Dover, Timon to the cave, Macbeth to the heath to revisit the witches, Antony to Rome and Athens, Coriolanus to Antium.[129] Such journeys, we rightly say, are called for by the plots. But perhaps we should not be wrong if we added that Shakespearean plotting tends to call for journeys, conceivably for discernible reasons. For one thing, journeys can enhance our impression that psychological changes are taking place, either by emphasizing a lapse of time, or by taking us to new settings, or by both. I suspect we register such effects subconsciously more often than we think.

Furthermore, though it would be foolish to assign to any of the journeys in Shakespeare's tragedies a precise symbolic meaning, several of them have vaguely symbolic overtones — serving as surrogates either for what can never be exhibited on the stage, as happens with the mysterious processes leading to psychic change, which cannot be articulated into speech, even soliloquy, without losing their formless instinctive character; or for the processes of self-discovery, the learning processes — a function journeys fulfill in many of the world's best-known stories (the *Aeneid*, the *Divine Comedy*, *Tom Jones*, etc.) and in some of Shakespeare's comedies. Hamlet's abortive journey to England seems to be an instance of the first category. After his return, and particularly after what he tells us of his actions while at sea, we are not surprised if he appears, spiritually, a changed man. Lear's and Gloucester's journey to Dover is perhaps an instance of the second category, leading as it does through suffering to insight and reconciliation.

During the hero's journey, or at any rate during his over-all progress in the second phase, he will normally pass through a variety of mirroring situations of the sort formerly discussed (though it will be by us and not him that the likeness in the mirror is seen). In some of these, the hero will be confronted, so to speak, with a version of his own situation, and his failure to recognize it may be a measure of the nature of the disaster to ensue. Coriolanus, revolted from Rome and now its enemy, meets himself in Aufidius's embrace in Antium. Hamlet meets himself in Fortinbras as the latter marches to Poland but does not see the likeness — only the differences. Lear goes to Goneril's and there meets, as everyone remembers, images of his own behavior to Cordelia. Thrust into the night he meets his own defenselessness in Edgar and is impelled to pray. Encountering in Dover fields, both Lear and Gloucester confront in each other an extension of their own experience: blindness that sees and madness that is wise. Macbeth revisits the witches on the heath and finds there (without recognizing them) not only the emblems of his death and downfall to come but his speciousness and duplicity. Antony encounters in Enobarbus's defection his own, and possibly, in Pompey, his own later muddled indecision between "honor" and *Realpolitik*. Othello hears the innocent Cassio set upon in the dark, then goes to re-enact that scene in a more figurative darkness in Desdemona's bedroom.

Sometimes, alternatively or additionally, the hero's way will lie through quasi-symbolic settings or situations. The heath in both *Macbeth* and *King Lear* is infinitely suggestive, even if like all good symbols it refuses to dissipate its *Dinglichkeit* in meaning. The same is true of the dark castle platform in Hamlet, and the graveyard; of the cliff at Dover and Gloucester's leap; of the "monument," where both Antony and Cleopatra die; and of course, as many have pointed out, of the night scenes, the storm, the music, the changes of clothing, the banquets. So much in Shakespeare's tragedies stands on the brink of symbol that for this reason, if no other, the usual terms for describing their construction and mode of action need reinforcement.

After the hero has reached and passed through his own antithesis, there comes a third phase in his development that is extremely difficult to define. It represents a recovery of sorts — in some cases, perhaps even a species of synthesis. The once powerful, now powerless king, will have power again, but of another kind — the kind suggested in his reconciliation with Cordelia and his speech beginning "Come, let's away to prison" (5.1.8); and he will have sanity again, but in a mode not dreamed of at the beginning of the play. Or, to take Othello's case, it will be given the hero to recapture the faith he lost[130], to learn that the pearl really was richer than all his tribe and to execute quite another order of justice than the blinkered justice meted out to Cassio and the blind injustice meted out to Desdemona. Or again, to shift to Antony, the man who has so long been thrown into storms of rage and recrimination by the caprices of his unstable mistress receives the last of them without a murmur of reproach, though it has led directly to his death, and dies in greater unison with her than we have ever seen him live.

I believe that some mark of this nature is visible in all the tragedies. Coriolanus, "boy" though he is and in some ways remains, makes a triumphant choice (detract from his motives as we may), and he knows what it is likely to cost. Moreover, he refuses the way of escape that lies open if he should return now with Volumnia and Vergilia to Rome. "I'll not to Rome, I'll back with you," he tells Aufidius, "and pray you Stand to me in this cause" (5.3.198). The young man who after this dies accused of treachery — by Aufidius's treachery and the suggestibility of the crowd, as slippery in Corioli as Rome — cannot be thought identical in all respects with the young man who joined Menenius in the play's opening scene. He is that young man but with the notable difference of his triumphant choice behind him; and there is bound to be more than a military association in our minds when the Second Lord of the Volscians, seeking to quell the mob, cries, "The man is noble, and his fame folds in This orb o' th' earth"; and again too when the First Lord exclaims over his body, "Let him be regarded As the most noble corse that ever herald Did follow to his urn" (5.6.123, 140). Even the monster Macbeth is so handled by Shakespeare, as has been often enough observed, that he seems to regain something at the close — if nothing more, at least some of that *élan* which made him the all-praised Bellona's bridegroom of the play's second scene; and everything Macbeth says, following Duncan's death, about the emptiness of the achievement, the lack of posterity, the sere, the yellow leaf, deprived of "that which should accompany old age, As honor, love, obedience, troops of friends" (5.3.24), affords evidence that the meaning of his experience has not been lost on him.

To say this, I wish to make it clear, is not to say that every Shakespearean tragic hero undergoes an "illumination," or, to use the third term of Kenneth Burke's sequence, a Mathema or perception.[131] This is a terminology that seems to me not very useful to the discussion of tragedy as Shakespeare presents it. It is sufficient for my purposes to say simply that the phase in which we are conscious of the hero as approaching his opposite is followed by a final phase in which we are conscious of him as exhibiting one or more aspects of his original, or — since these may not coincide — his better self: as in the case of Antony's final reunion with Cleopatra, and Coriolanus's decision not to sack Rome.

Whether we then go on to give this phenomenon a specific spiritual significance, seeing in it the objective correlative of "perception" or "illumination," is a question that depends, obviously, on a great many factors, more of them perhaps situated in our own individual philosophies than in the text, and so, likely to lead us away from Shakespeare rather than toward him.

Clearly if Shakespeare wished us to engage in this activity, he was remiss in the provision of clues. Even in *King Lear*, the one play where some sort of regeneration or new insight in the hero has been universally acknowledged, the man before us in the last scene — who sweeps Kent aside, rakes all who have helped him with grapeshot ("A plague upon you, murderers, traitors all. I might have saved her . . ." [5.3.270]), exults in the revenge he has exacted for Cordelia's death, and dies self-deceived in the thought she still lives — this man is one of the most profoundly human figures ever created in a play; but he is not, certainly, the Platonic idea laid up in heaven, or in critical schemes, of regenerate man.

7

I have kept to the end, and out of proper order, the most interesting of all the symbolic elements in the hero's second phase. This is his experience of madness. One discovers with some surprise, I think, how many of Shakespeare's heroes are associated with this disease. Only Titus, Hamlet, Lear, and Timon, in various senses, actually go mad. But Iago boasts that he will make Othello mad and in a way succeeds. Antony, it will be recalled, after the second defeat at sea, is said by Cleopatra to be

more mad
Than Telamon for his shield; the boar of Thessaly
Was never so embossed. (4.13.1)

Caithness in *Macbeth* tells us that some say the king is mad, while "others, that lesser hate him, Do call it valiant fury." Romeo, rather oddly, enjoins Paris at Juliet's tomb to

be gone. Live, and hereafter say,
A madman's mercy bid thee run away. (5.3.66)

Even Brutus, by the Antony of *Antony and Cleopatra*, is said to have been "mad."

What, if anything, one wonders, may this mean? Doubtless a sort of explanation can be found in Elizabethan psychological lore, which held that the excess of any passion approached madness, and in the general prevalence, through Seneca and other sources, of the adage: *Quos vult perdere Jupiter dementat prius.*[132] Furthermore, madness, when actually exhibited, was dramatically useful, as Shakespeare's predecessor Thomas Kyd had shown. It was arresting in itself, and it allowed the combination in a single figure of tragic hero and buffoon, to whom could be accorded the license of the allowed fool in speech and action.

Just possibly, however, there is yet more to it, if we may judge by Shakespeare's sketches of madness in *Hamlet* and *King Lear*. In both of these, madness is to some degree a punishment or doom, corresponding to the adage. Lear prays to the heavens that he may not suffer madness, and Hamlet asks Laertes in his apology before the duel to overlook his conduct, since "you must needs have heard, how I am punished With a sore distraction" (5.2.218). It is equally obvious, however, that in both instances the madness has a further dimension, as insight, and this is true also of Ophelia. Ophelia, mad, is able to make awards of flowers to the King and Queen which are appropriate to frailties of which she cannot be supposed to have conscious knowledge. For the same reason, I suspect we do not need Dover Wilson's radical displacement of Hamlet's entry in 2.2, so as to enable him to overhear Polonius.[133] It is enough that Hamlet wears, even if it is for the moment self-assumed, the guise of the madman. As such, he can be presumed to have intuitive unformulated awarenesses that reach the surface in free (yet relevant) associations, like those of Polonius with a fishmonger, Ophelia with carrion.

Lear likewise is allowed free yet relevant associations. His great speech in Dover fields on the lust of women derives from the designs of Goneril and Regan on Edmund, of which he consciously knows nothing. Moreover, both he and Hamlet can be privileged in madness to say things — Hamlet about the corruption of human nature, and Lear about the corruption of the Jacobean social system (and by extension about all social systems whatever) — which Shakespeare could hardly have risked apart from this license. Doubtless one of the anguishes of being a great artist is that you cannot tell people what they and you and your common institutions are really like — when viewed absolutely — without being dismissed as insane. To communicate at all, you must acknowledge the opposing voice; for there always is an opposing voice, and it is as deeply rooted in your own nature as in your audience's.

Just possibly, therefore, the meaning of tragic madness for Shakespeare approximated the meaning that the legendary figure of Cassandra (whom Shakespeare had in fact put briefly on his stage in the second act of *Troilus and Cressida*) has held for so many artists since his time. Cassandra's madness, like Lear's and Hamlet's — possibly, also, like the madness *verbally* assigned to other Shakespearean tragic heroes — contains both punishment and insight. She is doomed to know, by a consciousness that moves to measures outside our normal space and time; she is doomed never to be believed, because those to whom she speaks can hear only the opposing voice. With the language of the god Apollo sounding in her brain, and the incredulity of her fellow mortals ringing in her ears, she makes an ideal emblem of the predicament of the Shakespearean tragic hero, caught as he is between the absolute and the expedient. And by the same token, of the predicament of the artist — Shakespeare himself, perhaps — who, having been given the power to see the "truth," can convey it only through poetry — what we commonly call a "fiction" and dismiss.

NOTES

CHAPTER 1: EVERYBODY'S SHAKESPEARE

1. This was formerly a joke, but reality has caught up with it. See *A Shakespeare Music Catalogue*, ed. Bryan N. S. Gooch and David Thatcher, 5 vols. (Oxford: Clarendon Press, 1991), 2847 pp.

2. *The Waste Land*, 404–5.

3. Tim Brassell, *Tom Stoppard: An Assessment* (New York: 1985), 60.

CHAPTER 2: AUDIENCE AND PLAY

4. For an interesting account of engagement as the Renaissance painter presents it, see Alberti's *On Painting*, ed. J. R. Spencer (1956), 56 ff. L. A. Heydenreich notes in his *Leonardo da Vinci* (1954), 1.38, that even the table linen and cutlery in Leonardo's *Last Supper* were modeled on those actually used in the refectory where the monks, seated at the table, looked up to see the disciples seated at theirs. A related point about Taddeo Gaddi's *Last Supper* and Ghirlandajo's is made in Eve Borsodi's *Mural Painters in Tuscany* (1960), 15, 131–2, and plate 13; 31, 158–9, and plate 79. (I am grateful to my sister, Mrs. Andrew Bongiorno, for the above references.) Sir Kenneth Clark in *The Nude in Art* (1956) 130, makes the point about Titian that I wish to make about Shakespeare: "he could maintain that balance between intense participation and absolute detachment which distinguishes art from other forms of human activity."

5. Published in 1647.

6. Shirley says "reads," but he is writing after the closing of the theaters.

7. I paraphrase loosely from accounts of the address appearing in French and English newspapers of the time.

8. "Kleines Organon für das Theater," *Brecht Versuche*, 12 (1948), par. 40.

9. *The Dry Salvages*, 95.

10. I owe the Shirley reference to my friend and colleague, Professor E. M. Waith.

11. *Select Poetry and Prose*, ed. Stephen Potter (1933), 342.

12. In *A Shrew*, Sly wakes up resolved to try out what he has gleaned of the play's purport before falling asleep, and tame his own shrew at home.

13. *Narrative and Dramatic Sources of Shakespeare* (1957), 68.

14. See *Stephen Hero*, ch.25.

15. *De architectura*, 6.1.

16. As recorded in Jean Fouquet's *Martyrdom of St. Apollonia*.

17. *English Works* (1557) leaf fg2v. More bears interesting witness to the sophistication of the Renaissance mind with respect to illusion. In his life of Richard III, he has a very fine passage on how the spectators at a stage play well know "that he that playeth the soldan [sultan] is perchance a souter [shoemaker]" (More is evidently thinking of a guild performance), yet if anyone should venture to address him in that identity, "one of his tormentors might hap to break his head, and worthy [rightly] for marring the play," fol. clv. I have modernized More's spelling in both passages.

18. Something related though not quite the same takes place in the Ronald Colman film *A Double Life* (1947), where Colman as a Shakespearean actor playing Othello actually kills the actress playing Desdemona, who in fact is his wife. (I am grateful for this reminder to Michael W. Young.)

19. This point of view is developed in Chapter Eleven.

20. For an account of this contrast from a different angle and using somewhat different terms, see W. H. Auden's valuable "Notes on the Comic," in *Thought* 27 (1952), 57–71, to which I am indebted.

CHAPTER 3: PLAY AND HISTORY

21. Richard Elder, "Can We Rethink Shakespeare without Submerging Him?" *NY Times*, 16 July 1978: Section D, 3.

22. Mel Gussow, "An Auspicious Year at Britain's Stratford." *Ibid.*, 4.

23. *The Go-Between* (London: Hamilton, 1953), 9.

24. I am particularly indebted in what follows to the brilliant work done

in Tudor history, social history, and demography by Joel Hurstfield, *The Queen's Wards: Wardship and Marriage under Elizabeth I* (London: Longmans, 1958); Peter Laslett, *The World We Have Lost* (London: Methuen & Co., 1965); *Family Life and Illicit Love in Earlier Generations* (Cambridge: Cambridge UP, 1977); Laurence Stone, *The Crisis of the Aristocracy, 1558–1641* (Oxford: Clarendon Press, 1965); and *The Family, Sex, and Marriage in England, 1500–1800* (New York: Harper & Row, 1977); and Keith Thomas, "The Double Standard," *Journal of the History of Ideas*, 20 (1959), 195–216 and "Age and Authority in Early Modern England," *Proceedings of the British Academy*, 62 (1976), 205–28.

25. G. Davies, ed., *Autobiography of Thomas Raymond and Memoirs of the Family of Guise* (London: Camden Society, 3rd ser., 28, 1917), 114.

26. Lloyd De Mause, "The Evolution of Childhood," *The History of Childhood*, ed. Lloyd De Mause (New York: Psychohistory Press, 1974), 36. The Elizabethan exception is John Jones, whose *The Arte and Science of Preserving Bodie and Soule, in Healthe, Wisedome, and Catholike Religion* (1579), 42–5, sets the weaning period between 7 and 36 months.

27. De Mause, 50.

28. De Mause, 32.

29. *Tudor Economic Documents*, ed. R. H. Tawney and Eileen Power, 3 vols., (London: Longmans, 1924), i, 358, 356, 354.

30. Stone, *The Family*, 127.

31. *The Catechism of Thomas Becon*, ed. John Ayre (Cambridge, 1844), 354; Ecclus., 30: 10–12. Compare the experience of Lady Jane Grey, confided to Roger Ascham when she was fifteen: "When I am in the presence either of father or mother, whether I speake, kepe silence, sit, stand, or go, eate, drinke, be merie or sad, be sowying, plaiying, dauncing, or doing anie thing els, I must do it, as it were, in such weight, mesure, and number, even so perfitelie, as God made the world, or els I am so sharplie taunted, so cruellie threatened yea presentlie some tymes, with pinches, nippes, and bobbes, and other waies which I will not name, for the honor I beare them, so without measure misordered, that I thinke my selfe in hell . . ." *The Scholemaster* (1570), *English Works*, ed. W. A. Wright (1904), 201–2.

32. Bartholomaeus Battus, *The Christian Man's Closet*, tr. William Lowth (1581), 26.

33. L. L. Schücking, *The Puritan Family: A Social Study from the Literary Sources* (London: Routledge, 1969), 91. Though it may or may not be significant, it is interesting that the childhood attachments Shakespeare describes so winningly never occur within the family. See *A Midsummer Night's Dream* (1.1.214) and (3.2.198); *As You Like It* (1.3.69); *The Winter's Tale* (1.2.67).

34. For an illuminating discussion of Juliet's age at marriage in the light of Elizabethan social history, see Laslett, *World*, 81–9.

35. Published in 1583.

36. Leaf H5, recto.

37. *A Discourse on Marriage and Wiving and of the Mystery Contained Therein* (1615); *Harleian Miscellany* (1744), ii, 147–8.

38. Antigonus in *The Winter's Tale* (2.1.147) sets the female breeding age at fourteen.

39. Additional pressures sometimes came from a father's determination to arrange his children's marriages himself; for if he died before they were of an age to inherit, they became wards of the crown, their guardianship purchaseable for a fee, and with it the privilege of choosing their marriage-partners.

40. Stone, *Crisis*, 638.

41. Milton, *Animadversions upon the Remonstrant's Defense against Smectymnuus, Complete Prose Works*, ed. D. M. Wolfe, (1953), i, 718.

42. Partly owing to the necessity of supporting her, but partly also to the loss of family advantage from marrying her well. See the comment of the Marquis of Argyle in 1661, quoted by Stone in *Crisis*, 646: "in great and noble families . . . interest forbids perpetual virginity."

43. Stone, *Crisis*, 643–5.

44. *Works* (Edinburgh, 1866–7), i, 29–30.

45. Published in 1524.

46. Tr. Richard Nerde (1557), leaf J4, verso.

47. "Age and Authority," 237. I am indebted to this essay for referring me to several of the works cited below.

48. *The Compleat Gentleman* (1622), 27.

49. John Christopherson, *An Exhortation to all menne to take hede and beware of rebellion* (1554), leaf T2, verso.

50. "The Young Man's Task," *Works*, 1, 228.

51. H[umphrey] M[ill]. *Poems* (1639), leaf M8, recto.

52. Foulke Robartes, *The Revenue of the Gospel Is Tythes* (Cambridge, 1613), 144–15.

53. Jack Goody, "Aging in Nonindustrial Societies," *Handbook of Aging and the Social Sciences*, ed. R. H. Binstock and E. Shanas (New York: Van Nostrand, 1976), 119.

54. *Plumpton Correspondence*, ed. T. Stapleton (Camden Society, 1839), 122–25.

55. *A Royalist's Notebook*, ed. Francis Bamford (London: Constable, 1936), 124.

56. *Middle English Sermons*, ed. W. O. Ross (Oxford: EETS, 1940), 89–90.

57. *Pasquils Jests, mixed with Mother Bunches Merriments* (1604). ed. W. C. Hazlitt. *Shakespeare Jest-Books*, 3 vols. (1864), 1, 61.

CHAPTER 4: *ROMEO AND JULIET*

58. Published in 1592.

CHAPTER 5: *JULIUS CAESAR*

59. *Shakespeare's Plutarch*, ed. C. F. Tucker Brooke, 2 vols. (Haskell House reprint, New York, 1966), 1:92.

CHAPTER 6: *HAMLET*

60. Caroline Spurgeon, *Shakespeare's Imagery and What It Tells Us* (Cambridge University Press, 1971), 123–24.

61. E. M. W. Tillyard, *Shakespeare's Problem Plays* (University of Toronto Press, 1949), 6.

62. "Unpublished notes for a lecture," quoted in Richard Ellmann, *Yeats: The Man and the Masks* (New York, 1948), 298.

CHAPTER 7: *OTHELLO*

63. Though it is possible to find many intervening shades of opinion, the two major schools of thought (on this play as on several others) are irrecon-

NOTES TO PAGES 129-130

cilable. One holds that Othello is a man essentially noble who is brought to ruin by the incongruity of his virtues with the circumstances in which for the tragic purposes of the drama he has been placed. In the background of this view lies the assumption that dramatic characters are created for particular dramatic ends and have no existence otherwise or elsewhere. The opposing view is that Othello is a man deeply flawed who is destroyed by his own inner defects or even vices, fed by a massive egotism attributable variously to the effects of a patriarchal culture, psychological woundings from his early childhood, the erotophobia of contemporary Puritanism, or twentieth century identifications of love and power. Here the assumption is that dramatic characters, once created, have an existence in the real world that renders them as liable to medical or political diagnosis as any man or woman encountered in the street.

The first Othello, sometimes called by those who see him differently "the sentimentalist's Othello," is by and large the Othello of nearly four centuries of theater history, and his career *there* has been brilliantly traced by Marvin Rosenberg in *The Masks of Othello* (University of California Press, 1961).

The other Othello is a comparatively new figure of the last four decades, deriving from the habits of an intensely verbal academic culture which is at the same time in many quarters heavily committed to one or other of the current group ideologies. How far it is possible deconstructively to develop an interesting Othello unimaginable historically and altogether incommunicable onstage may be profitably examined in Martin Elliot's *Shakespeare's Invention of Othello* (New York, 1988).

64. *Coleridge's Shakespearean Criticism*, 2 vols., (Harvard UP, 1930), 1: 47.

65. Herbert Beerbohm Tree's comment in a letter to his wife explaining his choice of make-up for his performance of *Othello* in 1912. (*Herbert Beerbohm Tree. Some Memories of Him and His Art Collected by Max Beerbohm* [London, 1920], 148.) Regardless of make-up, if the reviewer of that performance for the *Daily Telegraph* may be trusted, Tree's interpretation caught much in the play that is now frequently overlooked or disdained. "This Othello speaks as having authority, and not as the scribes. He has the habit of command and great affairs. He is past the passions of youth, as indeed he says. He has not much of the days of gallantry. He speaks of Desdemona with

great tenderness. He treats her with gentlest affection. He is plainly all in love with her, but not after a young man's fashion of love. Through the long battle with Iago, the slow irresistible onset of doubt was finely played" (*Ibid.*, 147).

66. The quarto reading, in favor of which I part here and elsewhere from the inferior folio reading "Judean."

67. Thomas Heywood, *The Fair Maid of the West*, ed. R. K. Turner, Jr. (Lincoln: University of Nebraska Press, 1967), Pt. 2: 1.1.329.

68. *Complete Works*, ed. P. P. Howe, 14 vols. (London, 1967), 4: 14–17, 200–09.

69. As far back as 1940, a famous essay by Joseph Wood Krutch in his *The Modern Temper* traces our century's shrinking from the idea of heroism and with it the disappearance of tragedy as Shakespeare knew it. See also, more recently, George Steiner, *The Death of Tragedy* (New York, 1961).

70. Iago's counterpart in Shakespeare's source (the seventh tale of the third decade in Giraldi Cinthio's collection: *Hecatommithi* [1565]) has no name but "the Ensign," as Othello has no name but "The Moor," and shares little beyond villainy with the Iago that Shakespeare conceived.

71. I adopt here the reading of the quartos, as does Robert Heilman in his *Wit and Witchcraft in Othello* (Lexington: University of Kentucky Press, 1961), 140 ff. The folio text has no interposition by Desdemona. There, a "Senator," not the Duke, instructs Othello that he must away tonight, and Othello replies, as in the quarto, "With all my heart" (1.3.278). Considering what we have seen already of Desdemona's courage, her defiance of protocol in eloping, and her frank concern right now about "the rites for why I love him" (1.3.257), I find it impossible to imagine her standing in submissive silence while her new husband receives an order to leave her on her wedding night.

Heilman cites Othello's four words in support of his belief that Othello is immature about matters sexual and happy to be despatched on the Cyprus mission. It is a belief difficult to share in view of the commanding stature given Othello throughout the play and the preconceptions of Jacobean audiences about the sexuality of Moors. If Othello is a sexual cripple, much in the passion he later turns against Desdemona and in the erotic fury of the act with which he murders her, becomes inexplicable.

As evidence of Othello's lack of interest in the "rites" of which his new wife wishes not to be "bereft" (1.3.257), some cite his lines in support of her plea to be allowed to accompany him to the wars (1.3.260). There he assures the Senators that he seconds her request "Not to comply with heat—the young affects In me defunct" (1.3.263)—and that they need not fear he will "scant" (1.3.267) his responsibilities as their officer. "No," he adds, "when light-winged toys Of feathered Cupid" (1.3.268) so dull my faculties that pleasure interferes with duty, "Let housewives make a skillet of my helm" (1.3.272), and let all ill fortunes overtake me.

It is difficult to imagine a high service officer of mature years making any very different reply to his civilian superiors even today, and one notices, lurking in the background as he speaks, the traditional Renaissance topos of Mars feminized by Venus, lying languidly by while her Cupids—in Othello's version, the housewives—try on or sport with the pieces of his armor. Othello's message is that nothing of the sort will ever happen to *him*.

72. Preface to *The American*, vol. 2 (New York Edition, 1907).

73. George Santayana, *Interpretations of Poetry and Religion* (New York: Harper Torchbooks, 1957), 284.

74. Throughout this scene, as I see it, we are as much in the presence of a stage convention as we are in the Edmund-Gloucester episode mentioned above, or the radical conversion of Lady Anne from loathing to love in *Richard III*, or, to turn to another playwright, the fall of Mrs. Frankford in *A Woman Killed with Kindness*. It is also useful to recall that Renaissance drama, like Greek drama, is normally more concerned with actions and their effects than with speculation about their sources, and that when such speculation does appear it is quite unlike our own, being on the one hand more formulaic and on the other allowing greater scope to the inexplicable (See *Hamlet*, 1.4: "some vicious mole of nature," "the o'ergrowth of some complexion," "some habit that too much o'erleavens," "the dram of evil," etc.).

75. Harley Granville-Barker, *Prefaces to Shakespeare*, 2 vols. (Princeton: Princeton UP, 1951), 2: 114.

76. The content of this scene is discussed further in Lorne M. Buchman's

Still In Movement: Shakespeare on Screen (New York: Oxford University Press, 1991), 127. (For the Buchman reference I am indebted to Stephen M. Buhler.)

77. Diels, *Fragmente der Vorsokratiker*, 1: 169 (frag. 80).

78. *Canzoniere*, No. 21.

CHAPTER 8: *KING LEAR*

79. In his sonnet: "No worst, there is none."

80. The reference to the poet is, of course, to Wordsworth, and the critic is Hippolyte Taine.

81. Quoted from a course paper by Evelyn Hooven. Written many years ago, this remains a sensitive observation.

82. Quoted from a course paper by Leslie Epstein, catching both the troubled mood of the late 1960s and an aspect of the permanent grandeur of *King Lear*.

83. Spurgeon, *Shakespeare's Imagery and What It Tells Us*, 338–39.

84. *King Lear* (W. P. Ker Memorial Lecture) 48.

85. "The Two Techniques in *King Lear*," *Review of English Studies*, 18 (1942) 1–26, reprinted in enlarged form as chap. 3 of his *Shakespeare and Spenser* (1950).

86. A. C. Bradley, *Lectures on Shakespearean Tragedy* (1904), 319; he is corrected on this point by Granville-Barker (*Prefaces to Shakespeare*, 1, 281).

87. *Ibid.*

88. "Some Aspects of the Style of *King Lear*," *Shakespeare Survey*, 13 (1960), 51.

89. *Ibid.*, 52.

90. Enid Welsford, *The Fool: His Social and Literary History* (1935), 258.

91. *Op. cit.*, 56.

92. Michael Chekhov, *To the Actor on the Technique of Acting* (New York, 1953), 134.

93. W. H. Auden, *The Dyer's Hand* (1962), 107–8.

94. "*King Lear* at Stratford-on-Avon, 1959," *Shakespeare Quarterly*, 11 (1960), 198.

95. G. R. Kernodle, "The Open Stage: Elizabethan or Existentialist," *Shakespeare Survey*, 12 (1959), 3.

96. Crane Brinton, *Ideas and Men* (1950), 269.

97. *Anatomy of Criticism* (Princeton: Princeton University Press, 1957), 212–3.

98. *The View of Worldly Vanities: Complete Works*, ed. J. W. Cunliffe, 2 vols. (Cambridge: Cambridge University Press, 1907), 2: 220.

99. *Op. cit.*, 326.

100. O. J. Campbell, "The Salvation of Lear," *ELH*, 15 (1948), 107.

101. J. Stampfer, "The Catharsis of *King Lear*," *Shakespeare Survey*, 13 (1960), 4, 10.

102. Nicholas Brooke, *Shakespeare: King Lear* (1963), 60.

CHAPTER 9: *MACBETH*

103. *Chronicles of England, Scotland, and Wales*, 6 vols. (London, 1807–08), 5: 271.

CHAPTER 10: *ANTONY AND CLEOPATRA*

104. *Coleridge's Shakespearean Criticism*, 2 vols., (Harvard University Press, 1930), 1: 86.

105. Rosalie Colie, *Paradoxia Epidemica* (Princeton: Princeton University Press, 1966), 8. This is a fascinating exploration of the uses of paradox in the Renaissance, to which I am indebted. See also Janet Adelman's superb study of *Antony and Cleopatra* (New Haven: Yale University Press, 1973).

106. *Op. Cit.*, 290.

107. *Lives* (London, 1612), 951. See also Ernest Schanzer's *Problem Plays of Shakespeare* (New York: Schocken Books, 1963) which discusses, with an emphasis quite different from mine, the analogies to Hercules, Aeneas, and Mars.

108. Edgar Wind, *Pagan Mysteries in the Renaissance* (Harmondsworth: Penguin, 1967), 85–86.

109. Love's fetters are vividly allegorized in the chains that bind Spenser's Amoret to the brazen pillar in the House of Busyrane (*Faerie Queene*, 3.12. 30, 37, 41).

110. Spenser allegorizes these in the thunder, lightning, earthquake, and "hideous storme of winde" surrounding the House of Busyrane (*Faerie Queene* 3.12.2).

111. Donne, *Elegie 19: To His Mistris Going to Bed*. In *To Althea, from Prison*, Lovelace has: "When I lie tangled in her hair, And fettered to her eye, The gods that wanton in the air Know no such liberty."

112. Donne, *Elegie 20: Love's Warre*, and Lovelace, *To Lucasta, Going to the Wars*.

113. Shakespeare, *Venus and Adonis*, 1.231.

114. Donne, *Elegie 19: To His Mistris Going to Bed*.

115. Donne, *The Good-Morrow*, 10–14.

116. *Language as Symbolic Action* (Berkeley: University of California Press, 1966), 101.

117. Respectively, *Paradiso*, 33: 145, *Faerie Queene*, Canto 7: 59; Keats's so-called "last" sonnet: "Bright star"; *Burnt Norton*, 66–7.

CHAPTER 11: SHAKESPEAREAN TRAGEDY

118. *Op. Cit.*, ch 1.

119. The flexibility of the structure is witnessed by the amazing differences between the tragedies, of which it is, however, the lowest common multiple. In my discussion, I shall necessarily take the differences between the tragedies for granted and stress simply the vertebrate characteristics they share.

120. *The Development of Shakespeare's Imagery* (1951), 122.

121. F. P. Wilson, *Elizabethan and Jacobean* (1945), 122.

122. See an important comment on this by H. Levin in *Kenyon Review* (1950), 273–96.

123. I have commented on this point in Chapter Six.

124. *Magic in the Web*, 180.

125. Another emblematic entrance is the first entrance of the soothsayer in *Julius Caesar*. See Chapter Five.

126. *Duchess of Malfi*, 1.1.11.

127. By H. T. Price, in *Joseph Quincy Adams Memorial Studies*, ed. J. Mc-Manaway (1948), 101 ff.

128. See P. J. Aldus, *Shakespeare Quarterly* (1955), 397 ff. Aldus deals suggestively with the opening scene of *Julius Caesar.*

129. These are merely samples; other journeys occur that I have not named here.

130. See Helen Gardner's *The Noble Moor* (1956) and Chapter Seven.

131. *A Grammar of Motives* (1945), 38 ff.

132. "Whom Jove wishes to destroy he first makes mad."

133. *What Happens in* "Hamlet" (1935), 103 ff.

INDEX

Note: Apart from the titles of Shakespeare's plays, which are listed here individually, this is an index of authors. The page numbers following any author's name, or the title of any play by Shakespeare, record all mentions of, quotations from, characters in, and allusions to that play or the work of that author.